The Road to Gon

The Road to Gomorrah

Britain's War 1939 - 1943

Kenneth Duthie

Published by Kenneth Duthie.

ISBN: 978-1-3999-1460-4

Maps by Tez at Iolaire.

Cover design by Spiffing Covers.

Table of Contents

What is it then, poor mortal, that hath cast thee into lamentation and mourning? Some strange, unwonted sight, methinks, have thine eyes seen. Thou deemest Fortune to have changed towards thee; thou mistakest. Such ever were her ways, ever such her nature.

- Boethius.[1]

Onde è necessario ad un principe, volendosi mantenere, imparare a potere essere non buono, ed usarlo e non usarlo seconda la necessità.

– Niccolo Machiavelli.[2]

1 Chamberlain's Guarantee

On Friday 31st March 1939, Neville Chamberlain stood in the House of Commons and spoke the words that would oblige him to declare war on Germany some five months later: "In the event of any action which clearly threatened Polish independence, and which the Polish Government accordingly considered it vital to resist with their national forces, His Majesty's Government would feel themselves bound at once to lend the Polish Government all support in their power."[1]

At the subsequent debate in the House of Commons on Monday 3rd April, Chamberlain said,

> The declaration that I made on Friday has been described, in a phrase so apt that it has been widely taken up, as a cover note issued in advance of the complete insurance policy. I myself emphasised its transitional or temporary character, and the description of it as a cover note is not at all a bad one so far as it goes; but where I think it is altogether incomplete is that, while, of course, the issue of a cover note does imply that it is to be followed by something more substantial, it is the nature of the complete insurance policy which is such a tremendous departure from anything which this country has undertaken hitherto. It does really constitute a new point – I would say a new epoch – in the course of our foreign policy.[2]

Chamberlain was never going to be able to honour the guarantee he had just given to Poland. The British government had decided in 1937 that it was more important to create a defensive fighter force and to maintain Britain's naval power than it was to send an expeditionary force abroad to defend the territory of any of Britain's allies.[3] The British army had been starved of funding for years,[4] its soldiers were often desperate young men from the roughest areas in Britain with no other options in life,[5] and even its own officers acknowledged the moral and intellectual limitations of some of the upper ranks.[6] There had been no desire to fight another war on the European mainland after the country had experienced the horrors of the Somme and Passchendaele,[7] so creating a powerful army had not been a priority. The scaled-down British land forces may have been capable of suppressing poorly armed native people around the world, a form of duty known as imperial policing,[8] but that was a far cry from taking on the *Wehrmacht* in a full-scale land war.

When the former Prime Minister, David Lloyd George, arose in the House on 3rd April, he was critical of the new foreign policy:

> The Prime Minister said to-day that he has spoken plain words. That is not enough. You must make it clear that you have the means of implementing those words. . . . If war occurred tomorrow, you could not send a single battalion to Poland. . . . I am sorry to speak what is unpalatable, but I owe a duty to myself and to the country. . . .
>
> It is an assumption that Russia will come in sooner or later. I will give at once my definite suggestion to the Government and the House, and I urge it upon them. If we are going in without the help of Russia we are walking into a trap. It is the only country whose armies can get there. . . .
>
> I cannot understand why, before committing ourselves to this tremendous enterprise, we did not secure beforehand the adhesion of Russia. . . . I ask the Government to take immediate steps to secure the adhesion of Russia in a fraternity, an alliance, an agreement, a pact, it does not matter what it is called so long as it is an understanding to stand together against the aggressor. Apart from that we have taken a frightful gamble, a very risky gamble. With Russia you have overwhelming forces which Germany with her inferior army cannot stand up against. I appeal to the Government with all the earnestness I can command to take steps immediately. If Russia has not been brought into this matter because of certain feelings the Poles have that they do not want the Russians there, it is for us to declare the conditions, and unless the Poles are prepared to accept the only conditions with which we can successfully help them, the responsibility must be theirs.[9]

Lloyd George was experienced enough to realise that any British guarantee to Poland should be contingent upon their acceptance of Soviet military assistance. If the aim of the guarantee really was to protect Poland from a German invasion, then the Red Army would have to engage with the *Wehrmacht* on Poland's western border. If the Poles refused to let the Red Army into their country, then it would not be possible for the Soviet Union to do anything to defend them against German aggression.

Lloyd George was not the only politician who was prepared to speak out about the problems with the new foreign policy. The Labour MP Arthur Greenwood also laid out the case for recruiting the Soviet Union:

> In recent months and weeks there has been in Europe a more widespread feeling of uncertainty, uneasiness and apprehensiveness than before the days of Munich. Switzerland, Holland, Denmark and

> other smaller nations all feel that they may be suddenly struck down without warning by the assassin's hand.
>
> We have now reached the stage where there is a declaration regarding Poland, a declaration which must, without delay, be fully clothed with meaning and made capable of instant application. . . . I ask the Prime Minister whether he will make it the basis for the broadest possible brotherhood of nations to stand against aggression. . . .
>
> I would urge . . . that steps should be taken now to build up a clearly defined system of mutual aid. I say "clearly defined" because we must realise the duties and obligations that are imposed upon those who enter into that system; and into that system all should be invited to enter, all nations who are prepared to do what they can to increase world opinion against aggression with a view to deterring those who have been guilty or may be guilty of aggression . . .
>
> In this connection we cannot ignore the Union of Soviet Socialist Republics. . . . I realise that there are all kinds of ideological objections to the Union of Soviet Socialist Republics. . . . but in these times, it is important to mobilise in the cause of peace all States which are prepared to stand for peace. However you may assess the military value of the Union of Soviet Socialist Republics, there can be no question that she might well prove to be the final, decisive and smashing factor on the side of keeping the peace in the world.[10]

Sir Archibald Sinclair also spoke in the House of Commons on 3rd April. "Unless I have mistaken the aim of the policy," he said, "the object of the Government is less to make sure of victory in a possible war than to stop war breaking out."[11] However, if Chamberlain wanted to issue a military threat to Germany that would stop a war from breaking out, then the Germans would have to believe that they would end up on the losing side in any military conflict between the two countries. Without the military alliances necessary to ensure a British victory in the end, Chamberlain could only hope that his guarantee would be an effective deterrent. "It is clear," said Sinclair, "that the only way of stopping war is to build up an invincible resistance to aggression and to make it clear beyond a shadow of a doubt to Herr Hitler and his generals that if he attacks any of his neighbours he will have to face war on two fronts."[12] Sinclair stressed how important it was to recruit the Soviet Union to the cause:

I am impressed with what the Prime Minister has rightly described this afternoon as the momentous character of the departure in policy which the Government have made. I am impressed with the danger of the situation with which we are faced and with the immense practical difficulties in the present situation of giving effect to that policy. . . .[13]

Incomparably greater and more difficult than it would have been a year, or even seven months ago – is the task of establishing collective security in Europe to-day. It is now clearly a military problem and in the East of Europe Russia is obviously the key. . . .

The task of bringing Russia into co-operation with us in resistance to aggression is one of supreme importance.[14]

In the House days later, on 6th April, the Conservative MP Leo Amery emphasised the problems facing the British government as they entered what Chamberlain had called a "new epoch" in foreign policy, where the threat of military action would be used to influence other nation states:

I think it would be wrong, at a time so grave as the present, if one or two voices were not raised in order to draw attention to the implications of our present foreign policy and of the foreign situation in the sphere of defence. . . . The question we are bound to ask ourselves, and the House is bound to ask itself, is whether the preparations made by the Government to meet these dangers and to honour our commitments, are in any sense commensurate with our present national policy. . . .

We are bound to ask ourselves what is the military force which we have behind these commitments, and, more particularly, what is the military force we shall have available at the outbreak of war, the vital moment, the moment when everything may be decided one way or the other. What is the force we shall have available then? Let us face the actual facts of the situation. There is a force of, perhaps, five Regular Divisions. That is all we shall have – I am not quite sure we shall have even that – available at the time of war. . . .

I may be told that we are going to raise a great new force. Such terms are very relative in the world of to-day. The new force may be a great force, relative to what we have done in the past, but it will be very small, relative to the forces with which we shall have to deal. This so-called great force is to consist of a further 13 Territorial Army divisions, making 26 divisions altogether. Now it is essential that we should face the facts about this. I hope we may get the men. I hope that the patriotism of this country, even under the

> adverse conditions of so-called voluntary service, will find the men prepared to join. But what is the position to be when it comes to the outbreak of war? Will any of these divisions be ready to take the field? Of course not. To send troops with the kind of training which it is possible to get in spare time - an occasional evening's drill and a week or two in camp - to send troops with that amount of training, to face trained armies with modern equipment would just be [a] massacre. . . .
>
> That is one aspect of the matter. Again, it would be criminal to send troops into the field if there were no reserves behind them. Has anything been done to provide reserves for any of these Territorial divisions? We know quite well that there are neither reserves nor cadres in which trained reserves are being provided. Is it not perfectly obvious that so far as a force available at the outbreak of war is concerned, these 26 Territorial Divisions are just eyewash? They may form a nucleus for training, for sending divisions to the front some months after war has begun, but that is all. They will not be available at the outbreak of war.[15]

The prospect of fighting a war had also been considered by the British military. The Chiefs of Staff had prepared a memorandum on 15th February 1937 entitled "Planning for a war with Germany." For the purposes of their analysis, it was assumed that the war would begin in late 1939. The Chiefs of Staff argued that Britain did not have the military strength to take on the *Wehrmacht,* so she would have to fight a long, three-phase war. First, Britain would have to withstand an initial attack by Germany. Secondly, she could use her economic and industrial resources to develop a military force capable of fighting against the *Wehrmacht*. Only in the third phase of a long war could a counter-offensive be launched. The Chiefs of Staff recognised that supplies from the United States and direct military assistance from the Soviet Union "would go far towards making the Allied [not British] counter-offensive possible."[16]

The necessity of having the Soviet Union fighting on Britain's side in a war against Germany was once again brought to the government's attention in the House on 6th April, when Vernon Bartlett, the MP for Bridgwater in Somerset, said that

> as far as foreign policy is concerned, there are obviously two things we ought to do, in my opinion. One is, with the very greatest speed, to make an alliance with Russia . . .
>
> The second thing that ought to happen is, surely, that our foreign policy should be one that wins the fullest confidence of the

> American people. . . . The realisation that even if Germany were to succeed in a Blitzkrieg, in a lightning war, and in frightening the British and French people so much that they would demand peace, which I do not believe would happen, the knowledge and realisation that behind the British and French people were the great people of the United States would be the greatest of all deterrents for Germany. In other words, it seems obvious that our foreign policy must make quite sure that if Germany tried to declare war she would have to fight on two fronts, and would have the prospect of having to face the great resources of the United States.[17]

The man who ended up being responsible for forming a wartime alliance with the Soviet Union and the United States was Winston Churchill, who would become Prime Minister in May 1940. When he arose in the House on 3rd April 1939, Churchill was still MP for Epping. "I find myself in the most complete agreement with the Prime Minister," he stated. "I listened to his speech with the greatest attention, and both in its assertions and its reservations, in its scope, in its emphasis, and in its balance, I find myself entirely in accord with what he said."[18] However, Churchill understood that issuing a "cover note" to Poland would not deter Hitler, or anyone else for that matter, from doing whatever they pleased in Eastern Europe. If the British government really wanted to enter a "new epoch" in foreign policy where threats of military action were to be employed as levers of influence, then they were going to have to form an alliance with the most powerful military force in the region – the Soviet Union:

> Having begun this policy there can be no turning back. There is no halting-place. . . . To stop here with a guarantee to Poland would be to halt in no-man's Land under fire of both trench lines and without the shelter of either. That is why it seems to me that the announcement of the Prime Minister on Friday, which is explained and emphasised by his statement today, constitutes a milestone in our history. We must go forward now until a conclusion is reached. Having begun to create a Grand Alliance against aggression, we cannot afford to fail. . . .
>
> The worst folly, which no one proposes we should commit, would be to chill and drive away any natural co-operation which Soviet Russia in her own deep interests feels it necessary to afford. Primarily we must rely upon our own strength, but we welcome cordially the aid of all who stand for the main cause now at stake. . . .
>
> The attitude of His Majesty's Government towards Russia appears to me . . . to be well conceived. Russia is a ponderous

> counterpoise in the scale of world peace. We cannot measure the weight of support which may be forthcoming from Soviet Russia.[19]

It may have been recognised by many of Britain's politicians that an alliance of some kind with the Soviet Union was a necessary condition of being able to honour Chamberlain's guarantee, but there was no such agreement between the two states. As Lloyd George pointed out, even if Chamberlain had managed to reach an agreement with the Soviets, any offer of a guarantee ought to have been contingent upon the Polish leadership agreeing to let the Red Army move across Polish territory so the Soviet forces could engage with the *Wehrmacht* at the German border. Chamberlain had issued his guarantee to the Poles without first securing the necessary conditions for success in a war with Germany. Churchill recognised the danger:

> The men at the head of Germany are not restrained by any scruples. They have risen to their power by violence, cruelty and murder. Herr Hitler plumes himself particularly upon the lightning character of the blows which he strikes. These are men in the path of whose ambition it is very dangerous to stand, and we have taken up our stand right in their path.[20]

Churchill may have publicly supported Chamberlain's decision to give a guarantee to Poland at the time, but when he was writing the first volume of his history of the war years later, Churchill admitted that "no one who understood the situation could doubt that it meant in all human probability a major war, in which we should be involved" and that this war "must surely lead to the slaughter of tens of millions of people."[21]

At a Cabinet meeting on 20th March, Chamberlain had discussed the possibility of trying to interfere with Germany's *Drang nach Osten* (drive to the east) by entering into some form of agreement with other countries. "If the little States were all to become parties to the arrangement entered into," he warned the Cabinet, "they would be tempted to adopt a very rigid line about minor matters, and this might precipitate the very situation we wished to avoid."[22] Chamberlain never spoke a truer word.

The political relationship between Poland and Germany had been relatively stable since they signed a non-aggression pact in 1934,[23] but the people of Danzig wanted to live under German rule, and the German government had been trying to get permission to build an *Autobahn* (road or motorway) connecting Germany to East Prussia for years. If the Poles chose to "adopt a very rigid line" over these two "minor matters" after Chamberlain issued his guarantee, then the relationship between Germany and Poland could easily deteriorate. Instead of treating the Poles as potential allies in any conflict against the Soviet Union, Hitler could end up viewing Poland as an obstacle that stood in the way of his ultimate goal - obtaining sufficient *Lebensraum* (living space) in the east to ensure his people's survival. If that happened, then a war would be inevitable.

2 Germany Prepares for War

The National Socialist movement in Germany had always been steeped in darkness. When Hitler was on trial in February 1924, Lieutenant-General Otto von Lossow, the former chief of the *Reichswehr* in Bavaria, said that Hitler's followers considered him the German messiah, and Hitler himself spoke openly in court about his followers walking in the streets carrying the *Hakenkreuz* (crooked cross.)[1] This was symbolised as a black swastika on a white disc, with a red background.[2] At party rallies, Hitler would use what became known as the *Blutfahne* (bloody banner), which was stained with the blood of some of Hitler's followers who had been killed during the failed *putsch* of November 1923, to anoint the banners of his followers. All carried the image of the crooked cross. In such a wicked environment, it is not surprising that willing servants like Joachim von Ribbentrop would rise to prominence.

Ribbentrop, who had replaced Konstantin von Neurath as Foreign Minister on 4th February 1938,[3] had arranged to meet with Josef Lipski, the Polish ambassador, at the Grand Hotel in Berchtesgaden on 24th October that year. Ribbentrop let Lipski know that a lasting political arrangement between the two countries was a real possibility. "It was time to arrive at a general settlement of all possible points of friction between Germany and Poland," he told the ambassador.[4] However, "it was necessary to speak with Poland first of all about Danzig, as one part of a large settlement between the two nations. Danzig was German – had always been German and would always remain German."[5]

Ribbentrop proposed that

1. The Free State of Danzig would revert to the German Reich.
2. An extra-territorial *Reichsautobahn* belonging to Germany and likewise an extra-territorial, multiple-track railroad would be laid through the Corridor.
3. Similarly, Poland would receive in the Danzig area an extra-territorial road or *Autobahn*, a railroad, and a free port.
4. Poland would receive a guarantee of a market for her goods in the Danzig area.
5. The two nations would recognise their common boundaries (guarantee) or each other's territories.
6. The German-Polish treaty would be extended [from] 10 to 25 years.
7. Poland would accede to the Anti-Comintern Pact.
8. The two countries would add a consultation clause to their treaty.[6]

The possibility of building a road that would connect East Prussia to the rest of Germany had been put to the Poles on several occasions over the years. The German ambassador to Poland, Hans-Adolf von Moltke, had spoken to Josef Beck, the Polish Foreign Minister, about the construction of an *Autobahn* (road or motorway) through the Corridor in May 1935. Fritz Todt, the Nazi engineer in charge of the German roadway system, had been in Warsaw at a Polish exhibition in September that year. He had spoken with the Deputy Minister in the Ministry of Transportation about having experts from both sides meet to discuss the matter. Moltke believed that the Germans should go ahead with the project and build the road up to the edge of the Corridor on both sides. As Moltke put it, "This method of procedure would put the Poles under pressure to the extent that they would certainly find undesirable the impression which travellers would inevitably obtain, in passing between the Reich and its East Prussian territory, from the condition of the Polish roads in comparison with that of the German *Reichsautobahn*."[7]

Todt wrote to Ribbentrop on 27th October 1938 to remind him that

> we spoke once several years ago in the Hotel Viktoria in Stuttgart about the Führer's idea of connecting East Prussia with the Reich through a Corridor road (*Reichsautobahn* through the Corridor.) Ambassador Count von Moltke has made several attempts over a period of years toward realization of this plan, but so far without success. Last Sunday the Führer informed me of various aspects of his policy in order that we may adjust our highway construction program accordingly. He mentioned again that if there was to be any guarantee of the Corridor, Germany would have to be granted a traffic corridor for an *Autobahn* and if possible, also for a railway. Nothing could more effectively lend force to a guarantee of the Polish Corridor than the elimination, through such a corridor highway, of the economic disadvantage of the Corridor for Germany, namely the interruption of traffic between East Prussia and the Reich. I request that you keep these ideas in mind during the present negotiations.[8]

Another high-level political meeting was held at Berchtesgaden on 5th January 1939. In attendance were Hitler, Ribbentrop, Moltke, Beck and Lipski. Hitler had met Beck a year earlier, and he had "described at length his attitude toward Bolshevism and the Bolshevist danger which was still threatening Europe. . . . He repeatedly stressed that – aside, of course, from a further strengthening of Germany – the struggle against Bolshevism was the unalterable aim of his policy."[9]

Now Hitler told the Polish diplomats that

for a settlement of all existing difficulties it was first of all necessary to go back to the basic orientation of German-Polish relations. On the part of Germany he could state emphatically that there had not been the slightest change in Germany's relations with Poland as based on the nonaggression declaration of 1934. Germany would under all circumstances be interested in maintaining a strong nationalist Poland, quite irrespective of developments in Russia. Regardless of whether Russia was bolshevist or czarist, or something else, Germany's attitude toward that country would always be one of the greatest caution and for that reason she was decidedly interested in seeing Poland's position preserved. Purely from the military point of view the existence of a strong Polish Army meant a considerable easing of Germany's position; the divisions which Poland stationed at the Russian frontier saved Germany just so much additional military expenditure. . . .

As for the details of German-Polish relations, he wished to repeat once more that since 1934 there had been no change in the German attitude toward Poland. In order to arrive at a definitive settlement of the questions still pending between the two countries, one ought not to confine oneself to the rather negative agreement of 1934, but should try to bring the individual problems to a definitive settlement by treaty. From the German point of view the remaining problem in direct German-Polish relations . . . was that of the Corridor and Danzig, which was psychologically very difficult for German sensibilities. In his opinion it was necessary to depart from old patterns here and seek solutions along entirely new lines. Thus, for example, in the case of Danzig there might conceivably be a settlement by which this city would be brought into the German political community again in accordance with the will of its population; naturally the Polish interests, especially in the economic field, would have to be fully protected. This was after all in the interest of Danzig as well, for Danzig could not live economically without Poland, either, and so he, the Führer, was thinking of a formula by which Danzig would come into the German community politically but remain with Poland economically.

Danzig is German, will always remain German, and will sooner or later become part of Germany. He could give the assurance, however, that no *fait accompli* would be engineered in Danzig.

> With regard to the Corridor, which, as stated, was a difficult psychological problem for Germany, the Führer pointed out that it was of course completely absurd to want to deprive Poland of her outlet to the sea. . . . The necessity for Poland to have access to the sea definitely had to be recognized. In the same way, however, having a connection with East Prussia was a necessity for Germany; here too, by using entirely new methods of solution one could perhaps do justice to the interests of both.[10]

The Germans had been cultivating their relationship with the Polish leaders for several years.[11] Hitler had told Lipski prior to the signing of the non-aggression pact in January 1934 that he saw Poland as an important bulwark against the spread of Communism, and when he met with Beck in January 1938, he assured him that his primary mission was the long-term fight against Communism. The Polish leaders had been invited on several occasions to join the Anti-Comintern Pact, which Germany and Japan had signed in November 1936.[12] Although the Germans wanted to right the wrongs of the Versailles Treaty, at least from the German perspective, the records show that they had offered to guarantee the Polish borders, make sure that the Poles had access to the sea, and protect Polish economic interests in the port of Danzig. They had also offered to extend the non-aggression pact between the two countries for at least 10 years.

As one might expect, the negotiations between Germany and Poland over these minor issues had caused no problems whatsoever for Britain. After all, what business was it of anyone else if the Germans wanted to build a road to East Prussia? Why should it matter to anyone riding on the Clapham omnibus if the people of Danzig wanted to live their lives as Germans? The British government had made it known that they would have no objections if a German flag ended up flying over Danzig. Edward Wood,[13] who had become Viscount Halifax after his father died in January 1934,[14] travelled to Berchtesgaden to meet with Hitler on 19th November 1937.[15] Halifax said later that "he had encountered friendliness and a desire for good relations."[16]

Halifax explained the British position to the Nazis: "On the English side it was not necessarily thought that the *status quo* must be maintained under all circumstances. It was recognised that one might have to contemplate an adjustment to new conditions, a correction of former mistakes and the recognition of changed circumstances when such need arose." Regarding any "possible alterations in the European order which might be destined to come about with the passage of time," Halifax specifically mentioned Danzig, Austria and Czechoslovakia. "England was interested to see that any alterations should come through the course of peaceful evolution and that methods should be avoided which might cause far-reaching disturbances," he told Hitler. The British government were portrayed as rational people who the Nazis could work with. "Changes should only take place upon the basis of reasonable agreements reasonably reached," Halifax stated. "If on both sides there was agreement that the world was not static, one should try to put the recognition of this fact into practice so that the energies at the disposal of mankind should be directed in mutual confidence to a common objective."[17]

In February 1938, Hitler had also been visited by Sir Neville Henderson, the British Ambassador in Berlin, who told him that the British government was not unsympathetic towards Germany's desire to alter the political landscape in Eastern Europe.[18] The military historian Basil Liddell Hart has pointed out that these visits from prominent British figures could only have given Hitler the impression that there would be no objections from the British government if he kept on trying to get a road to East Prussia built, or if he kept pressing the Poles on the issue of Danzig.[19]

At a Cabinet meeting held on 19th April 1939, it was acknowledged that when Chamberlain performed a *volte-face* and issued a guarantee to Poland, this had made a negotiated settlement to these issues less likely:

> If the Polish Government were prepared to treat with Germany for a settlement of the Danzig question, it might be well if they could cut the ground from under the feet of the German Government by showing their disposition to negotiate. . . . At a later stage in the Meeting, the Foreign Secretary reported that he had now received a telegram from Berlin in regard to relations between Germany and Poland. In effect, the upshot of the report was that Herr Hitler was now dealing with these negotiations himself, but that not much progress was being made. This was attributed to the fact that the Poles were adopting a more intractable attitude since they had obtained our guarantee.[20]

On 31st March, Hitler had been on his way to Wilhelmshaven to attend the launch of the *Tirpitz*, which was Germany's second largest battleship. When he heard about the British guarantee, he flew into a rage,[21] and when he gave a speech at the launching ceremony the following day, he warned that Germany would not stand by and allow Poland to become a satellite state of the British.[22] On 3rd April, as Chamberlain's guarantee was being debated in the House of Commons, Hitler issued a directive to the German armed forces tasking them to prepare for an invasion of Poland, codenamed "Case White," that would begin no later than 1st September 1939.[23] When Chamberlain issued his guarantee, his intention may have been to prevent the Germans from advancing into Eastern Europe, but his actions only made that more likely to happen. The Polish leaders were now less inclined to negotiate a solution to the Danzig problem, and Hitler was more likely to use military means to force the issue.[24]

After the first world war, the German military had been severely limited under the terms of the Versailles Treaty, and another positional war of attrition against any numerically superior force would almost certainly have ended in a defeat. However, under the command of General Hans von Seeckt, the army had started to develop new military tactics so they would be able to fight a different kind of war - a *Bewegungskrieg* (war of movement) - in the future.[25] To that end, in the field service regulations (*Führung und Gefecht der verbundenen Waffen*, known as the *F.u.G.*) that were issued in 1921,[26] it was emphasised that soldiers had to be able to react to a change in circumstances on the battlefield by employing the principle of *Auftragstaktik*, which meant that individual soldiers were expected to do whatever was necessary to successfully complete their mission.[27]

Seeckt had set up an organisation called *Sondergruppe R* (Special Group R) to collaborate with the Soviet Union. In April 1926, the *Kampffliegerschule Lipezk* (Lipetz flying school) was opened, and Germany began to secretly train pilots in the Soviet Union. German officers were also sent to train at the *Panzerschule Kama* (Kama tank school) near Kazan, in Tatarstan, after the facility opened in the summer of 1929.[28] In 1930, General Kurt von Hammerstein-Equord became head of the German army, and Major General Oswald Lutz, who had run the *Panzerschule Kama*, was put in charge of a new army motorisation programme in early 1932. Lutz drew up specifications for a training tank, and Krupp was awarded a contract to build a prototype that would eventually become the Pz I tank.[29] In June 1932, Kurt von Schleicher, who had also been involved with *Sondergruppe R*, became the new defence minister. Schleicher authorised a programme to expand the army beyond the limits laid down by the Versailles Treaty.[30]

Lutz had only intended for the lightweight Pz I tank to be used for training, and the *Heereswaffenamt* (Army Weapons Department) requested an improved model with a 2cm cannon, which would give them a limited anti-armour capability. This light tank, which was classified as the Pz II, was produced by Daimler-Benz and MAN. By the end of 1938, the army had 800 of these 8.9 tonne tanks, and 250 more were produced in early 1939.[31] On 11th January 1934, the *Heereswaffenamt* issued a requirement for two medium tanks, which were intended to be the main tanks used in the army. Krupp was awarded the contract to develop the Pz IV, which was to be armed with a low velocity 7.5cm howitzer, to be used to engage buildings and fortified positions. Their first model was based on sound engineering principles and by September 1938, a year before the invasion of Poland, the

Pz IV Auf C was beginning low-rate production. When war broke out in September 1939, a total of 211 Pz IV tanks were in service in the Germany army.[32]

The contract for the development of the Pz III, which was to be fitted with a high velocity 3.7cm anti-tank cannon, was given to Daimler-Benz and Rheinmetall-Borsig. The first four models of the Pz III had four different suspension systems, and a basic production model, the Pz III Auf E, was not ready for low-rate production until December 1938. By September 1939, only 98 Pz III tanks had been built, 50 of which were the Pz III Auf E models.[33]

The Germans had managed to capture some of Czechoslovakia's military hardware when they took over the country in March of that year, so they also had over 200 LT vz. 35 tanks in their possession, and they had control of the production facilities for the new Czech LT vz. 38 tank.[34] One of the hallmarks of the German forces during the war was that they used the hardware and personnel of other countries to augment their own military forces. In the case of the Czechoslovakian tanks, this was done out of necessity, for the Pz 1 and Pz II tanks would soon be obsolete,[35] and the newer medium tanks were just starting to come off the production line in meaningful numbers in the autumn of 1939.

One of the significant properties of the army that Germany developed in the years prior to the outbreak of the second world war was that its two main components ran at different speeds.[36] The tanks could operate as a semi-independent force with the ability to break through the enemy lines and drive forward into the enemy's rear, but the army did not have enough motor vehicles to transport its troops and supplies, so most of the infantry following the tanks could only move at walking speed. The infantry would also have to fight the enemy forces left behind by the advancing tanks, which would be time consuming in and of itself. If these two components of the German army advanced at significantly different speeds for too long, then they would inevitably separate, and each would be left to fight without the support of the other. This property of Germany's under-mechanised army was to become more significant as the war progressed. However, in the summer of 1939, the Germans were confident that they would be able to defeat Poland without too much difficulty. On 22nd August, with the invasion of Poland in the offing, Hitler met with his military commanders at the Berghof and let them know what he expected of them.[37] The records available from that meeting show that Hitler said,

> Quick decision necessary. Unshakeable faith in the German soldier. A crisis may happen only if the nerves of the leaders give way. First aim: advance to the Vistula and Narew. Our technical superiority will break the nerves of the Poles. Every newly created Polish force

> shall again be broken at once. Constant war of attrition. . . . Complete destruction of Poland is the military aim. To be fast is the main thing. Pursuit until complete elimination. Conviction that the German *Wehrmacht* is up to the requirements.[38]

Hitler did not expect the British government to do anything to help Poland. "The probability is great that the West will not interfere," Hitler stated. "On the other side, a negative picture as far as decisive personalities are concerned. There is no outstanding personality in England or France." Hitler went further: "Our enemies are little worms. I saw them in Munich."[39] From the German perspective, if the British government wasn't prepared to do anything to help the Polish people, then the conflict could be contained, and if the *Wehrmacht* could be tasked with nothing more than an invasion of western Poland, then the Polish forces could be defeated quickly. If that could be achieved, then the country could be taken over and, to all intents and purposes, the Polish nation would cease to exist. The British government would be faced with a *fait accompli,* and there would be no point in fighting for Polish independence then.[40] However, Hitler acknowledged that "it may also turn out differently regarding England and France. One cannot predict it with certainty."[41] The rules of engagement for the upcoming conflict were established. The records show that Hitler instructed his commanders that afternoon to "have no pity. Brutal attitude. 80 million people shall get what is their right. Their existence has to be secured. The strongest has the right. Greatest severity."[42]

The Poles were about to experience a kind of war where the power of the German state would be used not just to invade and conquer another country, but to enforce the ideology of the victors upon the vanquished.

3 Anglo-Soviet Negotiations Fail

Hitler may have been confident that the *Wehrmacht* was more than a match for the Polish armed forces, but he understood as well as anyone that the guarantee issued by the British government in March 1939 meant nothing without a military agreement with the Soviet Union. If Germany could undermine any British efforts to parley with the Soviets and strike a deal of their own instead, then that would isolate Poland, and the Soviet Union would be able to provide Germany with supplies, which would render a British naval blockade ineffective.[1]

Churchill was aware of the problems the British government was facing. No British guarantee "had any military value except within the framework of a general agreement with Russia,"[2] he acknowledged in his history of the war:

> The obstacle to such an agreement was the terror of these same border countries of receiving Soviet help in the shape of Soviet armies marching through their territories to defend them from the Germans, and incidentally incorporating them in the Soviet-Communist system, of which they were the most vehement opponents. Poland, Roumania, Finland, and the three Baltic States did not know whether it was German aggression or Russian rescue that they dreaded more.[3]

The British government opened negotiations with the Soviets, but as the records of a Cabinet meeting on 19th July show, the Soviets insisted that there could be no political agreement until a military agreement had been concluded,[4] which was not an unreasonable position to take, given the circumstances. The records of that meeting show that

> in reply to questions, the Foreign Secretary [Halifax] said that he thought there was some evidence that Germany was trying to make matters as difficult for us as they could in our negotiations with the Soviet Union. It seemed that discussions of some kind were proceeding between the German government and the Soviet Government. It was impossible to assess their real value, but it seemed likely that these discussions related to industrial matters.
>
> The Prime Minister said that he could not bring himself to believe that a real alliance between Russia and Germany was possible.[5]

The British government did not understand that they were now engaged in a bidding war for Stalin's favour, and when an Anglo-French delegation was finally sent to Moscow to negotiate a deal with the Soviets, the naval officer in charge of the British contingent, Admiral Sir Reginald Plunkett-Ernle-Drax,[6] was told by Halifax to try to stretch the negotiations out until winter arrived. It was thought that this would make a German military operation in Poland less likely.[7] The British party boarded a merchant ship on 5th August that took them to Leningrad and from there, they travelled on to Moscow, finally reaching the Soviet capital on 11th August.[8]

Once the negotiations began, the Soviets, who were led by Marshal Kliment Voroshilov, the Commissar for Defence,[9] pressed Drax for direct answers to very specific questions.[10] When asked how many troops Britain had available to participate in a war on the European mainland, Drax admitted that they only had five infantry divisions and one mechanised division ready to fight alongside the French Army.[11] If the Soviet Union was going to have to do most of the fighting against the *Wehrmacht* in the event of a war against Germany, and the reason for the war was to protect Poland, then the Red Army would have to engage with the *Wehrmacht* as close to Poland's western border as possible. Voroshilov wanted to know if the Poles had given permission for Soviet forces to enter Polish territory.[12]

This issue was always going to arise and the best that Drax could do was argue that, although he could not say at this time that the Poles had given permission for the Soviets to enter Polish territory, he had been instructed by his government to point out that, in their opinion, an invasion would inevitably alter the outlook of the Polish leadership.[13]

Voroshilov was unimpressed with the British response. He wanted a straightforward answer to the question: Would Poland allow the Soviet Union to send its troops into Polish territory?[14] Drax now argued that this was a political matter, so it should be addressed at that level. He suggested that the Soviet government put the question directly to the Polish leadership. The Soviet negotiators put the ball back in the Anglo-French court, and insisted that they should be the ones to approach the Poles.[15]

The British and French ambassadors visited Beck in Warsaw on 19th August, and asked if the Soviets could have permission to cross to the western border of Poland, which was the only way that Poland could have any direct military assistance in the event of a German invasion.[16] Beck said that he would give a formal reply the next day and on the morning of 20th August, the British military attaché in Warsaw was informed that under no circumstances would the Poles agree to let Soviet troops enter Polish territory.[17]

The British government had only issued Poland with a verbal "cover note" at this time. They could have made issuing a hard copy of the "complete insurance policy" contingent upon the Poles allowing the Red Army to fight alongside the Polish armed forces on the country's western border. If the Poles refused military assistance from the only country in the region that could possibly help them in the event of a German invasion, then the British could have refused to issue a formal guarantee, backed away from the situation entirely, and blamed the Poles for sabotaging the Anglo-French talks with the Soviet Union. There was still a way to avoid what Churchill called "a major war, in which we should be involved,"[18] but Chamberlain and Halifax chose not to take it.[19]

The following day, Voroshilov told the British and French military delegations that if their governments had really wanted the Soviet Union to help defend Poland against a German invasion, then the question of whether the Red Army could move troops and tanks to the front lines would have been addressed beforehand. According to Voroshilov, the failure of the British and French governments to do this showed that they had never really been serious about coming to an arrangement with the Soviet Union.[20] On that note, the negotiations were formally concluded, with no agreement having been reached.[21]

Chamberlain and Halifax may have found it difficult to believe that Germany would form a military alliance with the Soviet Union, but that is exactly what happened as the British were struggling to find a way out of the situation they had created. They had issued a war guarantee to an Eastern European country that they could not honour unless the Soviet Union agreed to do their fighting for them. The Soviets had no interest in preserving the independence of Poland, and the Polish leadership refused to let the Red Army cross Polish territory to engage with the *Wehrmacht*. As Churchill acknowledged after the war, none of the countries along the border with the Soviet Union wanted to give the Soviets an excuse to enter their country, because they knew exactly what would happen if they did.[22] The British strategy was an exercise in futility. The only thing Chamberlain had guaranteed was a war against Germany – a long war that would last for years, which could only be won with the assistance of allies that Britain did not have.

The Nazis may have been confident in the abilities of their armed forces, but they were also prepared to use diplomatic means to prevent Britain from recruiting the ally they needed in Eastern Europe. Their own negotiations with the Soviet Union concluded in the early hours of 24th August, when Ribbentrop and Molotov signed a non-aggression pact.[23] This included a secret protocol that dealt with the Soviet Union extending its influence into the countries along its border:

The Government of the German Reich and The Government of the Union of Soviet Socialist Republics,

Directed by the wish to strengthen the cause of peace between Germany and the U.S.S.R. . . . have reached the following agreement:

Article 1. The two contracting parties undertake to refrain from any act of violence, any aggressive action, or any attack against one another, whether individually or jointly with other powers.

Article 2. In case any of the contracting parties should become the object of warlike acts on the part of a third power, the other contracting party will not support that third power in any form. . . .

Secret Additional Protocol
On the occasion of the signature of the Non-Aggression Treaty between the German Reich and the Union of Soviet Socialist Republics, the undersigned plenipotentiaries of the two parties discussed in strictly confidential conversations the question of the delimitation of their respective spheres of influence in Eastern Europe. These conversations led to the following result:

1. In the event of a territorial and political transformation in the territories belonging to the Baltic States (Finland, Estonia, Latvia, Lithuania), the northern frontier of Lithuania shall represent the frontier of the spheres of interest both of Germany and the U.S.S.R.. In this connection the interest of Lithuania in the Vilna territory is recognised by both parties.

2. In the event of a territorial and political transformation of the territories belonging to the Polish State, the spheres of interest of both Germany and the U.S.S.R. shall be bounded approximately by the line of the rivers Narew, Vistula and San.

The question of whether the interests of both parties make the maintenance of an independent Polish State appear desirable and how the frontiers of this State should be drawn can be definitely determined only in the course of further political developments. In any case both Governments will resolve this question by means of a friendly understanding.[24]

When the signing of the Nazi-Soviet Pact was announced, Chamberlain had another opportunity to avoid a war with Germany. It had been made clear to him during the debate in the House of Commons on 3rd April that without the promise of direct military assistance from the Soviet Union, his verbal guarantee to Poland was worthless. Now that the Polish leadership had refused to let the Red Army cross Polish territory and the Soviets had signed a non-aggression pact with the Nazis, Chamberlain could have withdrawn his original offer and blamed the political choices made by the Soviets and the Poles. The worst thing that could have happened was that Chamberlain might have had to do the honourable thing and fall on his sword. Chamberlain had said on 19th July that "he could not bring himself to believe that a real alliance between Russia and Germany was possible,"[25] but his inability to conceive of such an alliance did not mean it would not become a reality. The plain fact was, Chamberlain had been outmanoeuvred by both the Nazis and the Soviets, and now he had to respond to the new situation. On 24th August, he spoke in the House of Commons:

> The question that the Government had to consider when they learned of this announcement was what effect, if any, this changed situation would have upon their own policy. In Berlin the announcement was hailed, with extraordinary cynicism, as a great diplomatic victory which removed any danger of war since we and France would no longer be likely to fulfil our obligations to Poland. We felt it our first duty to remove any such dangerous illusion.
>
> The House will recollect that the guarantee which we had given to Poland was given before any agreement with Russia was talked of, and that it was not in any way made dependent upon any such agreement being reached. How then could we, with honour, go back upon such an obligation, which we had so often and so plainly repeated? Therefore, our first act was to issue a statement that our obligations to Poland and to other countries remained unaffected. Those obligations rest upon agreed statements made to the House of Commons, to which effect is being given in treaties which are at present in an advanced stage of negotiation.[26]

Instead of admitting that there was no way to live up to his self-created obligation to provide British military assistance to Poland, Chamberlain perpetuated the "dangerous illusion" that Britain would help Poland in the event of an invasion. A hard copy of Chamberlain's verbal "cover note" was issued on 25th August 1939, the day after the Nazi-Soviet Pact was signed in Moscow. The key text from this formal agreement between the British and Polish governments reads as follows:

Article 1
Should one of the Contracting Parties become engaged in hostilities with a European Power in consequence of aggression by the latter against that Contracting Party, the other Contracting Party will at once give the Contracting Party engaged in hostilities all the support and assistance in its power.

Article 2.
(1) The provisions of Article I will also apply in the event of any action by a European Power which clearly threatened, directly or indirectly, the independence of one of the Contracting Parties, and was of such a nature that the Party in question considered it vital to resist it with its armed forces. . . .

Protocol
The Polish government and the Government of the United Kingdom of Great Britain and Northern Ireland are agreed upon the following interpretation of the Agreement of Mutual Assistance signed this day as alone authentic and binding –

1 – (a) By the expression "a European Power" employed in the Agreement is to be understood Germany.[27]

Chamberlain had been told several times in the House of Commons that he would need the military backing of the Soviet Union if he was going to honour his guarantee to Poland, and with the signing of the Nazi-Soviet pact, it was clear that this would not happen. Undeterred, Chamberlain formally issued a hard copy of his initial "cover note" and thereby ensured that Britain would have to go to war. By including a secret protocol that limited the British government's obligations so that the Soviet Union would be free to act however she pleased in Eastern Europe and Scandinavia, Chamberlain had, perhaps inadvertently, left the door open for the Soviet Union to switch sides later in the war. Not everyone saw the wisdom in what Chamberlain had done. The Labour MP Nye Bevan stood in the House on 24th August and said,

> It must be present in the mind of every Member of this House that a guarantee to Poland is very difficult of execution without the assistance of Russia. When the guarantee to Poland was discussed in the House, immediately after it was given, the right hon. Gentleman the Member for Carnarvon Boroughs (Mr. Lloyd George)

> pointed out that the military assistance that Britain and France could render to Poland was very little indeed in the absence of an agreement with Russia . . .
>
> If Russian assistance to Britain would have been of no value, Germany would not have been so anxious to buy Russia off. The fact that Germany has turned off the tap of her propaganda, that Hitler has swallowed his words and falsified five years of anti-Bolshevik propaganda in Germany is evidence of the value that Germany attaches to Russian military assistance. It is one of our chief indictments against the Government that their policy has thrown away assistance of that kind. . . .
>
> The Prime Minister said that he bore a very great share of the responsibility; that upon his shoulders rested a heavier burden than upon the shoulders of anybody else. I think the guarantee to Poland, in the absence of an agreement with Russia, was a mistake. It was militarily silly. It should have followed, and not preceded, negotiations with Russia. . . . I do not accept the statement that the Prime Minister of Great Britain has a heavier burden upon his shoulders than anybody else. His is the easiest job in the House of Commons. The more blunders he makes, the more necessity there is for unity and for no criticism to be heard. The bigger the catastrophe of which he is the architect, the safer he is. This is the same Government, its personnel is the same, as that which was the architect of Munich. The suggestion is that the people of my constituency, the colliers, steelworkers and railwaymen, should offer their bodies as a deterrent to German aggression. There is one man over there whom you could offer - offer him. Let the Conservative party, if it wants to convince us that it is in earnest, call a Carlton Club meeting, and get rid of the Prime Minister. He is the man upon whom Hitler relies; he is the man responsible for this situation.[28]

Chamberlain had managed to paint his country into a corner so that Britain had to stand alone against Nazi Germany until 22nd June 1941, when Germany turned on their partners in crime and launched Operation Barbarossa. Churchill took that opportunity to form an alliance with the Soviet Union, but there was a price that had to be paid for Soviet participation in the second world war. Churchill recognised in his book, *The Gathering Storm*, that people who lived in countries that shared a border with the Soviet Union "did not know whether it was German aggression or Russian rescue that they dreaded more,"[29] and events during and after the war proved that their concerns were well founded. The Nazi-Soviet pact had split the area between the two countries into "spheres of influence," and from that moment forward, the Soviet Union did everything in its power to exert control over the countries along its border. One of the first countries to discover what it meant to have "Soviet armies marching through their territories . . . and incidentally incorporating them in the Soviet-Communist system"[30] was the very country whose independence the British government was supposed to have guaranteed – Poland.

4 Poland is Invaded

The war that followed the German invasion of Poland on 1st September 1939 had an ideological component that motivated its participants to act in ways that, in previous military conflicts, would have been considered beyond the pale. The Polish people were caught between two totalitarian regimes that were determined to expand their territories at the expense of the Polish nation, and both the Soviet Union and Germany were going to impose their ideological beliefs upon any newly occupied territory.

Hitler's first experience of warfare had been a gruelling, bloody affair. In October 1914, the regiment he served in, the 16th Reserve Infantry Regiment, which was part of the 6th Bavarian Reserve Division, was sent forward into the middle of the first battle of Ypres.[1] On 29th October, Hitler and his comrades were ordered to take part in an assault on the Flemish village of Gheluvelt.[2] As they tried to advance across a stretch of farmland, they came under fire and took significant casualties before reaching the British trenches, where they were forced to engage in brutal hand to hand combat.[3] Their casualty rate over the next few days was so high that the regiment was recalled from the front on 1st November, after losing approximately 2,900 out of 3,500 men.[4] The war of attrition that followed resulted in death and loss on an unprecedented scale. The effect of the first world war on the British people may have been to make them reluctant to even consider fighting another war on the European mainland, but Hitler's wartime experience taught him an entirely different lesson. Hitler acknowledged, in discussions with his inner circle, that there were times during the war when he had been afraid, but he claimed to have gained control of his emotions after becoming psychologically hardened to the death and destruction he saw around him.[5] Hitler developed a worldview based on his experiences during the war, and came to believe that human beings were engaged in a life or death struggle for finite resources in the natural world, and that individuals sometimes had to die for their race to prosper.[6]

Hitler believed that in such an environment, his primary mission as the leader of Germany was to secure sufficient *Lebensraum* (living space) for the country to become self-sufficient. If Germany could produce enough food to feed her own people, then no one would ever be able to starve the country into submission. Germany would be invulnerable to economic sanctions, and the British government would no longer be able to use a naval blockade as a weapon of war.

Hitler may have tasked his military commanders with planning an invasion of Poland, but the *Wehrmacht* was not going to be the only organisation operating on Polish territory in late 1939. Heinrich Himmler, the head of the SS *(Schutzstaffeln)*, had been appointed Chief of the German Police in June 1936. Himmler had reorganised the German police force so that it was divided into two sections, the *Orpo (Ordnungspolizei)* and the *Sipo (Sicherheitspolizei)*. The *Sipo* was composed of two further components, the *Kripo (Kriminalpolizei)* and the *Gestapo (Geheime Staatspolizei)*. Reinhard Heydrich, who was already in command of the SD *(Sicherheitsdienst)*, the intelligence agency of the SS, was given command of the *Sipo* as well.[7]

In May 1939, Heydrich was tasked with setting up special military units known as *Einsatzgruppen*.[8] These units were to work with the German military to secure the areas between the German border and the front lines.[9] Heydrich was able to select candidates for the *Einsatzgruppen* not just from the SS and the SD, but also from the *Kripo* and the *Gestapo*.[10] According to the historian Alexander Rossino, a meeting took place on 18th August 1939 which was attended by Heydrich and several of his *Einsatzgruppen* men, including *SS-Brigadeführer* Dr. Lothar Beutel of *Einsatzgruppe* IV and his aide Dr. Ernst Gerke.[11] At this meeting, Heydrich spoke about atrocities that were being perpetrated against ethnic Germans in Poland, then explained that the *Einsatzgruppen* would be responsible for dealing with anyone who committed such crimes against Poland's ethnic German population, as well as partisans and saboteurs.[12] The names of some 61,000 Poles who had been targeted by the Nazis was distributed to the *Einsatzgruppen* commanders in the *Sonderfandungsbuch* (special prosecution book.) The compilation of this list had been a collaborative effort involving several German organisations, among them the *Sipo* and the *Abwehr*, the German military intelligence service.[13]

On 1st September 1939, when the invasion began, the German army was divided into *Heeresgruppe Nord* (Army Group North) under the command of Colonel General Fedor von Bock, and *Heeresgruppe Süd*, (Army Group South) which was commanded by Colonel General Gerd von Rundstedt.[14] In the south, the 14th Army would invade from Slovakia, the 10th Army would invade from the south-west and head north-east towards Warsaw, and the 8th Army would invade from the west and head towards Lódź.[15] In East Prussia, the 3rd Army under Lieutenant General Georg von Küchler would head directly south towards Warsaw, and in the north of Germany, the 4th Army under the command of Lieutenant General Günther von Kluge was tasked with taking control of the corridor between north-east Germany and East Prussia.[16]

Einsatzgruppe IV had been assigned to support the 4th Army,[17] and within days, they were fighting in the city of Bydgoszcz alongside the regular military forces. The Polish militia in the city surrendered on 5th September, but German troops continued to be attacked by armed locals.[18] When Hitler learned that armed Polish citizens were resisting German rule, *Einsatzgruppe* IV was ordered to carry out a reprisal action.[19] On 10th September, *Einsatzgruppe* IV, led by *Sturmbannführer* Helmut Bischoff, pacified the *Schwedenhöhe* district of Bydgoszcz. The German soldiers entered the residents' houses and, after shooting between 50 and 60 people where they stood, they rounded up approximately 900 prisoners.[20] Anyone who was suspected of harming ethnic Germans or whose name was found in the *Sonderfahndungsbuch* was separated from the other prisoners. Dr. Beutel and *SS-Sturmbannführer* Hammer, the leader of *Einsatzkommando* 2/IV, conferred with the military commander in charge of security, Lieutenant General Walter Braemer, to decide what should be done with the prisoners. Beutel and Braemer agreed that they be liquidated.[21] Over the next two days, Hammer and his men took approximately 120 people into the forest beside Bydgoszcz and shot them beside an anti-tank ditch.[22]

The historian Richard Evans, in the final part of his trilogy on the Third Reich, provides a translation of a German soldier's account of the invasion of Poland. The soldier asserts that his unit set fire to individual houses, and sometimes entire villages, as a matter of course.[23] In his history of the second world war, Martin Gilbert describes an incident that occurred on 6th September near the town of Mrocza, in which Polish officers were shot after they had surrendered, and enlisted prisoners-of-war were locked inside a wooden hut and burned to death.[24] In Rossino's account of the Polish campaign, he describes an incident that took place near Ciepelów on 9th September 1939. A Colonel in the 15th Motorized Infantry Regiment, who was angry because he had lost 14 men in a firefight, ordered his soldiers to strip approximately 300 prisoners of war of their uniforms so they looked like partisans. The POWs were then machine gunned to death and left in a ditch at the side of the road.[25]

The German war machine had been set in motion and from the first days of the war, the Poles were dehumanised and treated with the utmost cruelty by Heydrich's *Einsatzgruppen* and at least some of the soldiers of the German Army. On 7th October, the situation for the Poles worsened, if that was possible, when Heinrich Himmler was appointed Reich Commissioner for the Strengthening of German Nationality.[26] At the Nuremberg Trials, Himmler was quoted as saying that the purpose of establishing the SS had been "to create an order which will spread the idea of Nordic blood so far that we will attract all Nordic blood in the world, take away the blood from our adversaries, absorb it so that never again - looking at it from the viewpoint of the grand Policy – will Nordic Germanic blood in great quantities and to an extent worth mentioning fight against us. We must get it and the others cannot have it."[27]

The Soviets had agreed to let ethnic Germans from the Baltic States move to the territory now occupied by Germany. Himmler was now responsible for making sure the lives of these German colonists would not be tainted by the influence of lesser races.[28] The occupied territory was divided into new districts. The *Reichsgau* of Danzig-West Prussia was created in what had been the Polish corridor. The *Reichsgau* of Posen was south of Danzig-West Prussia, reaching east to just beyond the city of Lódź. These two districts were formally incorporated into the Reich on 26th October 1939.[29] The remainder of the occupied territory, from Warsaw in the north to the river Bug in the east,[30] was known as the General Government.[31] This was used by the Germans as a dumping ground for people who could have no place in the new Germany that was now being created.[32] Tens of thousands of people were dispossessed and transported to the General Government during the first winter of occupation in 1939-1940. Many people died in freezing railway carriages that were left to stand on side tracks, sometimes for days at a time.[33] This was not something that would have troubled Himmler, who told a group of SS men on 4th October 1943, "We must be honest, decent, loyal and comradely to members of our own blood and to nobody else. What happens to a Russian, to a Czech, does not interest me in the slightest. . . . Whether nations live in prosperity or starve to death interests me only in so far as we need them as slaves for our culture; otherwise, it is of no interest to me."[34]

The actions of the German forces in western Poland were widely reported in the British press. On 30th November, General Sikorski, the head of the Polish government in exile, was quoted in the Nottingham Journal as saying:

> The unrestrained violence with which the Germans made war on Poland in September aroused the indignation of the civilised world. Never had anyone acted with such savagery towards a disarmed people against whom guns, machine guns, incendiary bombs and bombs were used. One would have thought that on the day when the Germans imposed their yoke on Poland they would be glutted with blood and cruelty. Far from it.
>
> From every part of occupied Poland where the German authorities speak so freely of honour and justice and where the Gestapo and the storm troopers reign, reports reach us which fill us with horror.
>
> Never a day passes, whether in Warsaw, Gdynia, Bydgoszcz, Poznan, Katowice or Cracow, that individual or mass executions do not take place, that people are not expelled from their homes and their property pillaged or confiscated, and that individuals are not

brutalised so that the Germans well merit the name of 'butchers' which has been given them.

Not within memory, never in the worst moment of the most horrible wars have such atrocities been committed as are occurring daily in Poland."[35]

The records in the National Archives for 16th November 1939 show that Sikorski told Halifax that some people were being forced to evacuate their homes at 24 hours' notice so that incoming Germans could take over their properties, some were being forced to take refuge in marshes and forests and many of the leading Poles had simply been shot.[36]

The British government may have been aware of what was happening in the occupied territory, but they did nothing to help the Polish people. When Chamberlain declared war on Germany on 3rd September 1939, Arthur Harris, the man who would eventually lead the bombing war against Germany, was in a friend's house in Norfolk. They listened as Chamberlain delivered an "uninspired and uninspiring broadcast; when he announced that we were now at war with Germany he was about as stirring as a schoolmaster confirming the fact that mumps had broken out in his prep. school."[37]

Chamberlain attended a meeting of the War Cabinet at 5 p.m. that evening so that he could decide upon an appropriate course of action, and according to the records held in the National Archives, "Consideration was given to the question whether we should drop propaganda leaflets over Germany. It was believed that these leaflets would have an important effect on German public opinion." The War Cabinet agreed that this project should commence that night. It was believed that "the dropping of leaflets might well have its maximum effect during the first few hours of war."[38]

The RAF were sent out to drop leaflets over Hamburg, Bremen and the Ruhr on 3rd September.[39] The bombers went back to Germany twice more that week, on 4th and 7th September.[40] At a further meeting of the War Cabinet on Friday 8th September, "a discussion took place as to whether the dropping of leaflets should be continued." Apparently, "there was good reason to believe that the German authorities feared the effect of our propaganda, and the fact that our aircraft were able to fly with impunity all over the North-West of Germany would have a depressing effect on the morale of the German people." It was therefore agreed that "the distribution of propaganda leaflets by the Royal Air Force was a viable operation which should be repeated from time to time as and when opportunity offered."[41]

Although it was initially thought that dropping leaflets for German citizens to read "might well have its maximum effect during the first few hours of war," it was still considered "a viable operation" by the British almost five months later. At a War Cabinet meeting on 29th January 1940, Halifax, now the Foreign Secretary, "made a statement regarding Nazi views on the relative potentialities of Allied leaflet and broadcast propaganda."[42] Halifax read to the other members of the War Cabinet from a report "which he had received from a secret source." The author of the report stated that "any kind of printed matter has an attraction for the average German. The German is a born book-worm and has a natural penchant for reading." A possible defence for any book-worms who may have found themselves in trouble with the German authorities after reading a British leaflet was provided in the report: "If a man finds a piece of printed paper on the ground he may think it is an advertisement for liver pills, and if he is found reading it he cannot easily be convicted of a deliberate act." Halifax did not provide any examples of anyone successfully employing this form of defence, although if the author of the report was to be believed, it was likely that German citizens who were "somewhat tired of the spoken word" and could not resist reading British propaganda leaflets could very well find themselves in trouble with the authorities, for the report noted that "the Gestapo hates leaflets."[43]

The RAF was sent to Wilhelmshaven to carry out an actual bombing raid on German ships tied up at the port, but the raid was not a success. When they returned the following day, more damage was done to the pocket battleship *Admiral Scheer* by one of the British planes crashing into it than by any of their bombs actually hitting their target.[44] An attempt was made to blockade Germany, but the Nazis had already signed trade deals with the Soviet Union, so this was ineffective. On 17th September 1939, the Soviet Union went beyond providing supplies to Germany and invaded Poland themselves, attacking their neighbour from Byelorussia in the north-east and Ukraine in the south-east.[45] The Poles were unable to resist a second invasion, and the Red Army soon overran the territory that had been allocated to the Soviet Union under the terms of the Nazi-Soviet Pact. Ivan Maisky, the Soviet Ambassador to Great Britain, wrote in his diary on 18th September, "What will be the response to our actions in England? – I expect a note of protest, an angry speech in Parliament by the prime minister, and campaigns in the press, but nothing more."[46]

When Chamberlain finally issued a written copy of his war guarantee to Poland the day after the Nazi-Soviet Pact was signed, he had included a secret protocol, which said that the British government was only obliged to assist Poland in the event of German aggression. Chamberlain made no mention of this when he spoke in the House of Commons on 20th September:

> On 17th September, an event occurred which has inevitably had a decisive effect upon the war on the Eastern Front. On the morning of 17th September Russian troops crossed the Polish frontier at points along its whole length and advanced into Poland. . . . The effects of the Russian invasion upon the hard-pressed Poles have naturally been very serious. Caught between two vast armies, and with their communications to the South cut off, the Polish forces are still continuing their courageous resistance. . . . It is still too early to pronounce any final verdict on the motives or consequences of the Russian action. For the unhappy victim of this cynical attack the result has been a tragedy of the grimmest character. The world which has watched the vain struggle of the Polish nation against overwhelming odds with profound pity and sympathy admires their valour which even now refuses to admit defeat.[47]

Chamberlain may have uttered a few descriptive words about the Soviet invasion of Poland, but all that he had done was fulfil Maisky's expectations. The truth is, the British government failed to provide any meaningful support or assistance to Poland in September 1939, despite Poland being invaded not once, but twice.

On 27th September 1939, Ribbentrop flew back to Moscow to reinforce the relationship with the Soviets by signing a further agreement, the Boundary and Friendship Treaty.[48] Under the terms of this agreement, the Nazis and Soviets agreed to collaborate to prevent the Polish state from ever being re-established and to move the border between Nazi and Soviet occupied territory to the east, so that it ran along the river Bug. The Soviets took Lithuania as compensation for the loss of territory.[49] One of the first things the Soviets did to transform the territory they controlled was have sham elections, in which only their own approved candidates ran for office. Once in power, their political puppets asked for the occupied territory to be incorporated into the Soviet Union. On 28th November, everyone in what used to be the eastern part of Poland officially became a citizen of the Soviet Union, and choosing any other form of government was no longer possible.[50] With that political escape route closed off, the Soviets began to deconstruct Polish society. The Polish currency was devalued by setting the exchange rate at one-to-one. People's savings became worthless overnight, and the concept of owning their own property was also destroyed by the Soviets. Their soldiers walked into people's homes and took them over, then stole their belongings.[51] Leaflets had been distributed by the advancing Soviets calling on working people to turn against landowners and the wealthy. In his diary entry for 27th September, Maisky described a meeting with Halifax:

At Halifax's request, I gave a brief description of Polish landownership and the poverty and exploitation of the Polish, Ukrainian and Belorussian peasantry.

'And what do you do with the landlords' land?'

'It is confiscated without exception and distributed among the peasants.'

Halifax shook his hand [*sic*] and uttered gloomily: '*A grim tale*'.

His landlord's heart couldn't bear it.[52]

Anyone in a position to resist the Soviet occupation was targeted for arrest or deportation. In December 1939, Lavrenty Beria, the head of the NKVD (*Narodny Komissariat Vnutrennikh Del*), the Soviet secret police, wrote to Stalin and was given approval to carry out a series of deportations.[53] The first of these deportations took place in the early hours of 11th February 1940. Thousands of people were forced to leave their homes in the middle of the night. They were taken to the nearest railway station, put aboard freight cars, and taken to work camps in the farthest reaches of the Soviet Union.[54]

On 19th September 1939, Beria had set up an administrative department within the NKVD to deal with the prisoners of war that were being captured during the invasion of Poland. This department was commanded by Major Pyotr Soprunenko.[55] In February 1940, Soprunenko sent Beria proposals for dealing with the POWs being held in Soviet camps. Beria sent these proposals up his chain of command, and both Molotov and Stalin signed off on them.[56] When the Soviet armed forces had invaded Poland, in accordance with the secret protocol of the Nazi-Soviet pact, approximately 125,400 prisoners had been taken. Some 42,500 of these prisoners of war were of Ukrainian or Belorussian ethnic origin, and they were released and allowed to go back home. The same number of POWS had lived in the west of the country before the war, and they were handed over to the Nazis. Some 25,000 of the POWs were used as labourers on a road being built in Ukraine, from Novohrad-Volinsky to Lviv. The prison camps at Starobilsk, Ostashkov and Kozelsk were used to hold state and military officials who had been captured during the invasion, as well as military officers and policemen. NKVD agents interrogated these prisoners to establish their political and moral standing in the eyes of the Soviet government. Any individuals who continued to display patriotic or religious beliefs, which indicated to the NKVD that they would never give their allegiance to the Soviet state, were sentenced to death.[57]

At Starobilsk and Ostashkov, the condemned prisoners of war were executed using the same technique. A prisoner's name would be checked off a list, then he would be taken into a room where two NKVD agents grabbed him by the arms. The executioner would approach the prisoner from behind and, using a pistol, shoot a bullet into the base of his neck.[58] The prisoners held in the camp at Kozelsk were executed after they were taken to the forest at Katyn, rather than being shot first, then taken to the burial site on the back of a lorry.[59] According to figures uncovered in the Soviet archives by the researcher Eugenia Maresch, 15,131 prisoners of war from the Kozelsk, Ostahkov and Starobilsk camps, and approximately 7,000 prisoners from other camps,[60] were executed by the NKVD in April and May 1940.[61]

The family members of the victims were then targeted for deportation by the NKVD. All these people were guilty of was being related to the prisoners of war who had been eliminated by agents of the Soviet state. The mothers, children and other relatives of the people buried in the Katyn forest were taken from their homes and transported against their will to collective farms spread throughout the Soviet Union, from Kazakhstan to Siberia. The British government could not claim to be ignorant of this. On 6th April, an article from Reuters was printed in newspapers throughout Britain. According to the article, a Polish communique had been issued stating that "the Russians are carrying out a reign of death and terror in Soviet-occupied Poland." It was asserted that hundreds of people were being arrested and tortured by the Soviet authorities every day. "Whole families were awakened in the middle of the night and forcibly taken to the nearest railway station where they are crowded into cattle trucks and driven into the interior of Russia," it was reported. "Over 200,000 have been deported."[62]

If you are abducted by agents of the state and abandoned in the middle of nowhere with nothing but the clothes on your back, then it does not matter if those agents were wearing a swastika or a red star on their uniform. Your life is over, and the state took it. The fundamental nature of a society can be discerned not by listening to the ideological statements made by its politicians, but by considering the limits placed on the negative liberty of its citizens and the ruthlessness by which those limits are enforced by agents of the state. In this regard, there was very little difference between the National Socialist and the Soviet regimes.

On 3rd April 1939, Churchill had said in the House of Commons that issuing a guarantee to Poland without any military allies in the region to do the heavy lifting had left the British government "in no-man's Land under fire of both trench lines and without the shelter of either." If the *Wehrmacht* was ever going to be defeated, then the Soviet Union would have to join what Churchill called a "Grand Alliance" of countries that would fight against Nazi Germany.[63] When Chamberlain issued a hard copy of his guarantee to Poland on 25th August 1939, he made sure that it would only apply in the event of a German invasion. This meant the British government was under no obligation to respond militarily when the Soviet Union invaded Poland on

17th September. Since Britain and the Soviet Union were not at war, the Soviets could still become part of Churchill's "Grand Alliance" at some point in the future. The problems that this would bring were acknowledged by some people within the British government. The head of the British Military Mission to Moscow, Lieutenant General Noel Mason MacFarlane, said in a report sent to London on 7th August 1941 that

> I am frankly terribly worried about the Russo-Polish business. I see innumerable snags ahead. . . .
>
> We are going to find ourselves being pulled in as mediators in a situation which holds promise of developing in the most awkward way. I only hope the business won't sow a lot of discord.
>
> What is going to happen when the Poles find out the number of Poles who have been 'lost' since 1939 is clearly an awkward one to answer. What will the British Press want to say when they find out? We've got to keep out of the affair as much as we can, and when we do intervene we must remember that Russia can help us to beat Hitler, and not Poland.[64]

The fate of Poland, or any other nation state for that matter, was of secondary importance to the main problem facing the British government. An alliance with the Soviet Union was a necessary condition of Britain ending up on the winning side at the end of the war against Germany. As the war progressed, the decisions made by the British government showed just how far they would go to secure Soviet participation in the tripartite military alliance that would eventually bring Nazi Germany down.

5 Churchill Becomes Prime Minister

The phoney war ended on the morning of 10th May 1940, when Germany invaded western Europe. A total of 136 divisions advanced into Belgium and Holland, 2,500 German aircraft attacked airfields in Belgium, Holland, France and Luxembourg, and 16,000 airborne troops, led by General Kurt Student, parachuted into Rotterdam, Leiden and The Hague.[1] On the same day, Chamberlain's term as Prime Minister came to an end, and Winston Churchill was invited to Buckingham Palace to meet privately with the King. According to Churchill's record of the encounter,

> His Majesty received me most graciously and bade me sit down. He looked at me searchingly and quizzically for some moments, and then said, "I suppose you don't know why I have sent for you?" Adopting his mood, I replied, "Sir, I simply couldn't imagine why." He laughed and said, "I want to ask you to form a Government." I said I would certainly do so.[2]

Churchill had finally become Prime Minister, at the age of 65.[3] There were some who doubted whether Churchill could lead the country successfully[4] but as we shall see, Churchill accepted the responsibilities that came with the office of Prime Minister, and he did what was necessary to defeat Nazi Germany.

On the mainland, the British Expeditionary Force responded to the German invasion by advancing into Belgium to meet the oncoming threat. The French 7th Army, which was on the left flank of the BEF, advanced to Breda in Holland, and the BEF moved forward to the river Dyle, just east of Brussels, with the French 1st Army on their right flank.[5]

As the British and French forces advanced to meet Army Group B in the north, Colonel General Gerd von Rundstedt's Army Group A, consisting of 37 infantry divisions and 7 Panzer divisions,[6] entered French territory through the Ardennes forest.[7] By selecting this as their *Schwerpunkt* (point of attack) the Germans had given themselves an opportunity to breach the French defences at a lightly defended point, then use their mobile armoured forces to drive forward and do what had not been possible in the first world war, and take the enemy in the rear. On 11th May, Guderian's 1st Panzer Division broke through the French defences where the 11th *Cuirassier* (Dragon) Regiment and the 60th Reconnaissance Battalion met, and together with the 2nd Panzer Division, forced the surrender of the French garrison at Neufchâteau.[8] Guderian headed towards the Meuse, and made use of two crossing points over the Semois to get there before the French established their defences.[9] On 13th May, Major General Erwin Rommel's 7th Panzer division, which was part of Lieutenant General Hermann Hoth's XV Motorised Corps, crossed the Meuse at Dinant, and Guderian's Panzers crossed at Sedan.[10] The Germans intended to push forward, with their tanks in the vanguard, then swing north and trap the BEF and the French armies with the sea at their backs.[11]

On 16th May, General Billotte of the French army instructed the BEF to withdraw to the Escaut river,[12] which they did over the following two days.[13] Lord Gort, the Commander-in-Chief of the BEF,[14] recognised that the German forces could advance and cut the BEF off from the rest of the French army, and he ordered General Pownall, his Chief of Staff,[15] to contact the War Office.[16] The records of a War Cabinet meeting held on 19th May 1940 show that General Pownall had "rung up the War Office and said that if the gap on the right of the BEF widened, the Commander-in-Chief had it in mind to withdraw towards Dunkerque, resting his right on the canal running through St. Omer, and to fight it out there."[17]

The Chief of the Imperial General Staff at that time was General "Tiny" Ironside. He told Pownall that "this proposal could not be accepted at all."[18] As the records held in the National Archives show, Ironside thought that if the operation was attempted, then "we could certainly never evacuate the force complete."[19] Churchill agreed: "In such a position the British Expeditionary Force would be closely invested in a bomb-trap, and its total loss would be only a matter of time."[20]

The War Cabinet agreed that the best course of action at that time was for the BEF to head south-west, towards Arras and then Amiens.[21] The British fought on, but the writing was on the wall. By 18th May, Rommel's 7th Panzer Division had reached Cambrai,[22] where they fought alongside the SS Death's Head Division,[23] and Guderian's armoured forces had reached St. Quentin.[24] On 21st May, the enemy reached the French coast at the mouth of the Somme.[25] In just eleven days, the *Wehrmacht* had cut the Allied forces in two.

Lord Gort gave the order to evacuate the BEF from France on 26th May.[26] Churchill may initially have been pessimistic about the operation's prospects of success, but in the event, most of the troops of the BEF were successfully evacuated through Dunkirk and across the English Channel.

Not all the British troops managed to escape from the French mainland. In early May, the 51st (Highland) Division, which included the 1st and 5th Battalions of the Gordon Highlanders, had been sent to help defend the Maginot Line.[27] The Scots had been cut off from the rest of the BEF after the German advance through the Ardennes, and they had been sent to assist the French 2nd Army fight the German advance along the Somme.[28] In the early hours of 4th June, the French launched a counterattack, and although the 1st Battalion Gordon Highlanders acquitted themselves well and achieved their assigned military objectives, the French armour was largely destroyed and the counterattack failed.[29]

The Germans renewed their attack the following day.[30] The British and French forces planned to withdraw towards Le Havre on the French coast[31] but the German forces managed to close off the road to Le Havre[32] and the harbour at Dieppe was blocked,[33] so the only option left to the Scottish and French troops was to reach St. Valéry-en-Caux and hope that they could be evacuated from there by the Royal Navy.[34] This was not to be. Upon reaching St. Valéry-en-Caux, the Scottish soldiers soon found themselves under fire from German positions on the surrounding cliffs.[35] They had no option but to surrender.[36] Thousands of British and French soldiers, including approximately 1,500 Gordon Highlanders, were forced to march east, away from the coast, into captivity.[37]

On 4th June 1940, less than a month after he became Prime Minister, Winston Churchill stood up in the House of Commons and acknowledged that "what has happened in France and Belgium is a colossal military disaster."[38] The German forces had "swept like a sharp scythe around the right and rear of the Armies of the north,"[39] leaving evacuation as the only option. Although many British and French soldiers had been uplifted from the Dunkirk beaches, the BEF had been equipped with the best military equipment that Britain had, "and that is gone."[40]

Churchill acknowledged that "wars are not won by evacuations."[41] Nevertheless, he argued that the RAF and Royal Navy had done an exceptional job, and this augured well for the future. Winston concluded his speech with some of the most memorable words ever spoken in the English language:

> Even though large tracts of Europe and many old and famous states have fallen or may fall into the grip of the Gestapo and all the odious apparatus of Nazi rule, we shall not flag or fail. We shall go on to the end, we shall fight in France, we shall fight on the seas and oceans, we shall fight with growing confidence and growing strength in the air, we shall defend our island, whatever the cost may be, we shall fight on the beaches, we shall fight on the landing grounds, we shall fight in the fields and in the streets, we shall fight in the hills: we shall never surrender . . .[42]

These were fine words, but if Churchill was going to be a successful wartime leader, then he was going to have to do more than make good speeches. The BEF may have been expelled from France and a lot of military hardware may have been lost, but the Royal Navy was still a powerful force, and it had the potential to destroy any Nazi troop transports attempting a Channel crossing. One of the first things Churchill had to do as Prime Minister was preserve Britain's naval superiority by making sure the French fleet could not be used by Germany.

At a meeting of the War Cabinet on 24th June 1940, Churchill said that "we could not be expected to release ships, aircraft and gold, all of which would be afterwards turned against us by the enemy."[43] During the ensuing discussions, it was considered "a wise move" to repatriate the crews of any French ships currently in a British harbour, and keep the ships tied to the pier for the duration of the war.[44] Any ships in foreign ports would be dealt with in a more robust manner. The War Cabinet discussed how they would prevent these French ships from ever coming under German control: "If necessary, we should not scruple to use force to secure this end."[45]

On 27th June 1940, the War Cabinet discussed what should be done about the French ships at Mers-el-Kébir, the port at Oran, in Algeria.[46] If the *Hood, Nelson, Valiant, Resolution* and the *Ark Royal* set sail for North Africa, then they could arrive at Oran as early as the 3rd July. The British could then demand that the French leave North Africa and set sail for British ports, "demilitarise" their ships under British supervision, or scuttle their ships altogether. Failure to comply would mean that "we should bombard them."[47] As the records in the National Archives show, "The view was expressed that it was most important to take action to ensure that the French Fleet could not be used against us."[48]

Churchill summed up the meeting by saying that he believed that the War Cabinet had approved in principle what would come to be known as Operation Catapult: British ships would sail to Oran and give the French an ultimatum. If the French did not comply, then the British ships would open fire.[49] Churchill may have used bureaucratic language to express himself, but his meaning was clear: We are going to do this. The War Cabinet formally approved the operation, and "invited the First Lord of the Admiralty and the Chief of Naval Staff to arrange for the planning of the operation to be taken in hand at once."[50]

On the morning of 3rd July 1940, Captain Holland, the former British Naval Attaché in Paris,[51] sailed into Mers-el-Kébir aboard the destroyer *Foxhound*, and attempted to contact the French Admiral,[52] Marcel Gensoul.[53] The Admiral waited until the middle of the afternoon before inviting Captain Holland to come aboard the *Dunkerque*.[54] Despite Captain Holland's best efforts, an agreement could not be reached with the French.[55] At 17:25, Holland boarded a motor boat to sail back to the *Foxhound*,[56] and at 17:55, Admiral Sir James Somerville, in charge of the British Fleet, gave the order to open fire.[57] The bombardment lasted for just nine minutes. At

18:04, Admiral Somerville gave the order to cease fire.[58] Several of the French ships had been hit, including the *Dunkerque.*

Admiral Somerville was ordered to return to Oran on 6th July to ensure that the *Dunkerque* was out of action.[59] An air torpedo attack was launched, the target was hit six more times, "and one heavy explosion was heard." The notes of the War Cabinet meeting on 6th July state that "it had not been thought necessary to give warning of this attack."[60]

Niccolo Machiavelli wrote in *The Prince* that "a man who wants to profess goodness in all parts of his life will bring about his own ruin among so many who are not good. Therefore, it is necessary for a prince who wants to maintain his position to learn how not to be good, and to use that whenever he needs to."[61] This is what is known in philosophy as the dirty hands problem. A political leader may find themselves in a situation where they must choose between acting in a way that is considered "not good," when that will avoid a disastrous outcome, and acting in a way that will let them maintain their sense of moral integrity, when that will help to bring that disaster about.

The situation Churchill inherited on 10th May 1940 was a difficult one, but at Mers-el-Kébir, he showed the world that he was a war leader who was not afraid to get his hands dirty. Churchill may have been a magnificent orator who was able to inspire his country, and he may have been able to make hard choices when he had to, but he also knew that Britain could not prevail in a war against Germany without allies.

The attack on the French fleet not only removed the danger of those ships falling into German hands, which would help the British to maintain naval superiority in the English Channel. It also let the Americans see that with Churchill as its wartime leader, the British government would go to any lengths to see Nazi Germany defeated.

6 The United States

Churchill may have understood that he needed to recruit a powerful ally in the war against Nazi Germany, but persuading the President of the United States to become that ally would prove difficult. In February 1940, Franklin Roosevelt sent Sumner Welles, his undersecretary of state, on a fact-finding mission to Europe. At a press conference on 9th February 1940, Roosevelt stated that "this visit is solely for the purpose of advising the President and the Secretary of State as to present conditions in Europe."[1] Welles visited Italy, France, Germany and Great Britain and spoke to numerous prominent people, including Churchill, who at that time was First Lord of the Admiralty. This is how Welles described meeting Churchill on 12th March 1940:

> I called on Mr. Winston Churchill at the Admiralty at 5 P.M. When I was shown into his office Mr. Churchill was sitting in front of the fire, smoking a 24-inch cigar, and drinking a whisky and soda. It was quite obvious that he had consumed a good many whiskeys before I arrived.[2]

If Churchill wanted to make a good impression on the President's man, this may not have been the best way to go about it. Welles did say that by the end of their meeting, Churchill had become "quite sober."[3] Welles also stated that the War Maps Room at the Admiralty, which Churchill showed him, was "one of the most impressive things I have seen."[4] Churchill showed that he had a thorough knowledge of Britain's maritime affairs, and Welles acknowledged the efficacy of Britain's efforts to protect their merchant ships, but the encounter could hardly be described as auspicious.

Roosevelt's correspondence with Churchill during the war years had begun in September 1939, after Churchill had been reinstated as First Lord of the Admiralty. Roosevelt had seen an opportunity to establish communications with a member of the British government who was not associated with the failed policy of appeasement, so he sent Churchill a congratulatory telegram.[5] After Churchill became Prime Minister in May 1940, his personal correspondence with Roosevelt became one of the most important channels of communication between the two governments, and Churchill used it as part of the British strategy to bring the United States into the war.[6] On 15th May, as the German forces were advancing into French territory and it was becoming clear that the BEF would be forced back to the sea, Churchill wrote directly to Roosevelt and informed him that

> the enemy have a marked preponderance in the air, and their new technique is making a deep impression upon the French. . . . If necessary, we shall continue the war alone, and we are not afraid of that.
>
> But I trust you realise, Mr. President, that the voice and force of the United States may count for nothing if they are withheld too long. You may have a completely subjugated Nazified Europe established with astonishing swiftness, and the weight may be more than we can bear. All I ask now is that you should proclaim non-belligerency, which would mean that you would help us with everything, short of actually engaging armed forces.[7]

The British government had always understood that Britain could not defeat Germany without support from America and the Soviet Union. As we have seen, the British Chiefs of Staff produced a memo entitled "Planning for a war with Germany" on 15th February 1937, two full years before Chamberlain gave his guarantee to Poland, which laid out the British strategy for ending up on the winning side in such a conflict.[8] The Chiefs of Staff had concluded that Britain would have to fight a long war by resisting an initial attack by the enemy, then using Britain's economic and industrial base to build up military resources over time until a counterattack could be launched. It was noted that material assistance from the United States and the intervention of the Soviet Union "would go far toward making the Allied counter-offensive possible."[9]

On 25th May 1940, ten days after Churchill sent his telegram to Roosevelt, the War Cabinet met to discuss a report prepared by the Chiefs of Staff, entitled "British Strategy In A Certain Eventuality." The object of this report was to "investigate the means whereby we could continue to fight single-handed if French resistance were to collapse completely, involving the loss of a substantial proportion of the British Expeditionary Force, and the French government were to make terms with Germany."[10] The Chiefs of Staff had based their findings on the assumption that the "United States of America is willing to give us full economic and financial support, without which we do not think we could continue the war with any chance of success."

It was asserted that the British ability to resist an air offensive would depend on "whether our fighter defences will be able to reduce the scale of attack to reasonable bounds." Consequently, it was recommended that "we must concentrate our energies primarily on the production of fighter aircraft and crews, and the defence of those factories essential to fighter production should have priority. At the same time it is clear that we cannot afford to neglect our bomber force or to expend it on operations that are not of first importance." This report is significant because it clearly states, almost two years before Arthur Harris took over at Bomber Command, that "Germany might still be defeated by economic pressure, by a combination of air attack on economic objectives in Germany and on German morale . . ." In an appendix to their report, the Chiefs of Staff again stated that they had assumed that "we could count on the full economic and financial support of the United States of America," before adding the rather telling phrase: "possibly extending to active participation on our side."[11]

When he wrote to Roosevelt on 15th May, Churchill may have portrayed the situation in a way that made it appear critical, but the British had enough resources in the air to defend themselves against a German attack. The previous British governments, under Stanley Baldwin and Neville Chamberlain,[12] had authorised a series of expansion programmes for the RAF, and ever-increasing percentages of the defence budget had been allocated to the air service.[13] Baldwin had appointed Sir Thomas Inskip as Minister for the Co-ordination of Defence, and Inskip had agreed with Air Chief Marshal Hugh Dowding, who had been put in charge of Fighter Command in July 1934. Dowding believed that fighters were far more important to the defence of Britain than the deterrent threat of retaliatory bomber raids.[14] A fighters-first air defence policy suited Chamberlain, since he was reluctant to engage in an airborne war of attrition in which civilians would be targeted.[15]

On 28th March 1938, the Cabinet discussed the latest expansion programme, known as Scheme L, which would provide the RAF with a front-line strength of 1,352 bombers and 608 fighters by the end of March 1940. The programme would need a total of 12,000 aircraft to be built in the next two years. The newly knighted Sir Charles Bruce-Gardner had spoken with the owners of the different businesses that made up the British aircraft industry. He estimated that approximately 4,000 aircraft could be produced in the next twelve months and a further 8,000 could be built by 31st March 1940. Bruce-Gardner concluded that "the plan for securing the first 2 years of Scheme L by 31st March, 1940, ought to be substantially achieved" and that this could be done without putting undue strain on Britain's industrial infrastructure, although the construction of several shadow factories throughout the UK had been planned "for the purpose of increasing the war potential" should this become necessary. Bruce-Gardner made a point of informing the Cabinet that his conclusions had been reached "exclusive of the possibility of American purchases of special types which it had been thought wiser to treat, for the purposes of estimate, as a contingent reserve."[16]

In April 1938, the British government had sent a mission to the United States to buy American aeroplanes. This was led by Group Captain Weir, the brother of Lord Weir, who was the industrial advisor to the Air

Ministry. He was accompanied by Sir Henry Self, who would go on to lead the British Air Commission in America during the war,[17] and Group Captain Arthur Harris, who had been in command of No. 4 Bomber Group in Yorkshire.[18]

After touring the American plants, the mission rejected the Boeing B-17 bomber and the Consolidated "Catalina" amphibious patrol bomber, and placed orders instead for 200 NA-16 Harvard I single engine, low wing training aircraft from North American Aviation and 200 Lockheed Hudsons, with an option to buy 50 more of the latter.[19] Harris wrote later that

> my reason for giving the order for Lockheed Hudsons was not only that I was much impressed with the aircraft itself and thought it highly suitable for reconnaissance work; it was also that I was immensely struck by the ability and energy of the comparative youngsters who were running this then very small factory, and I could see they obviously knew their business from A to Z.[20]

Although the British purchases from America only constituted one thirtieth of the total amount of aircraft that would be produced as part of Scheme L, the Hudson contract alone had cost the country $25 million.[21] The purchases from North American Aviation and Lockheed were discussed at a Cabinet meeting on 25th May. Halifax argued that "the idea of purchasing American machines with its implication that America was behind us had had a useful effect in Germany. There would be a certain contrary effect if we dropped the proposal."[22] The limited purchases from American companies in 1938 showed that the government at that time had confidence in Britain's own aircraft industry. However, the political benefit of buying aircraft from the United States was undeniable. On 12th November, then Group Captain John Slessor wrote in a paper for the Air Ministry that

> the recent Air Mission has shown that it is easy to exaggerate the existing capacity of the US aircraft industry to provide immediate assistance to British air rearmament . . . [but] to decry the value of American support merely on the grounds that they cannot at present supply us with aircraft in sufficient quantities or of adequate quality, is obviously to take a ludicrously short view.[23]

The historian Gavin Bailey has argued in his book, *Arsenal of Democracy*, that the British were paying a lot of money for American planes and declaring themselves to be in a military crisis to make sure they got them as quickly as possible, in the hope that they would benefit from being customers of the United States during a long war.[24] On 20th May 1940, Churchill wrote to Roosevelt again:

> Though we have taken heavy toll of the enemy in the air and are clawing down two or three to one of their planes, they still have a formidable numerical superiority. Our most vital need is, therefore the delivery at the earliest possible date of the largest possible number of Curtiss P.40 fighters, now in course of delivery to your Army.[25]

On 24th May, a telegram sent by Arthur Purvis, the director general of the British Purchasing Commission, to Jean Monnet, who was working with Purvis to co-ordinate the war effort of Britain and France, contained an assessment of American aircraft at that time:

> 1. Our experts have studied very carefully aircraft types, particularly fighters now in service with United States Army or on order for United States Navy.
>
> 2. Regarding types now in service it is unanimous opinion of British and French experts that nothing is suitable for European combat conditions. Types are obsolete and this fact is acknowledged by Army itself. No planes are armoured, no self-sealing tanks, and insufficient fire power. Only planes which could be of some value in Europe are a score of troop carrier planes.[26]

In the next paragraph of that same document, it was stated that the United States Army had ordered 524 P-40 fighters, but the British had "obtained release of 324 Curtiss P.40 delivery of which will begin within two or three months."[27] If the British government believed that American fighters were not fit for purpose at that time, then why were they paying for those P-40s, and why was Churchill pressing Roosevelt to release them as soon as possible? The Chiefs of Staff had already laid out the overall strategy that Britain would have to employ in a war with Germany: First, resist an initial attack. Britain was always going to be reliant on its own resources to complete this stage of the plan, because the American fighters available at that time were not fit for purpose, and it was simply too late to get enough of these sub-standard P-40s built in the United States then shipped over to the UK and adapted for use in the European theatre to make a difference.

However, the British government had to take into account the fact that American assistance would be necessary if the final stage of the plan laid out by the Chiefs of Staff in 1937, which was to launch an Allied (not British) counter-offensive at some point, was ever going to be carried out. The British used the fact that they were under pressure to their advantage and claimed that the military situation was so critical that the Americans had to join in the war effort, or there could be dire consequences. In the second part of his telegram of 20th May, Churchill said,

> Our position is, whatever happens, to fight on to the end in this island, and, provided we can get the help for which we ask, we hope to run them very close in the air battles in view of individual superiority. Members of the present Administration would go down during this process should it result adversely, but in no conceivable circumstances will we consent to surrender. If members of the present Administration were finished and others came in to parley amid the ruins, you must not be blind to the fact that the sole remaining bargaining counter with Germany would be the Fleet, and if this country was left by the United States to its fate no one would have the right to blame those then responsible if they made the best terms they could for the surviving inhabitants. Excuse me, Mr. President, [for] putting this nightmare bluntly. Evidently I could not answer for my successors, who in utter despair and helplessness might well have to accommodate themselves to the German will. However, there is happily no need at present to dwell upon such ideas. Once more thanking you for your goodwill . . .[28]

Churchill not only gave Roosevelt the impression that things might turn out badly for Great Britain, but by raising the possibility of the Royal Navy ending up in the hands of the Nazis, he had made it seem that the United States, and indeed the whole world, could be in danger as well. Once he had painted this rather alarming picture for the President, he assured him that there was no need to dwell on these possibilities. After all, none of this would happen if the United States joined in the war against Nazi Germany. Churchill's telegrams in late May 1940 can be seen as part of an overall strategy that sought to tap into the industrial potential of the United States as soon as possible, so that the military hardware necessary to win the war would be available in the future.[29]

However, in the summer of 1940, Britain was relying almost entirely on her own resources. The British government had initiated a series of expansion schemes that would see the RAF almost reach numerical parity with the *Luftwaffe* by the end of 1939,[30] but the British aircraft industry had not simply worked to increase the production figures of existing models. The development of new types of aircraft had been prioritised.[31] As the Battle of

Britain loomed ever closer, this meant that Fighter Command would have a qualitative advantage over the enemy that would prove to be decisive.

One of the unsung heroes of the second world war was the engineer R. J. Mitchell, who had won the Schneider Trophy three years in a row with his S5 and S6 racing seaplanes, beating the Italians and Americans so that the trophy would reside permanently in the UK.[32] Mitchell had undergone surgery for cancer in 1933, and knew there was a chance the disease could return in the next few years. He had taken a holiday in Europe after his surgery and had spoken with some German pilots, which had convinced him that Germany was gearing up for a war. Mitchell decided to do everything in his power to provide his country with a new aeroplane.[33]

When the Air Ministry issued specification F10/35 for a new single engine fighter,[34] Mitchell's experience of competing at the Schneider Trophy helped him to design and build a new high speed fighter at the Supermarine plant in Southampton.[35] Named after the daughter of Sir Robert McLean, the chairman of Vickers, the new aeroplane was to be called the Spitfire.[36] The test flights were promising, and on 6th June 1936, the Air Ministry placed an order with Supermarine for 310 of the new fighters. On the same day, a contract was signed for the delivery of 600 Hawker Hurricanes.[37]

On 17th May 1940, three days before he sent his telegram to Roosevelt asking for American Curtiss P-40s, Churchill had put his old acquaintance Beaverbrook in charge of the Ministry of Aircraft Production,[38] and the Canadian millionaire had set about increasing the number of Spitfires and Hurricanes available to Fighter Command with the "vital and vibrant energy" ascribed to him by his sponsor.[39]

Beaverbrook immediately limited all production to five models – the Spitfire and Hurricane fighters, and the Blenheim, Whitley and Hampden bombers.[40] Managers throughout the industry were replaced with people Beaverbrook knew personally, and employees around the country were made to work seven days a week. Inevitably, the rate of production throughout the industry increased and at the end of June, Fighter Command had over 600 aircraft available.[41] Churchill had to get his country ready for the upcoming conflict as a matter of urgency, and he could not wait for American military hardware to make its way across the Atlantic, then expend considerable time and effort trying to adapt it all to suit the conditions of modern warfare. When Churchill wrote to Roosevelt on 20th May claiming that Britain needed fighters from the United States, he had already put Beaverbrook in charge of the Ministry for Aircraft Production, and he was clearly relying on the sweat and ingenuity of the people working in the British aircraft industry to save the day.

The RAF had not been waiting around for suitable American fighters to arrive either. A lot of people in Britain had been working hard to get the country ready for a shooting war with Germany. A series of radar stations had been built around the coast, known as the Chain Home (CH) system. A lower level radar system called Chain Home Low (CHL) had also been constructed.[42] These radar systems would detect German raiders as they came across the sea, and once they crossed over the coastline and headed for their targets, the raiders were tracked by the 30,000 members of the Observer Corps, who were stationed throughout the country.[43]

The historian Stephen Bungay has noted that the British system that had been created to counter the inevitable attacks by the *Luftwaffe* functioned in much the same way as a modern intranet.[44] Data from the coastal radars was input to Fighter Command HQ at Bentley Priory, just north-west of London. Data was also collected by individual Observation Corps posts and input into the system by an Observer Corps Centre.

The RAF had divided the country into geographical areas and assigned responsibility for the protection of each area to a Fighter Command group. Number 10 group was responsible for the south-west of England, 11 was responsible for London and the south, 12 for central England and Wales, and 13 for northern England and Scotland.[45] Each of these groups had smaller geographical sectors under them, and each sector in turn controlled several airfields.

The defensive system had a hierarchical structure, which allowed Dowding to keep control of his fighters and ensure that their time in the air was used as efficiently as possible by sending them out to meet the enemy.[46] The incoming data from the Observer Corps centres was available to all levels of the system. Once Fighter Command HQ had processed the raw data it received from the coastal radar systems and the Observation Corps, it passed on all relevant information to the groups, which allowed them to keep each of their sectors up to date with the latest time-sensitive information. The controllers at the sector level could then direct their fighters into the air to intercept the enemy and bring him down.[47]

An American military attaché who was stationed in London, General Raymond E. Lee, visited the Fighter Command HQ at Bentley Priory and described the British defensive system as one of "the most intricate and modern organizations in the world." Lee described the hub of the Dowding System in operation. It was "almost silent – only a soft murmur of voices as messages come and go over headsets, and only a little movement as operators move counters and markers from point to point and others tend electric bulleting and switch-boards . . . I had no idea that British could evolve and operate so intricate, so scientific and rapid an organization."[48]

As Churchill wrote later, the Germans had to attempt to destroy the Royal Air Force before launching a land invasion, because without achieving air supremacy, there would be no way they could prepare their embarkation points on the French coast, assemble their fleet, sweep clear any minefields that were in their path, or ultimately cross the Channel.[49] Churchill warned that this could be the next military operation attempted by the Germans. "Either Hitler must invade and conquer England," Churchill wrote, "or he must face an indefinite prolongation of the war, with all its incalculable hazards and complications."[50] It is a matter of history that the RAF managed to hold off the *Luftwaffe* after Britain was attacked. On 20th August, Churchill said in the House that

> the enemy is of course far more numerous than we are. But our new production already largely exceeds his, and the American production is only just beginning to flow in. Our bomber and fighter strengths now, after all this fighting, are larger than they have ever been. We believe that we should be able to continue the air struggle indefinitely and as long as the enemy pleases, and the longer it continues the more rapid will be our approach, first towards that parity, and then into that superiority in the air upon which in large measure the decision of the war depends.[51]

The order of battle for Fighter Command on 1st September 1940 lists a total of 351 Hurricanes, 197 Spitfires, 77 Bristol Blenheims and 9 Boulton Paul Defiants.[52] Unfortunately, R. J. Mitchell had passed away on 11th June 1937[53] after his cancer returned, so he never got to see what became of the aeroplane he built for his country, or the impact it had on the world.

The American P-40 fighters may not have been necessary for Britain to successfully defend herself in the summer of 1940, but the British were going to need help to fight a long war, and in January that year, orders had been placed for another 200 Lockheed Hudsons and 600 Harvards from North American Aviation. New contracts had also been signed for 120 Brewster Buffalo fighters and 50 Consolidated "Catalina" seaplanes.[54] By March, a total of 4,600 aircraft had been ordered from the United States, and this increased to 10,800 aircraft by June of that year. By November 1940, the total value of all of the orders placed for American aircraft came to 1,262 million dollars.[55] Churchill had also written to Roosevelt and asked for "the loan of forty or fifty of your old destroyers to bridge the gap between what we have now and the large new construction we put in hand at the beginning of the war."[56] He wrote again after Italy had joined forces with Germany: "Nothing is so important as for us to have the thirty or forty old destroyers you have already had reconditioned. We can fit them very rapidly with our Asdics . . . The next six months are vital."[57]

On 27th May, the War Cabinet discussed a proposal from Philip Kerr, the Marquess of Lothian, who was the British ambassador in the United

States at that time. According to Lothian, "Various suggestions had been made that we should cede some of our possessions in the New World to the United States as part payment of our war debt . . ." It was Lothian's opinion that "we should consider making a formal offer to the United States government that, while we were not prepared to discuss any question of sovereignty, we were prepared to lease to the United States landing grounds on British territory, in view of the importance of such facilities to U.S.A. security." Lothian suggested that British-held territories in Trinidad, Bermuda and Newfoundland might be used for this purpose.[58]

This proposal was not well received by Sir Dudley Pound, who was now the First Lord of the Admiralty. "We must not bargain away facilities essential for the defence of our Empire," he stated. Churchill was not keen either. According to the records of the meeting, "The Prime Minister said that he would be opposed to a proposal that we should offer such facilities except as part of a deal. The United States had given us practically no help in the war, and now that they saw how great was the danger, their attitude was that they wanted to keep everything which would help us for their own defence."[59]

In the first week of August, the Americans let Lothian know that they were prepared to supply the destroyers Churchill had asked for in exchange for military bases in the Caribbean.[60] According to Lothian, the only way such a significant amount of military hardware could be signed over to Britain was if the Americans could demonstrate that the deal would enhance the security of the United States.[61] Churchill understood that "there was of course no comparison between the intrinsic value of these antiquated and inefficient craft and the immense permanent strategic security afforded to the United States by the enjoyment of the island bases."[62] Churchill would end up writing to Roosevelt on 31st December to let him know that the American destroyers still had not seen action, because they were not fit for purpose when they arrived and they had been tied up until the necessary repair work had been carried out.[63] The fact that the American destroyers were still not seaworthy at the end of the year shows that they were not needed to defend the country in the summer of 1940. However, when the arms-for-property deal was being drawn up, Churchill accepted the terms of the exchange because it served his long-term interests. On 20th August, he stood in the House of Commons and explained why he believed that leasing naval bases to the United States was the right thing to do:

> These are important steps. Undoubtedly this process means that these two great organisations of the English-speaking democracies, the British Empire and the United States, will have to be somewhat mixed up together in some of their affairs for mutual and general

advantage. For my own part, looking out upon the future, I do not view the process with any misgivings. I could not stop it if I wished; no one can stop it. Like the Mississippi, it just keeps rolling along. Let it roll. Let it roll on – full flood, inexorable, irresistible, benignant, to broader lands and better days.[64]

The Americans may have been prepared to send some of their old destroyers across the Atlantic in exchange for a series of naval bases that they could use to defend their east coast, and they would naturally be happy to fulfil any orders placed by the British government, so long as they were managing to pay the invoices when they came due. But it would not be possible for the British government to sustain this incredible rate of expenditure indefinitely. The time would inevitably come when the British would struggle to pay the bills they were still running up. On 17th December, as factories all over America were gearing up to mass-produce the military hardware that would be needed to go on and win the war, Roosevelt held a press conference at the White House and explained how he intended to deal with the looming financial crisis. "What I am trying to do is eliminate the dollar sign," he said. According to Roosevelt, America could either lend Britain the money to buy American goods or take over British orders and manufacture goods which would then be gifted to Britain. However, Roosevelt dismissed these options and presented a third possibility, using a simple analogy that everyone could understand. What would anyone do if their neighbour's house was on fire, and they had a garden hose? They would lend them the hose and worry about getting it back after the fire had been put out. Who could argue with that? What Roosevelt was proposing was that America would take over British orders for military hardware and

when they came off the line, whether they were planes or guns or something else, we would enter into some kind of arrangement for their use by the British on the ground that it was the best thing for American defense, and that when the show was over we would get repaid in kind sometime, thereby leaving out the dollar mark in the form of a dollar debt and substituting it for a gentleman's obligation to repay in kind. I think you all get it.[65]

This may have been a good informal explanation of how the Americans could help Britain to carry on fighting against Germany, but there remained the question of why they should do so. Roosevelt addressed the issue in a radio broadcast twelve days later. "This is not a fireside chat on war," he assured his audience. "It is a talk on national security." The President told the American people that their country was under threat because the Nazis preached world domination, and America's wealth made her a prime target:

> The Nazi masters of Germany have made it clear that they intend not only to dominate all life and thought in their own country, but also to enslave the whole of Europe, and then to use the resources of Europe to dominate the rest of the world . . . The plain facts are that the Nazis have proclaimed, time and again, that all other races are their inferiors and therefore subject to their orders. And most important of all, the vast resources and wealth of this American hemisphere constitute the most tempting loot in all the round world.[66]

To use Roosevelt's own analogy, what the American people were being told was that the home of their "neighbours" on the other side of the Atlantic had not caught fire due to faulty electrics, it had been deliberately set alight by an arsonist. According to Roosevelt, that same arsonist was going to cross the Atlantic Ocean and burn down America. "Our national policy is not directed toward war. Its sole purpose is to keep war away from our country and our people," said Roosevelt. "We are planning our own defense with the utmost urgency, and in its vast scale we must integrate the war needs of Britain and the other free nations which are resisting aggression." Roosevelt explained what was needed:

> American industrial genius, unmatched throughout the world in the solution of production problems, has been called upon to bring its resources and its talents into action. But all our present efforts are not enough. We must have more ships, more guns, more planes – more of everything. We must be the great arsenal of democracy. For us this is an emergency as serious as war itself. We must apply ourselves to our task with the same resolution, the same sense of urgency, the same spirit of patriotism and sacrifice as we would show were we at war.[67]

When Welles visited Europe in the spring of 1940, he wrote in his report to Roosevelt that

> if the present situation continues to drift, no matter whether a war of devastation breaks out in the immediate future or not, I doubt whether the present generation will again see a world in which there exists any real security, national, physical or economic.

What is imperatively required is statesmanship of the highest character, marked by vision, courage and daring.

I saw no signs of statesmanship of that kind in any of the countries I visited, nor do I know of any of that character in any other European country.[68]

The reality of eight months of war under Churchill's leadership had refuted Welles' analysis. Britain had defied Germany, and she had prevailed in the Battle of Britain. Operation Sealion, the Nazis' plan to invade the British Isles, had come to naught. The British had shown that they were worth backing, so in January 1941, Roosevelt sent his right-hand man, Harry Hopkins, across to Britain to reassess the situation. Hopkins had undergone surgery for cancer in 1937, and still had significant health problems, but he did not let that stop him from travelling the world in the service of the President. Hopkins' arrival in Britain was recorded by Churchill in *The Grand Alliance:*

> On January 10 a gentleman arrived to see me at Downing Street with the highest credentials. Telegrams had been received from Washington stating that he was the closest confidant and personal agent of the President. I therefore arranged that he should be met by Mr. Brendan Bracken on his arrival at Poole Airport, and that we should lunch together alone the next day.[69]

Hopkins' ongoing health problems meant the journey had been difficult for him. When Bracken came aboard the plane to greet Hopkins, he found him slumped over in his plane seat, so exhausted he was barely able to unfasten his seatbelt. However, Hopkins was nothing if not resilient, and once he regained his strength, he managed to pay a visit to the Prime Minister at 10 Downing Street. The pair had a long lunch together,[70] and Hopkins let his host know that the President wanted the two countries to work together to defeat Germany.[71]

When the War Cabinet was discussing what to do about the French fleet on 3rd July 1940, a telegram from Washington had been read out which showed how concerned Roosevelt had been about the fate of the French ships. Lothian had asked the President if American public opinion would support the seizure of the ships by force. According to the telegram, "He said certainly. They would expect them to be seized rather than that they should fall into German hands and that he would do everything in his power to help this solution."[72] As we now know, the British government used military force to prevent the French ships at Mers-el-Kébir from being used against them. What is not so well known is that during his trip to Britain in January 1941,

Hopkins told Jock Colville that the bombardment of the French fleet was what had convinced Roosevelt that the British would fight on against Germany, and that America should provide them with all possible support:

> The United States Administration now saw that the British were seriously determined to continue the struggle. One evening at Chequers, in the following January, Mr. Harry Hopkins told me it was Oran which convinced President Roosevelt, in spite of opinions to the contrary sent by Ambassador Joseph P. Kennedy, that the British really would go on fighting . . . Thenceforward it was the President's primary interest to see how, in spite of Congressional doubts, all assistance short of war could be made available to the United Kingdom.[73]

As we have seen, Machiavelli argued that a political leader had to be able to get their hands dirty if they wanted to be successful. Churchill understood that Britain was at war and dropping leaflets for German "book-worms" to read simply would not do. Stern measures would have to be taken, and they were. The bombardment of the French fleet and the follow-up attack on the *Dunkerque* three days later showed that Churchill could act in ways that were "not good" when it was necessary. These actions may have stopped the French fleet from falling into German hands, but according to what Hopkins told Colville in January 1941, the attacks also gave Great Britain a pipeline to the military hardware that would be needed to fight a long war against Germany.

7 The Soviet Union

On 22nd June 1941, Germany invaded the Soviet Union.[1] The *Luftwaffe* sent 500 bombers and 270 dive-bombers to strike at the Soviet airfields,[2] and approximately 1,200 Soviet aircraft were destroyed on the first morning of the invasion.[3] The cities of Kaunas (Kovno), Minsk, Rivne (Rovno), Odessa and Sevastopol were also bombed.[4] The *Ostheer* (Eastern Army) advanced into Soviet territory with Army Group North, led by Field Marshal von Leeb, heading towards the Baltic States, then Leningrad. Army Group Centre, led by Fedor von Bock, headed east towards Minsk and Smolensk and Army Group South, led by Gerd von Rundstedt, headed into Ukraine.[5] It had always been Hitler's intention to capture *Lebensraum* in the east. On 21st June 1941, the day before the invasion began, Hitler wrote to Mussolini and told him, "The partnership with the Soviet Union, in spite of the complete sincerity of the effort to bring about a final conciliation, was nevertheless often very irksome to me, for in some way or other it seemed to me to be a break with my whole origin, my concepts, and my former obligations. I am happy now to be relieved of these mental agonies." Now that the invasion was just hours away, Hitler said, "I again feel spiritually free."[6]

Churchill's mood also improved when news of the German invasion of the Soviet Union reached Britain on the morning of 22nd June, and he immediately sent his valet round to Anthony Eden's room at Chequers with a big cigar on a silver plate.[7] The British government may have failed to recruit the Soviets after Chamberlain issued his war guarantee to Poland, but they would now be able to get the military assistance they needed. Churchill spent the rest of the day preparing for a radio broadcast on the BBC.[8] At 9 p.m. in the evening, he addressed the British people:

> I have taken occasion to speak to you tonight because we have reached one of the climacterics of the war. The first of these intense turning-points was a year ago when France fell prostrate under the German hammer, and when we had to face the storm alone. The second was when the Royal Air Force beat the Hun raiders out of the daylight air, and thus warded off the Nazi invasion of our island while we were still ill-armed and ill-prepared. The third turning-point was when the President and Congress of the United States passed the Lease-and-Lend enactment, devoting nearly 2,000 millions sterling of wealth of the New World to help us to defend our liberties and their own. Those were the three climacterics. The fourth is now upon us.[9]

Churchill told his audience that the Soviet Union had been invaded by Germany in the early hours of that morning. Hitler was described as a "bloodthirsty guttersnipe" in charge of a "group of villainous men" who had launched a "cataract of horrors upon mankind." The *Wehrmacht* was a "terrible military machine" led by "clanking, heel-clicking, dandified Prussian officers" which was "in continual motion, grinding up human lives and trampling down the homes and the rights of hundreds of millions of men."

In this broadcast, Churchill acknowledged that "no one has been a more consistent opponent of Communism than I have for the last twenty-five years" and asserted that "the worst features of Communism" were "indistinguishable" from those of the Nazi regime.[10] The Soviet Union may have been no better than the National Socialist regime in Germany when it came to its treatment of individuals or its desire to control other nation states, but the fact was, the Soviet Union was now at war with Britain's enemy. As Prime Minister, Churchill was responsible for charting Britain's course through a world war, and he could not afford to let his opposition to the Soviet political system influence any decisions he made. Churchill had to take account of the latest change in circumstances and set his mind towards the Soviet Union in a way that would be of most benefit to his own country:

> I have to make the declaration, but can you doubt what our policy will be? We have but one aim and one single, irrevocable purpose. We are resolved to destroy Hitler and every vestige of the Nazi regime. From this nothing will turn us – nothing. We will never parley, we will never negotiate with Hitler or any of his gang. We shall fight him by land, we shall fight him by sea, we shall fight him in the air, until with God's help we have rid the earth of his shadow and liberated its peoples from his yoke. Any man or state who fights on against Nazidom will have our aid. Any man or state who marches with Hitler is our foe. . . . That is our policy and our declaration. It follows, therefore, that we shall give whatever help we can to Russia and the Russian people. We shall appeal to all our friends and allies in every part of the world to take the same course and pursue it, as we shall, faithfully and steadfastly to the end.[11]

On 7th July, at the urging of Stafford Cripps, the British Ambassador in Moscow,[12] Churchill followed up his speech of 22nd June by sending a message directly to Josef Stalin:

> We are all very glad that the Russian armies are making such strong and spirited resistance to the utterly unprovoked and merciless invasion of the Nazis. There is general admiration for the bravery and tenacity of the Soviet soldiers and people. We shall do everything to help you that time, geography and our growing resources allow. The longer the war lasts the more help we can give. We are making very heavy attacks both by day and night with our Air Force upon all German-occupied territories and all Germany within our reach. About 400 aeroplanes made daylight sorties overseas yesterday. On Saturday night over 200 heavy bombers attacked German towns, some carrying three tons apiece, and last night nearly 250 heavy bombers were operating. This will go on. Thus we hope to force Hitler to bring back some of his air power to the West and gradually take some of the strain off you.[13]

Cripps hand delivered the message to Stalin in Moscow, and the Soviet leader responded by asking for a formal agreement with Britain that would allow for mutual help and assistance and prevent either party from concluding a separate peace with Germany.[14] Churchill called a meeting of the War Cabinet on 9th July to discuss how he ought to respond, and the records in the National Archives state that

> some discussion followed as to whether the Prime Minister's message should include any reference to the settlement of frontiers at the Peace Conference, and the right of the ethnographical units then established to choose their own form of government and system of life. After some discussion, in which it was pointed out that this might make difficulties for the Poles in their negotiations with the Russians, it was generally felt that the wisest course would be to limit the answer to the two points covered by M. Stalin's proposal.[15]

The British government had issued a guarantee to Poland that obliged them to go to war if the independence of Poland was ever threatened, and now they refused to even mention the subject of political freedom in a telegram to the Soviets. In the summer of 1941, the British government had to make sure they got the military assistance they needed to fight their long war against Germany, so the independence of Poland was forgotten and, on 12th July, an agreement between Britain and the Soviet Union was signed by Cripps and Molotov in Moscow. It stated that

His Majesty's Government in the United Kingdom and the Government of the Union of Soviet Socialistic Republics have concluded the present Agreement and declare as follows:-

(1) The two Governments mutually undertake to render each other assistance and support of all kinds in the present war against Hitlerite Germany.

(2) They further undertake that during this war they will neither negotiate nor conclude an armistice or treaty of peace except by mutual agreement.

The present Agreement has been concluded in duplicate in the English and Russian languages.

Both texts have equal force.[16]

Churchill arose in the House of Commons on 15th July and, in response to a question from Hastings Lees-Smith, the acting Leader of the Opposition, who had asked if he could provide any information about the new Russian agreement, he made the following statement:

> Towards the end of last week it became possible to make a solemn agreement between the British and Russian Governments, carrying with it the full assent of the British and Russian people and all the great Dominions of the Crown, for united action against the common foe. Both the British and Russian Governments have undertaken to continue the war against Hitlerite Germany to the utmost of their strength, to help each other as much as possible in every way and not to make peace separately. My right hon. Friend the Foreign Secretary and the right hon. and learned Member for East Bristol (Sir Stafford Cripps), our Ambassador in Moscow, were indefatigable in carrying matters to a swift conclusion. The Agreement which has been signed, the text of which has been published, cannot fail to exercise a highly beneficial and potent influence on the future of the war. It is, of course, an Alliance, and the Russian people are now our Allies.[17]

Churchill had contacted Stalin prior to the launch of Barbarossa and warned him that the Germans were getting ready to invade.[18] According to Martin Gilbert, the British had cracked the communication code known as "Vulture," which was used by the Germans on the Eastern Front, and

Churchill ordered that the fruits of Bletchley Park's labours were to be shared with the Soviet Union.[19] The Soviets did receive some military intelligence from Great Britain then. However, as Churchill wrote later, "When Soviet Russia was attacked by Hitler the only way we and the Americans could help them was by sending weapons and supplies. These were given on a grand scale from United States and British production, and from American munitions already given to Britain."[20]

Maisky had met Harry Hopkins when he was visiting Chequers to hand a telegram to Churchill, and the two men had spoken briefly.[21] Maisky then contacted John Winant, the American Ambassador to Great Britain, and arranged a meeting with Hopkins on 25th July.[22] At their meeting, Hopkins assured Maisky that America would be willing to provide the Soviet Union with supplies,[23] and Maisky suggested a visit to Moscow so the President's man could deal directly with Stalin.[24]

Hopkins wrote to Roosevelt:

> I am wondering whether you would think it important and useful for me to go to Moscow. Air transportation good and can reach there in twenty four hours. I have a feeling that everything possible should be done to make sure the Russians maintain a permanent front even though they be defeated in this immediate battle. If Stalin could in any way be influenced at a critical time I think it would be worth doing by a direct communication from you through a personal envoy. I think the stakes are so great it should be done.[25]

Roosevelt replied on 26th July: "Welles and I highly approve Moscow trip and assume you would go in a few days. Possibly you could get back to North America by August eighth. I will send you tonight a message for Stalin."[26] Sumner Welles then sent a telegram to Laurence Steinhardt, the American Ambassador in Moscow: "The President has instructed Harry Hopkins, who is now in London, to proceed by air to Moscow. . . . The objective of his mission is primarily to investigate how best we can furnish material assistance to the Soviet Union at this time."[27]

According to the records held in the FRUS (Foreign Relations of the United States) archives, Hopkins flew out to Moscow and met with Josef Stalin on 30th July 1941. Hopkins wrote:

> I told Mr. Stalin that I came as personal representative of the President. The President considered Hitler the enemy of mankind and that he therefore wished to aid the Soviet Union in its fight against Germany. . . . I impressed upon him the determination of the

President and our Government to extend all possible aid to the Soviet Union at the earliest possible time.[28]

Stalin told Hopkins that he would need anti-aircraft guns and ammunition, heavy calibre machine guns and at least one million rifles that could fire Russian ammunition.[29] The Soviet Union also needed aluminium to build aeroplanes, and aviation fuel.[30] When Hopkins asked what would be the best route would be to transport this materiel to the Soviet Union, Stalin argued against using the overland route through Iran, because the railway system was not up to the task. Vladivostok on the Pacific coast could be cut off by the Japanese and was too far away from the front line. Stalin concluded that the best way to transport materiel to the Soviet Union was via the northern ports of Archangel, Murmansk and Kandalaksha.[31]

The meeting between Stalin and Hopkins marked the first step in the creation of the Arctic convoy system, which carried British and American supplies via naval bases in Iceland and the west coast of Scotland to the Soviet Union. It is notable that Hopkins, an American citizen acting as an unofficial fixer, met with Stalin before either Churchill or Roosevelt did and that the American offer to "extend all possible aid to the Soviet Union at the earliest possible time" was made before Roosevelt and Churchill's first wartime meeting, which took place after Hopkins had returned from Moscow. This secret rendezvous was scheduled to take place on the second week of August at Placentia Bay in Newfoundland, which was one of the bases the British had signed over to the Americans in exchange for their old destroyers.[32] Hopkins flew back from the Soviet Union aboard a Catalina seaplane[33] and when he landed at Scapa Flow, where he was due to meet Churchill and cross the Atlantic with him, he was exhausted by his travels and spent two days in bed before the Prime Minister and his entourage arrived.[34]

Churchill had travelled north on a sleeper train which dropped him and his entourage off at Thurso, where they were taken by car to Scrabster. There, local fishing boats took Churchill and his party out to the destroyer *Oribi*, which took them all north to Scapa Flow.[35] The party then boarded the battleship *HMS Prince of Wales* and, with a destroyer escort, began their journey across the Atlantic. Churchill had written to the Queen before he set off: "I must say I do not think our friend would have asked me to go so far for what must be a meeting of world-wide notice, unless he had in mind some further step."[36] This was wishful thinking on Churchill's part, because Roosevelt had no intention of bringing America into the war at that time.[37] The President had made his position on this issue clear during a speech in Philadelphia on 23rd October 1940, as he ran for re-election:

> Truthful campaign discussion of public issues is essential to the American form of government; but wilful misrepresentation of fact has no place either during election time or at any other time. . . . The worst bombshell of fear which the Republican leaders have let loose on this people is the accusation that this Government of ours, a Government of Republicans and Democrats alike, without the knowledge of the Congress or of the people, has secretly entered into agreements with foreign nations. They even intimate that such commitments have endangered the security of the United States, or are about to endanger it, or have pledged in some way the participation of the United States in some foreign war. It seems almost unnecessary to deny such a charge. But so long as the fantastic misstatement has been made, I must brand it for what it is.
>
> I give to you and to the people of this country this most solemn assurance. There is no secret treaty, no secret obligation, no secret commitment, no secret understanding, in any shape or form, direct or indirect, with any other government, or any other nation in any part of the world to involve . . . no such secrecy that might or could in any shape involve this nation in any war or for any other purpose. Is that clear?[38]

Roosevelt had kept the meeting at Newfoundland secret from the American press by pretending that he was taking a trip on the presidential yacht *USS Potomac*. He had left Washington by train on 3rd August, then boarded the yacht at New London in Connecticut and headed north. He then transferred aboard the flagship of the Atlantic fleet, the *USS Augusta*, before heading to Newfoundland.[39] It was made clear to the President's military advisors, General Marshall, Chief of Staff of the U.S. Army, and Admiral Harold "Betty" Stark, Chief of Naval Operations, and Major General Henry "Hap" Arnold, Chief of the U.S. Army Air Forces,[40] that there was to be no organised group meeting between all of the American and British Chiefs of Staff. They were only to meet with their counterparts one on one, so they could find out what the British needed to fight against Germany. The larger strategic and political issues were not to be discussed. Nothing was to happen on this trip that could possibly be misconstrued by the President's political opponents.[41]

Roosevelt had given advance notice of his real intentions to Sumner Welles, who landed at Placentia Bay on 8th August.[42] Welles had been told that the President wanted a public statement of shared objectives to be drawn up. When Churchill arrived at Placentia Bay the next morning, he soon discovered that he was going to be inveigled in this scheme. The *Prince of Wales* arrived at Placentia Bay on the morning of 9th August, and

Churchill immediately went aboard the *Augusta* to meet Roosevelt, who stood to receive his visitor, holding the arm of his son, Elliot.[43] The two men shook hands, then went below for their first official meeting as leaders of their two countries.[44]

Roosevelt got straight down to business and let Churchill know his agenda for the conference. The President told Churchill that what he wanted to do at this first wartime summit was draw up a joint declaration of principles.[45] Churchill wrote in his history of the war that he provided a draft version of the document, which came to be known as the Atlantic Charter, to Roosevelt the next day,[46] and after it had been revised by Roosevelt and Welles,[47] a final version of the document was made ready, which read as follows:

> The President of the United States of America and the Prime Minister, Mr. Churchill, representing His Majesty's Government in the United Kingdom, being met together, deem it right to make known certain common principles in the national policies of their respective countries on which they base their hopes for a better future of the world.
>
> First, their countries seek no aggrandisement, territorial or other;
>
> Second, they desire to see no territorial changes that do not accord with the freely expressed wishes of the people concerned;
>
> Third, they respect the right of all peoples to choose the form of government under which they will live; and they wish to see sovereign rights and self-government restored to those who have been forcibly deprived of them;
>
> Fourth, they will endeavour, with due respect to their existing obligations, to further the enjoyment by all States, great or small, victor or vanquished, of access, on equal terms, to the trade and to the raw materials of the world which are needed for their economic prosperity . . .[48]

The document goes on to state that America and Britain desired to collaborate with other nations to improve labour standards and social security for all, and to create a peaceful environment that would allow everyone to "live out their lives in freedom from fear and want." According to the eighth principle listed in the document, any nations which "may threaten aggression outside their frontiers" should be disarmed, "pending the establishment of a wider and more permanent system of general security."[49]

Churchill, whose mother was American,[50] did everything he could to emphasise the cultural connections between Britain and the United States by arranging for a religious service to be held aboard the *Prince of Wales*. Roosevelt sat in a chair on the ship's deck, with Churchill seated beside him, as sailors from both countries joined together to sing a selection of hymns. Acting as lector, Jack Leach, the Captain of the *Prince of Wales*, read aloud from the first chapter of the book of Joshua.[51] Churchill may have hoped that the United States would agree to go beyond providing Britain with supplies and join in the war, but the President was not about to do that. American camera crews had been flown out to Newfoundland. Roosevelt had them film the religious service aboard the *Prince of Wales*, thereby ensuring that the lasting images of the conference would show the people of two nations coming together to worship, not to make war.

There may have been no place for religious services like the one held aboard the *Prince of Wales* in the atheistic Soviet Union, but that did not prevent Ivan Maisky from attending an Inter-Allied Council meeting in London on 24th September, along with representatives of Belgium, Czechoslovakia, Greece, Luxembourg, the Netherlands, Norway, Poland, Yugoslavia, and General De Gaulle's Free France. The statement released following this meeting stated that all parties present had "taken note of the declaration recently drawn up by the President of the United States and by the Prime Minister (Mr. Churchill) on behalf of His Majesty's Government in the United Kingdom, [and] now make known their adherence to the common principles of policy set forth in that declaration and their intention to cooperate to the best of their ability in giving effect to them." Maisky stated at this meeting that "the Soviet Government proclaims its agreement with the fundamental principles of the declaration of Mr. Roosevelt and Mr. Churchill."[52]

Churchill may have hoped to enlist America in the war against Germany, but he had been unable to persuade Roosevelt to have the United States join the war as a belligerent nation. As Churchill sailed back across the Atlantic, the Soviet Union was still Britain's only real military ally. On 25th August 1941, British and Indian forces launched Operation Countenance and occupied the south of Iran, while the Red Army invaded from the north. The British and Soviet ambassadors in Teheran presented the Iranian government with an ultimatum which required the Iranians to accept the "protection" of the two countries. A treaty was drawn up between the three governments, which gave the British and the Soviets unfettered access to the country. This allowed the British to transport approximately 41 million tons of materiel through the country by train between 1941 and 1945, which was almost a quarter of the total amount of Lend-Lease goods delivered to the Soviet Union during the war.[53]

On 4th November, Churchill offered to send two of his generals to Moscow to meet with Stalin:

> In order to clear things up and plan for the future I am ready to send General Wavell, the Commander-in-Chief in India, Persia and Iraq, to meet you in Moscow, Kuibyshev, Tiflis or wherever you will be. Besides this, General Paget, our new Commander-in-Chief designate for the Far East, will come with General Wavell. General Paget has been in the centre of things here, and will have with him the latest and best opinions of our High Command. These two Officers will be able to tell you exactly how we stand, what is possible and what we think is wise. They can reach you in about a fortnight. Do you want them?[54]

Stalin would not have forgotten the ill-fated visit to the Soviet Union by Admiral Drax in August 1939, and when he replied to Churchill, he made it clear that discussing purely military matters with the British generals would be a waste of his time. Stalin believed that the ultimate war aims of the Soviet Union and Britain should be addressed.[55] Cripps suggested that Anthony Eden should travel to the Soviet Union to speak directly with Stalin.[56]

Churchill wrote to Stalin on 21st November and formally offered to send Eden out to Moscow. "The fact that Russia is a Communist State and Britain and the United States are not, and do not intend to be, is not any obstacle to our making a good plan for our mutual safety and rightful interests," he assured the Soviet dictator. "The Foreign Secretary will be able to discuss the whole of this field with you."[57]

On 7th December, Eden departed from Euston Station in London and travelled north to Scotland,[58] where he boarded a ship for Murmansk, then travelled by train to Moscow.[59] Eden met with Stalin on 16th December 1941 and according to Sir Frank Roberts, a diplomat who had accompanied Eden, the first thing that Stalin wanted to discuss was the fate of the countries along the Soviet border.[60] Eden sent a report back to the Foreign Office in the early hours of 17th December: "M. Stalin handed me draft projects of two treaties, one to cover military assistance irrespective of war and [the] other political collaboration now and after the war." That was not all. According to Eden, "M. Stalin then suggested we should also sign a secret protocol which would embody our joint views for a settlement of post-war frontiers."[61] In a further telegram dated 18th December 1941, Eden elaborated: "I was summoned to meet Stalin at midnight and we had a discussion lasting three hours. At the outset Stalin said that he had examined the texts but what interested him was the question of the frontiers of the USSR after the war. He would agree that the Polish frontier might be left an open question but he wanted our immediate agreement of his territorial claims in Finland Baltic States and Roumania."[62]

Churchill recorded his reaction to Stalin's proposals in his history of the war: "As soon as I read the telegrams I reacted violently against the absorption of the Baltic States."[63] He wrote to Clement Attlee: "Stalin's demands about Finland, Baltic States and Roumania are directly contrary to the first, second and third articles of the Atlantic Charter, to which Stalin has subscribed. There can be no question whatever of our making such an agreement, secret or public, direct or implied, without prior agreement with the U.S."[64]

Churchill may have given voice to this position at the time, and he may have recorded it after the war, but within months of Stalin outlining his territorial demands, Churchill once again allowed the changing circumstances of the war to dictate the course of action he would take, as he sought to achieve the best possible outcome for his country.

8 The Winter War

The territorial demands that Stalin put to Eden in December 1941 had not come out of nowhere. The secret protocol of the Nazi-Soviet Pact, which had been signed in the early hours of 24th August 1939, had split Poland and the Baltic States into two "spheres of interest."[1] Ribbentrop had visited Moscow again on 27th September to negotiate the signing of the Boundary and Friendship Treaty. At this second meeting, the border in Poland was moved east to the river Bug. In return, Lithuania was also given over to the Soviet Union.[2]

Ribbentrop was not the only foreign dignitary to visit the Soviet Union in late September 1939. Karl Selter, the Foreign Minister of Estonia, had been invited to Moscow, and like old-time gangsters running a protection racket, the Soviets used strong-arm tactics to force compliance. At their first meeting, Molotov told Selter that a Polish submarine, the *Orzel*, had left Tallinn harbour and entered the Gulf of Finland. According to Molotov, the Estonian authorities should not have let this happen. Molotov proposed that a mutual assistance pact between the two countries should be drawn up and threatened to use force against Estonia if no arrangement could be reached.[3]

Selter returned to Tallinn and discussed the matter with his colleagues in the cabinet. They had signed a non-aggression pact with Germany in June 1939, but there was no sign of any assistance coming from that quarter. All they could do now was try to make the best deal possible with the Soviet Union.[4] On 27th September, Selter flew back to Moscow and met with Molotov again. Molotov now claimed that the submarine *OrzelI* had managed to sink a Soviet merchant ship, the *Metalisst*. Under pressure, Selter had no option but sign the proposed mutual assistance pact, which allowed the Soviets to establish 35,000 troops in Estonia.[5] A week later, a similar agreement was forced upon the Latvian government, which allowed 30,000 Red Army troops to be stationed there.[6] The Lithuanians were given control over the city of Vilnius, which the Soviets had taken over when they invaded Poland, but the agreement they signed also allowed Red Army soldiers to be stationed inside their borders. By mid-October, these countries were bound to the Soviet Union through mutual assistance agreements, and approximately 70,000 Red Army troops were stationed there.[7]

In May 1940, as the British and French were facing the *Wehrmacht* in western Europe, the Soviets moved to take the Baltic States over completely. On 25th May, Molotov told the Lithuanian ambassador in Moscow that a Red Army officer had recently died, and two others had gone missing while serving in Lithuania. Molotov blamed the Lithuanian authorities, who he accused of plying the soldiers with alcohol, then persuading them to desert.[8] Antanas Merkys, the Lithuanian Prime Minister, travelled to Moscow to meet with Molotov, but the outcome was a foregone conclusion. Molotov accused the Lithuanians of conspiring to form a military alliance with Latvia and Estonia and demanded the arrest of two Lithuanian cabinet members. Furthermore, a new Lithuanian government would have to be formed that could work with the Soviets and more troops would have to be allowed into the country. As this pressure was being applied at the political level, the Soviet military was preparing to invade and on 15th June, the Red Army advanced unopposed into Lithuania.[9] In a matter of days, similar ultimatums were put to the Estonian and Latvian governments, and as the British government was dealing with the evacuation of the BEF from French soil and planning for a possible German invasion, these three nation states were taken over by the Soviet Union.[10]

The people living in the Baltic States soon found out what it meant to be under Soviet control. All political parties that were thought to be unfriendly to the Soviet Union were banned, almost all members of the political class were arrested, and the concept of private property was abolished.[11] Rank and file soldiers were forcibly enlisted in the Red Army and thousands of officers were taken into the forest on lorries, then loaded on to cattle cars and deported to the Soviet interior, or simply shot. At the Litene Army base in Latvia, approximately two hundred officers were executed by the NKVD, and five hundred more were sentenced to hard labour at the nickel and copper mines at Norilsk, above the Arctic Circle, at the foot of the Putoran Mountains.[12]

In the north, the Finns had always understood that the Soviet Union would be the enemy in any war they would be involved in, and they had planned accordingly.[13] The Finnish Army only had ten divisions in November 1939[14] and their equipment and ammunition was limited,[15] but the Finns knew how to use the terrain to their advantage.[16] In the north of the country, invading Red Army soldiers would be forced to advance along the only roads available through dense forests.[17] Finnish ski patrols could ambush the invaders using weapons like the Suomi submachine gun, which they could hang round their shoulders then quickly bring to bear, opening fire at the enemy at close range.[18] In the south, the Finns relied on the Mannerheim Line, a series of defensive trenches, forts and bunkers running from the Gulf of Finland to Lake Ladoga,[19] to act as a more conventional defensive barrier.[20] The territory on the far side of the Mannerheim Line was mapped down to the last inch, so that the Finnish artillery could lay down accurate artillery fire on the enemy.[21] The Finns were under no illusions, however. They understood that in the event of a Soviet attack, the best they could do was hold out long enough for help from other countries to arrive. If none came, then the Finns would make sure that the enemy had to pay such a high price for every inch of Finnish territory that they would have to come to the negotiating table to end to the conflict.[22]

On 5th October 1939, the Soviets asked the Finns to send a delegation to Moscow to negotiate land concessions and a mutual peace agreement.[23] At a meeting on 12th October, the Finns were told that the border on the Karelian Isthmus would have to be moved west until it was only twenty miles east of Viipuri (now Vyborg),[24] all their fortifications on the Karelian Isthmus would have to be destroyed, which would mean dismantling the Mannerheim Line,[25] and they would have to allow the Soviets to build a base on the peninsula of Hanko, which is west of Helsinki, on the northern side of the Gulf of Finland.[26] The Finns refused, and at a subsequent meeting on 3rd November, Molotov threatened to use force to resolve the issue.[27]

Stalin was determined to get what he wanted, and he believed that a swift military victory over Finland was possible. The Soviet general staff had prepared an invasion plan, but Stalin was not pleased with it. Instead of using all the military resources that the plan had called for, operational responsibility for an invasion of Finland was given to Army Commander Cyril Meretskov, the senior officer in charge of the Leningrad Military District.[28]

On 26th November, following orders from Leningrad, the Soviet 221st Artillery Regiment, which was stationed just north of the Soviet village of Mainila, fired a salvo on the village.[29] The Soviets then claimed that the shells had been fired from across the border, although the Finns had moved their artillery weapons back out of range so that such an incident could not happen.[30] The Finns demanded an international investigation into the incident,[31] but the Soviets now had their *casus belli*, and they refused to co-operate.[32]

At a War Cabinet meeting on 27th November, Halifax noted that "the Soviet government, as a result of a serious incident on the Soviet-Finnish frontier, had addressed a note to the Finnish government demanding that the Finnish troops on the Karelian Isthmus should be withdrawn for a distance of 20 and 22 kilometres since, it was alleged, the presence of Finnish troops at their present strength so near to Leningrad represented not only a danger, but also a hostile act."[33] If the Soviets had their way, the consequences for the Finns were clear enough. As Halifax said, "It would not be possible for the Finnish army to withdraw the distance suggested in the Soviet note without abandoning the whole of their defensive system."[34]

On 29th November, Halifax drew the attention of the other members of the War Cabinet to a telegram sent by Sir William Seeds, the Ambassador to the Soviet Union. According to Seeds, the Soviet government had told the

Finns that "the refusal of the Finnish government to withdraw their troops for the distance suggested, and their proposal for mutual withdrawal of troops, expressed a hostile desire to keep Leningrad under threat."[35] Seeds went on: "Soviet papers appearing on the evening of 28th November published an order issued by the Commander of the Leningrad Military District instructing troops to fire back in case of further provocation by the Finnish forces."[36]

The Soviets understood very well that the Finns were on their own. Maisky's diary entry for 29th November reads:

> Don't the Finns understand that, if trouble comes, they can't count on anyone to help them? Who will help them? The Swedes? The British? The Americans? Like hell they will! A racket in the newspapers, moral support, oohing and aahing – yes. Troops, airplanes, cannons, guns – no. [Rab] Butler told me plainly yesterday: "Should anything happen, we wouldn't be able to send a single warship to Finland."[37]

On 30th November, Soviet bombers attacked Helsinki. At approximately 10:30 that morning, nine Soviet SB-2 bombers flew over the harbour and dropped several bombs into the water before heading towards the railway station, where they dropped more bombs into the public square in front of the main building, killing forty people. The Soviets then dropped incendiary bombs throughout the city and strafed the houses in a working class area,[38] before flying off to the east. The Finnish air raid sirens started to sound as the planes disappeared, and their anti-aircraft batteries sent a few shots into the sky, but it was too late. The Soviets sent a second bombing raid back to Helsinki that afternoon, after the all-clear had sounded. Another fifty people were killed, and over a hundred were injured.[39]

The records in the National Archives show that on 30th November, "the War Cabinet were informed that confirmation had been received that the Soviet Forces had crossed the Finnish Frontier north-east of Lake Ladoga, and that firing had taken place across the Karelian peninsula."[40]

Chamberlain had said back in March that Britain was about to enter a "new epoch" in its foreign policy,[41] where the threat of military action was to be used as a deterrent against territorially aggressive nation states. Now that Chamberlain was expected to respond to a formal question in the House of Commons about the Soviet Union's attack on Finland, he wondered what he should say.[42]

Halifax advised him that "the importance of the answer . . . would lie in the attitude which we took in regard to Russia's action. He thought that the reply should show our strong disapproval of Russia's action, but at the same time should not lose sight of the fact that there was no effective action which we could take in the matter."[43]

Chamberlain thought that "it would be very difficult to confine the reply to a strictly impartial statement of the Russian and Finnish cases. The situation demanded some expression of reprobation."[44]

The records of the meeting show that "after some further discussion, the War Cabinet invited the Prime Minister and the Secretary of State for Foreign Affairs, in drafting a reply to the Private Notice Question, to bear in mind the War Cabinet's view that expression should be given to our strong sense of disapproval of Russia's action."[45]

Churchill, who was present at the meeting, understood that this would not matter to Stalin: "*The First Lord of the Admiralty* thought that we ought not to be deterred from expressing disapproval by consideration of the possible effects on the Russians, who were impervious to words."[46]

In the House of Commons on 1st December, Chamberlain was asked by Clement Attlee, the leader of the Labour party, "whether he [could] give the House the latest information regarding the Russo-Finnish situation?"[47] Chamberlain gave his response:

> The House will be aware that for some time past there has been an exchange of views between the Soviet and Finnish Governments on certain questions, mainly of a strategic character, raised by the former. Some apprehension had been expressed by the Soviet Government at the proximity of Leningrad to the Finnish frontier, which is in fact only some 20 miles distant, and a proposal was made by them for the realignment of this part of the frontier in exchange for territorial compensation further North. Claims were also made for the acquisition of certain Finnish islands in the Gulf of Finland and of a Finnish port at the entrance to the Gulf, in order, it was stated, to assure the position of the Soviet Union in the Gulf of Finland. A further claim is believed to have been made for the Finnish side of the Rybachi Peninsula, which overlooks and dominates Finland's sole Arctic port of Petsamo. . . .
>
> His Majesty's Government have observed these developments with increasing concern and they have found it difficult to believe that strategic measures of such scope and importance as were suggested should have been considered necessary to protect the Soviet Union against a country as small as Finland.
>
> Late last night M. Molotov broadcast a statement in the course of which he is officially reported as having denied the suggestion, which he attributed to the foreign Press, that a Soviet

attack on Finland was intended. Yet, only a few hours after this broadcast, it is understood that Soviet forces have invaded Finnish territory on several sections of the frontier and have dropped incendiary bombs on an aerodrome in the neighbourhood of Helsingfors. It is later reported that Helsingfors, Viborg and other centres have been bombed, in some cases with loss of life.

His Majesty's Government warmly welcomed the offer of mediation made by the United States Secretary of State, since in their opinion the questions at issue between Finland and the Soviet Union were not of a nature to justify the resort to warlike measures. They deeply regret this fresh attack upon a small independent nation, which must result in fresh suffering and loss of life to innocent people.[48]

On 14th December, Chamberlain spoke in the House again:

The Finns have been defending their country with the courage and determination which were to be expected of that gallant people, and it is clear that the Finnish Army has proved itself by far the better fighting force in everything but numbers. It is too soon to attempt any forecast of the outcome of this unequal struggle, but its political consequences have already been far-reaching. By their act of aggression the Soviet Government have outraged the conscience of the whole world. . . .

I should like, further, to say a few words about the bearing of the Finnish conflict upon our war aims. The opportunity provided by this conflict has been eagerly seized upon by the German propaganda machine, and by many people acting consciously or unconsciously in its service, to deflect attention from the primary objective of the Allied war effort, which is the defeat of Nazi Germany. We must never lose sight of that objective. We must never forget that it was German aggression which paved the way for the Soviet attack on Poland and Finland, and that Germany, alone among the nations, is even now abetting by word and deed the Russian aggressor. We must all give what help and support we can spare to the latest victim of these destructive forces; but meanwhile it is only by concentrating on our task of resistance to German aggression, and thus attacking the evil at its root, that we can hope to save the nations of Europe from the fate which must otherwise overtake them.[49]

Chamberlain had managed to deflect attention away from Soviet aggression against several other nation states by focusing on the actions of Hitler's Germany. When Archibald Sinclair rose to speak, he agreed with Chamberlain's position:

> We have consistently condemned the many instances of aggression which have occurred in the last few years, and we condemn, no less forcibly and no less wholeheartedly, the aggression of which Finland has been the victim. . . . At the same time, I very strongly agree with the Prime Minister that our prime object at the moment must be the defeat of Nazi Germany. We must never allow ourselves to forget what a gigantic enterprise that is, and we must never allow the people of this country to forget it. If, therefore, His Majesty's Government have to follow a policy of non-intervention in Finland we hope that they will pursue it energetically and as vigorously as circumstances permit, and we shall give our full support to the Government in lending such help as they can to the Finnish people in their brave struggle to defend themselves against a powerful aggressor.[50]

In America, the tone of their government's response to the invasion of Finland was set by Roosevelt at a conference at the White House on 1st December. Roosevelt read out a prepared statement:

> The news of the Soviet naval and military bombings within Finnish territory has come as a profound shock to the Government and people of the United States. . . . It is tragic to see the policy of force spreading, and to realize that wanton disregard for the law is still on the march. All peace loving peoples in those nations that are still hoping for the continuance of relations throughout the world on the basis of law and order will unanimously condemn this new resort to military force as the arbiter of international differences.
>
> To the great misfortune of the world, the present trend to force makes insecure the independent existence of small nations in every continent and jeopardizes the rights of mankind to self-government. The people and government of Finland have a long, honorable and wholly peaceful record which has won for them the respect and warm regard of the people and government of the United States.[51]

The assembled journalists wanted to know what America was going to do about the latest Soviet invasion besides saying a few words about having “respect and warm regards” for the people of Finland. “There is a great deal of agitation, as far as I can hear, for the withdrawal of recognition of Russia, or rather, the severance of diplomatic relations,” said one journalist. “There is no news,” was Roosevelt’s response, which promptly ended this line of questioning.[52]

At a press conference held at the White House on 12th December, Roosevelt explained that the Red Cross was providing warm clothes and medicines to the Finns, and to refugees from Poland. Roosevelt also acknowledged the efforts of the former President, Herbert Hoover.[53] At the request of Risto Ryti, who was then the Prime Minister of Finland, Hoover had set up the Finnish Relief Fund, which went on to raise millions of dollars to help the Finnish people.[54] All around the world, politicians were speaking out in support of the Finns, and Churchill was no exception to that. On 20th January, he made a speech on the radio, and talked about the fate of the countries trapped between Germany and the Soviet Union:

> Only Finland – superb, nay, sublime – in the jaws of peril – Finland shows what free men can do. The service rendered by Finland to mankind is magnificent. . . . We cannot tell what the fate of Finland may be, but no more mournful spectacle could be presented to what is left to civilised mankind than that this splendid Northern race should be at last work down and reduced to servitude worse than death by the dull brutish force of overwhelming numbers.
>
> If the light of freedom which still burns so brightly in the frozen North should be finally quenched, it might well herald a return to the Dark Ages, when every vestige of human progress during two thousand years would be engulfed. . . .[55]

On the battlefield, the Finns were fighting desperately to save their country. When the Soviets began to advance along the Karelian Isthmus, they found that the Finns who lived there had already been evacuated, their houses had been burnt to the ground to deny the invaders shelter from the elements, and everything in sight had been booby trapped.[56]

The Soviets tried attacking the Mannerheim Line at Taipale, near Lake Ladoga,[57] but came to grief against the Finnish 10th Division.[58] The Finns had left the Koukunniemi peninsula in front of their position exposed, but they had surveyed and measured every inch of the peninsula before the invasion began. When the enemy started to advance, the Finns were able to bring their guns to bear upon the enemy with deadly accuracy.[59] The Red Army attacked using the same tactics the *Wehrmacht* would encounter in the summer of 1941, with no regard whatsoever for the lives of their own troops.[60] Waves of men were sent forward, only to be cut down by the waiting Finnish machine gunners.[61]

After the attempt to break through at Taipale had failed, the Soviets attacked the Summi sector of the line. After a five hour artillery barrage, the Soviets sent sappers forward to disable the Finnish anti-tank defences then sent in their tanks, but the attack was not co-ordinated with the infantry. The Finnish troops dug in and waited for the Soviet tanks to pass by, then opened fire on the infantry when they appeared.[62] When the advancing tanks realised their supporting troops were nowhere to be seen, some withdrew to their own lines, and some adopted a defensive position and tried to hold out against the Finnish tank-killer squads. The Finnish tactics had meant allowing tanks to fire on them and to move through their lines, but these tactics had successfully separated the enemy's armoured and infantry forces and prevented a breakthrough.[63] The Finns attacked the Soviet KV-1 tanks using any and all means available to them, firing their Suomi machine guns through the viewing slits, levering open the tanks' hatches and throwing in grenades, and using "Molotov cocktails" to set the tanks aflame.[64] The Soviets had thrown seven divisions, including two armoured brigades, against the Mannerheim Line, but they had failed to breach the Finnish defenses.[65]

The resourcefulness of the Finns was further demonstrated when their telephone lines were cut by Soviet artillery fire. Once the limitations of the insecure radio systems became apparent, the Finnish soldiers improvised by talking to one another over the radio using their local dialects.[66] The ability to use native linguistic skills to keep radio traffic secure against a listening enemy was used later on in the war by Navajo code talkers in the Pacific Theatre.[67] The Finnish use of local dialect during the winter war appears to be the first recorded instance of language being used in this way during the war years.

In the north of the country, the Finns' ability to operate in the winter environment served them well against the invaders. The Soviets tried to fight their own style of war without adapting to the local circumstances in the northern forests,[68] whereas the Finnish soldiers knew very well what winters could be like in their own country, and incorporated that knowledge into the tactics they used.[69] The winter of 1939 was one of the coldest on record,[70] and the Finns were dressed and equipped for Arctic warfare. The Finnish soldiers wore thick woollen underwear and sweaters, several pairs of socks, and boots lined with reindeer fur.[71] Just behind the front line, the Finns constructed shellproof dugouts with roofs made of logs and earth. These dugouts were lined with furs and animal skins and they had highly efficient stoves burning in them to keep the Finnish soldiers warm in the sub-zero temperatures.[72]

As the Soviets advanced through the thick northern forests, their lines were inevitably stretched out, and in a foreshadowing of the deadly tactics that would be employed by the Red Army a year and a half later, the Finns ambushed the invaders from the surrounding trees.[73] The soldiers in the Red Army called their enemy in the winter war *Belaya Smert* – White Death. Some men succumbed to the cold slowly and fell asleep, never to awaken. Others met their fate suddenly, at the hand of a sniper's bullet, or a burst of automatic fire from a Suomi.[74] As the invasion stalled in the face of the Finnish resistance, the *Stavka* (Soviet High Command) put Army Commander Simon Timoshenko in charge of military operations on the Karelian Isthmus, and increased the number of troops stationed there to 1.3 million.[75] Timoshenko also assembled a massive amount of artillery to bombard the Finnish defences. Approximately 2,800 cannons were brought forward so that on average, eighty guns would be firing on each mile of the Mannerheim Line. Behind the front lines, "ghost guns" that were so large they could only be transported by rail would be able to fire twelve inch shells into the Finnish rear.[76] Heavy KV-1 tanks were also brought up to replace those lost in the earlier fighting, and the tactics used by the Soviet tanks were changed. Tank commanders would now be given limited military objectives, and would be ordered to stay within reach of their artillery and infantry support.[77] The Soviets intended to drive into the Mannerheim Line in an armoured wedge, then force more troops into the breach until the Finns had no option but to give way.[78]

Knowing that they were facing a militarily superior force, the Finnish political leadership tried to open negotiations with the Soviets so they could bring the war to an end as quickly as possible. The Finns believed that the harder they fought and the more difficult and costly the war became for the Soviets, the more likely it would be that a political arrangement of some kind could be reached.[79] On 1st February 1940, Timoshenko led a new assault against the Mannerheim Line. The Finns managed to hold out for a few days,[80] but on 10th February another attack was launched, and this time the Finns were forced to retreat to a secondary line of defence.[81] The end was in sight for the Finns, who had very little military reserves left.[82] On 4th March, the Soviets attacked the Finnish city of Viipuri, with tanks approaching on the now frozen lakes, and bombers attacking the city from the air.[83] The next day the Soviets indicated that they would be willing to negotiate with the Finns, and on 7th March, Risto Ryti flew to Moscow.[84]

The Finns had no choice but to agree to the Soviet demands. To bring an end to hostilities, the Karelian Isthmus was signed over to the Soviet Union, along with Hanko at the entrance to the Gulf of Finland and the Rybachi Peninsula, which reached into the Barents Sea.[85] The Moscow Peace Treaty was signed in Moscow by Molotov and Ryti on 13th March. The winter war was over, and although the Soviets had managed to obtain a defensive perimeter north of Leningrad, they had paid a high price for it.

After the winter war, the Finns tried to form new political and military alliances to improve their defensive position, but the only country willing to fight against the Soviet Union was Germany.[86] On 22nd June 1941, the Germans launched Operation Barbarossa. The Soviets responded by shelling the border and launching a bombing raid on Finnish vessels and fortifications around Hanko and the Åland islands. On 25th June, a bombing campaign was launched against industrial and civilian targets throughout Finland. Along the south coast, Kotka, Helsinki and Turku were targeted, and farther inland, Lahti, Heinola and Varkaus were hit.[87]

The continuation war had begun.

9 The Continuation War

The Finnish government had been expecting the Soviets to revert to type and launch a second attack on their country. On 7th February 1941, the American Minister Plenipotentiary in Finland, Arthur Schoenfeld, had sent a telegram to Cordell Hull, the Secretary of State:

> The Finnish Government is fully aware of possibility of renewed aggression which depends largely upon development of the general war and on whether Russians are preoccupied at other points on their long frontiers. . . . The view here is evidently that present situation continues to depend upon arbitrary decisions of Soviet Government following its estimate of its own interests at any given moment. Foreign Minister pointed out that Finnish policy is based upon avoiding provocation while firmly maintaining essential rights and preparing to defend them, adding that if a policy of supine accommodation had been followed after last March, present position of Finland would be the same as that of Baltic States.[1]

The Finns were ready to defend their way of life, and when the Soviets attacked them again, the Finns let the American government know that they were going to fight back. On 25th June, Schoenfeld sent a telegram back to Washington:

> Ministry for Foreign Affairs informed me at 4:35 this afternoon that up to 3 p.m. today some 16 Soviet aircraft had been shot down in various parts of the country and one seaplane captured by a coast guard vessel after a forced landing. Bombing had been widespread in nearly all parts of the country with civilian casualties considerable, Soviet forces having been used in some places including groups of as many as 50 planes. . . . The Minister did not tell me what the official statement to be made by the Prime Minister in the Diet this evening will contain but he greeted me with the words: "We are in the war again."[2]

In Washington the next day, Sumner Welles wrote that

> the Minister of Finland called to see me this afternoon with the instruction from his Government to inform the United States Government that Finland has now been forced, in her own defense and as a result of attack from Russia, to undertake defensive military

measures. The Minister was further instructed to state that the Finnish Government over a period of two days, as a result of Russian attacks by sea and from the air, had requested an explanation from the Russian government and a disavowal of those responsible for these attacks. No reply had been received from the Russian government.[3]

In London, the latest act of Soviet aggression was discussed at the highest level. The conclusions of a War Cabinet meeting held on 26th June state that "the Russians had bombed Finnish aerodromes, and the Finns had declared that they would defend themselves against Russian attacks. The prospects of Finnish neutrality being maintained were not very bright."[4] There was no possibility of any military assistance being offered to the Finns at that time because the British government was actively supporting the other side. At a War Cabinet meeting on 30th June, "the Secretary of State for Foreign Affairs said that M. Maisky had asked him what was in the mind of His Majesty's Government regarding military, economic and political collaboration with Russia. He had assured M. Maisky that we were with them up to the hilt in all military and economic measures for the defeat of Germany."[5]

The British government had to support the Soviet Union, because they needed the Red Army to keep fighting against the *Wehrmacht* on the Eastern Front. The Finns needed to defend themselves against the Soviet Union, and Germany had been the only country willing to stand against their common enemy. The Finns made their position clear to the British and American governments. In the FRUS (Foreign Relations of the United States) archives, a memo written by Welles dated 28th June states that

> the Minister of Finland called to see me this morning at his request. The Minister left with me an *aide-memoire* giving a detailed account of the hostile acts committed by Russia within Finnish territory during the past few days.
>
> The Minister then read to me, by instruction of his Government, a statement of the policy of the Finnish Government as already communicated by the Finnish Minister in London to the British Government. The statement contained the following declaration: "The Government of Finland desires to maintain unaltered its relations with Great Britain. The Government of Finland is a co-belligerent with Germany solely against Russia."[6]

On 4th July, Schoenfeld met with President Ryti in Helsinki. The position adopted by the Finns was formally recorded in a telegram Schoenfeld sent back to Washington at 6 p.m. that evening:

> Following is text of my formulation, made at President Ryti's request, of his remarks to me today:
>
> In answer to my inquiry as to the policy of the Finnish Government in the present situation of hostilities with the Soviet Union, His Excellency President Ryti stated, and authorized me so to inform the President of the United States, that Finland was a co-belligerent with Germany in those hostilities and was seeking to achieve purely Finnish aims. The strategic position of Finland after the conclusion in 1940 of the previous hostilities with the Soviet Union was dangerously vulnerable and it would be the purpose of Finland to correct that condition for her own protection only. Aside from necessary military understandings, in connection with the parallel operations now proceeding in common with the German forces, no political agreements exist between the Finnish and the German Governments. . . .
>
> It is the view of President Ryti that the defeat of the Soviet Army and the complete crushing of Bolshevism as a consequence thereof are in the interest of the whole world, and particularly of Finland. But the Finnish people have not departed and have no intention of departing from their established national system of political and social organization."[7]

The Americans were not interested in fighting against Communism at that time because they were setting up one of the largest arms deals in history with the Soviet Union, and they were not going to allow the Finns to interfere with it. When the President's representative, Harry Hopkins, flew to Moscow and met with Stalin on 30th July, the continuation war was getting under way on the Finnish front. On behalf of the United States, Hopkins promised to supply the Soviet Union with materiel, despite the non-belligerent status of the United States at that time. After Hopkins flew back from Moscow, he travelled across the Atlantic to Newfoundland with Churchill's party and met face to face with Roosevelt aboard the *USS Augusta*. Hopkins reported to the President that, in his opinion, the Soviets would be able to fight on against the *Wehrmacht*. Roosevelt therefore agreed to send Averell Harriman, together with Lord Beaverbrook, on an Anglo-American Mission to the Soviet Union.[8] This mission arranged for the Soviets to receive a terrific amount of supplies, which Britain and the United States would now have to do without. Over the coming months, the Soviet

Union was to receive 1,800 Spitfires and Hurricanes, 900 American fighters and 900 American bombers, 150 Asdic submarine detection sets, 1,500 naval guns, 3,000 anti-aircraft machine guns, and eight destroyers. For the land war, the Red Army was to be supplied with 1,000 tanks together with the necessary spares and accessories, 300 anti-aircraft guns, 300 anti-tank guns and 2,000 armoured cars each month. General supplies were to include 4,000 tons of aluminium a month, along with 13,000 tons of steel bars and significant quantities of copper, tin, lead and brass. A huge amount of medical supplies was also to be provided, including 100 portable x-ray sets, 4,000 kg of local anaesthetics, over a million doses of antibiotics, sedatives, instruments for performing different operations, including 15,00 amputation saws, and half a million pairs of surgical gloves.[9]

Roosevelt made sure the Soviet Union would be able to pay for these supplies by authorising the purchase of 30 million dollars of Soviet gold and arranging for one billion dollars of credit to be extended to the Soviet Union under the Lend-Lease Act, with no interest required and repayment only beginning five years after the war ended.[10] With this gigantic arms deal in place, none of the parties involved were going to allow the Finns to sabotage the whole project.

With German military assistance, the Finns had been attempting to cut the railway heading south from Murmansk. In the far north, Operation *Platinfuchs* (Platinum Fox) was led by a German officer, Colonel General Eduard Dietl, the commander of Mountain Corps Norway.[11] Hitler had insisted that sufficient forces remain in Norway to defend against a possible British attack, so Dietl only had the 2nd and 3rd Mountain Divisions and the Finnish Task Force P at hand to carry out the operation.[12] On 29th June, Dietl sent the 3rd Mountain Division into the Kalastajasaarento Peninsula, where they were faced with the Soviet 14th Army, which put up a tough defence. The Soviet troops may have been cut off from any overland supply lines, but they were resupplied by sea from Murmansk, and they managed to hold out against Dietl's men.[13] To the south, the 2nd Mountain Division crossed the Titovkajoki River and tried to make their way east towards Murmansk.[14] Hitler was still concerned about defending the Norwegian coast, so he transferred one of the German battalions and three artillery batteries back to Norway. With his forces depleted, and facing determined Soviet resistance, Dietl was unable to advance beyond the Litsajoki River, and the attack slowly ground to a halt.[15]

The main German-Finnish effort to cut the Murmansk railway line was codenamed Operation *Polarfuchs* (Arctic Fox). The commander of the German contingent was General Hans Feige, who led XXXVI Army Corps.[16] The Finnish 6th Division, led by Colonel Verner Viikla, was to provide support on Feige's southern flank. The aim of the operation was to capture the town of Salla, then head towards Kantalahti, which lay on the westernmost point of the White Sea.[17] The attack was launched on 1st July, and the Soviet troops put up a fierce defence, then counterattacked. The Soviets were able to send reinforcements across the sea from Archangel to bolster their position, and the Germans suffered significant losses. It took six days before the Germans and the Finns, fighting together, managed to cross the Kuola River and capture the town of Salla.[18] The fighting raged on for several months, and the German casualties mounted. By the time they had reached the Vilmajoki River on 17th September, they decided to take advantage of the terrain, switched over to the defensive, and dug in.[19] The attempt to cut the Murmansk railway line was therefore a failure, but the Soviet resistance was only one reason why this was so. Since Hitler had thought it necessary to protect the Norwegian coastline, the resources and manpower that were available on the Finnish section of the Eastern Front were less than they might have been. Another factor that influenced events was the pressure applied to the Finns by the American and British governments.

On 25th October, Hull wrote to Schoenfeld in Helsinki, and had him explain America's foreign policy to the Finns:

> You are requested to inform at the earliest opportunity such members of the Finnish Government as you deem appropriate that if Finland desires to maintain our friendship now and later, satisfactory evidence must be given that it is the intention of the Finnish government to discontinue immediately all offensive operations against Soviet territory and that to that end Finnish troops in principle will promptly be withdrawn. You should also state that should war material despatched from this country via the Arctic Ocean to northern Soviet territory be attacked en route even allegedly or presumably from Finnish-controlled territory, such an incident in the present status of American opinion must be expected to create an immediate crisis in American-Finnish relations.[20]

President Ryti did not appreciate being threatened by the Americans, and he informed Schoenfeld "with great vehemence"[21] that Finland was not a vassal state, and that she was pursuing her own interests and her own policies. The Finnish President then told Schoenfeld a few home truths:

> Finland was best judge of needs of its own self-defense, but if he were to judge need of United States in respect of its own self-defense he would say our association with Communist Russia involved greater

danger through Communism in United States as well as in Britain than any threat emanating from Germany. . . . Nothing would now alter fixed resolve of Finnish people to gain security for themselves. It was apparent that people in United States did not understand necessity for this resolve to protect Finland against Bolshevik danger.[22]

Churchill had spoken out previously in support of Finland, and no doubt his words had impressed all who heard them, but what he said in private showed a different side to his character. In the final analysis, Churchill understood that he had to put British interests above all else. According to the record of the War Cabinet meeting on 16th November 1939,

> *The First Lord of the Admiralty* said that no doubt it appeared reasonable to the Soviet Union to take advantage of the present situation to regain some of the territory which Russia had lost as a result of the last war, at the beginning of which she had been the ally of France and Great Britain. This applied not only to Baltic territories, but also to Finland. It was to our interests that the U.S.S.R. should increase their strength in the Baltic, thereby limiting the risk of German domination in that area. For this reason it would be a mistake for us to stiffen the Finns against making concessions to the U.S.S.R. In general, it should be our policy to secure as much support as possible in this war from the U.S.S.R., China and the U.S.A.[23]

When Chamberlain assured the Poles that the British government would provide all the support in its power should Poland's independence ever be threatened,[24] that verbal guarantee was worthless without Soviet backing, which Chamberlain did not have.[25] The written version of this guarantee, which was only issued the day after the Nazi-Soviet pact was signed in Moscow, contained a secret protocol which made it clear the British government would not be obliged to help Poland in the event of Soviet aggression.[26] The underlying facts of the situation were the same in 1941. The British government was still not inclined to help the victims of Soviet aggression, because they needed Soviet military assistance to fight the war against Germany. In his history of the second world war, Churchill explained Britain's policy towards Finland:

> The Finns had taken the opportunity of the German attack on Russia to renew hostilities on the Karelian front in July 1941. They hoped to regain those territories lost by the Treaty of Moscow the previous

> year. Their military operations in the autumn of 1941 represented a grave threat not only to Leningrad, but also to the supply lines from Murmansk and Archangel to the Russo-German front. . . . Now that Russia was engaged in a life-and-death struggle with Germany it was clearly impossible for the Allies to allow the Finns, acting as a German satellite Power, to cut Russia's main northern lines of communication with the West.[27]

When Churchill wrote to Stalin on 5th September, he assured him that "we are willing to put any pressure upon Finland in our power, including immediate notification that we will declare war upon them should they continue beyond the old frontiers. We are asking the United States to take all possible steps to influence Finland."[28]

Anthony Eden noted in a telegram to Stafford Cripps on 17th October that

> in the course of a conversation with M. Maisky this evening, his Excellency told me that he had been asked by M. Molotov to raise with me the question of our relations with Finland, Roumania and Hungary. The Soviet Government would appreciate it if we could see our way to declare ourselves at war with these three countries. It would be regarded by Russia as a gesture of solidarity at this time. The Ambassador said that he imagined that it was unnecessary to give any elaborate reason for our action, but he presumed that we would make it plain that it was because these countries continued in a state of war with the Soviet Union.[29]

Eden went on to send a memo to the members of the War Cabinet on 23rd October, in which he laid out the arguments against declaring war on Finland at the request of the Soviets. At the beginning of the memo, Eden noted that Molotov had asked that Britain declare war not only on Finland, but on Hungary and Romania as well. "Although we should naturally wish to meet the Soviet Government's request," Eden wrote, "there are arguments of a practical nature against declaring war in the case of each of the three countries." In the case of Finland, Eden argued that a declaration of war would have no practical effect, it could make it easier for Germany to recruit Finnish troops to fight against Britain, and "would be likely to be distasteful to a large body of American public opinion, which still thinks of the Finns as a gallant little people, who alone paid their debts to the United States." Nevertheless, Eden concluded that "the importance at this juncture of not rebuffing or discouraging our Russian Allies outweighs the above arguments and I am in favour of declaring war on all three countries."[30]

On 21st November, Churchill sent a telegram to Stalin that said,

> About Finland. I was quite ready to advise the Cabinet to declare war upon Finland when I sent you my telegram of 5th September. Later information has made me think that it will be more helpful to Russia and the common cause if the Finns can be got to stop fighting and stand still or go home, than if we put them in the dock with the guilty Axis Powers by a formal declaration of war and make them fight it out to the end. However if they do not stop in the next fortnight and you sill wish us to declare war upon them we will certainly do so.[31]

Stalin responded on 26th November:

> On the question of Finland the U.S.S.R. never proposed anything else – at least in the first instance – but the cessation of the military operations and the de facto exit of Finland from the war. If however Finland refuses to comply even with this in the course of the short period you indicated, then I believe the declaration of war by Great Britain would be reasonable and necessary. Otherwise an impression may be created that there is no unity between us on the question of war against Hitler and his most ardent accomplices and that the accomplices of Hitler's aggression can do their base work with impunity. With regard to Hungary and Roumania we can perhaps wait a little while.[32]

When the War Cabinet met on 3rd December, it was decided to proceed with the declaration of war, although Churchill insisted that it was officially recorded "that in his view this declaration on Finland (and also Hungary and Roumania) would not assist either our cause or that of the Russians. The sole justification for it was that it was necessary in order to satisfy the Russian Government."[33]

The British government formally declared war on Finland on 6th December 1941,[34] an historical fact that is difficult to reconcile with the assertion that the British government declared war on Germany to protect countries like Poland from their territorially aggressive neighbours. The necessity of keeping the Soviets onside so that Great Britain would end up on the winning side at the end of the war meant that Churchill had no option in the winter of 1941 but to do Stalin's bidding and declare war on Finland. There was no chance of the British taking up arms against the Finns, but Stalin had successfully manipulated the situation so that it would be difficult to resist any territorial demands made by the Soviet Union in the future.

After all, the British government could hardly go against an ally and take the side of a nation they had declared war on.[35]

The day after the British government declared war on Finland, Eden left London and travelled to Moscow to meet with Stalin. As we have seen, Churchill had originally intended to send two of his generals to the Soviet Union, but Stalin had made it clear to the British government that he would rather hold meaningful political discussions, so they had agreed to send the Foreign Secretary instead. In the meantime, Stalin had made sure that the British government declared war on Finland. Once he had Eden in Moscow, Stalin made his next move on the geo-political chessboard. According to Eden's report of their first meeting on 16th December,

> As regards the special interests of the Soviet Union, M. Stalin desired the restoration of the position in 1941, prior to the German attack, in respect of the Baltic States, Finland and Bessarabia. The "Curzon Line" should form the basis for the future Soviet-Polish frontier, and Roumania should give special facilities for bases, &c., to the Soviet Union, receiving compensation from territory now occupied by Hungary.[36]

Stalin made it clear to Eden that the territorial expansion of the Soviet Union was the only real item on the agenda for these meetings. Everything else could wait until Britain had agreed that the Soviet Union could keep the territories it had already claimed under the terms of the Nazi-Soviet Pact. "What I want to underline is that I want to come to an agreement on this so as to have a united front on these problems," Stalin told Eden. "My desire is to establish that the war aims of our two countries are identical, as then our alliance will be all the stronger. If our war aims were different then there would be no alliance."[37]

Eden agreed on this point but told Stalin that he did not have the authority to reach such an agreement and that he would have to discuss the matter with his colleagues back in London. Stalin persevered, telling Eden at their meeting on 17th December that:

> You will remember that last night we talked of the possibility of doing something as regards the frontiers of the U.S.S.R. apart from the general question of Central and Western European frontiers. . . . Is it really necessary on this question of the Baltic States to have a Government decision? Surely this is absolutely axiomatic. We are fighting our hardest and losing hundreds of thousands of men in the common cause with Great Britain as our ally, and I should have

> thought that such a question as the position of the Baltic States ought to be axiomatic and ought not to require any decision.[38]

Eden let the Soviet dictator know that so far as the government of the United Kingdom was concerned, the fate of the Baltic States had already been settled, although this could not be admitted publicly for fear of offending the Americans:

> The present position is that we do not recognise the independent existence of any of these States. They have no diplomatic status with us, but we are committed to the United States of America not to bind ourselves as to any decision upon European frontiers before the end of the war without consultation with them. I am, however, prepared to seek a decision from my Government on this issue and also consult the Americans upon it as soon as I get back to London. I think it is most desirable that all three Governments should come to an agreement on this question.[39]

Stalin pressed Eden on the issue of the Baltic States being recognised by the British government, pointing out that "you still have their representatives in London."[40]

"We don't accept them as representatives," said Eden. "We neither accept notes from them nor allow them diplomatic status. The U.S.S.R. is, in fact, recognised as having the *de facto* sovereignty of the Baltic States."[41]

"That seems to be a rather curious situation," replied Stalin.

"I agree it may seem curious," said Eden. "But I don't really think that this is a very important political question. The present position is that there are no independent Baltic States and that in fact they do form part of the U.S.S.R. . . . Do you want me to say that they are recognised *de jure* as part of the U.S.S.R.?[42]

"We are in the midst of the greatest war in history," said Stalin, "and I think these nice formulae about *de jure* and *de facto* &c. are rather out of place." Now that Eden was on record acknowledging that the British government had to all intents and purposes given up on the Baltic States, Stalin applied even more pressure. "It is not only the question of the Baltic States, but of the whole of the Western frontiers of the Soviet Union," he told Eden. "I think that the whole war between us and Germany began because of these Western frontiers of the U.S.S.R., including particularly the Baltic States. That is really what the whole war is about, and what I would like to know is whether our ally, Great Britain, supports us in regaining these Western frontiers."[43]

"I had never heard of these western boundaries until I got here," said Eden, "and I cannot agree to them without first putting them to my own Government and to the Dominions and to America. But that does not in the least prevent us [from] being loyal allies or from doing all we can to help you defeat the Germans." Eden continued: "I have always, as you know, been very strongly in favour of promoting good relations between our two countries, but there are limitations to the power of a Minister in our country, and I cannot commit the country to your propositions without consulting my own Government, the Dominions and the United States of America."[44]

"I certainly do not want to demand the impossible from you and I fully realise the limitation of your powers," said Stalin. "But I am addressing myself to the British government and I am genuinely surprised. I thought that the Atlantic Charter was directed against those people who were trying to establish world dominion. It now looks as if the Charter was directed against the U.S.S.R."

"No, that is certainly not so," replied Eden. "It is merely a question of your putting forward certain views as to your frontiers and of my being unable to give you an immediate reply and asking you to allow me time to get the answer."

"Why does the restoration of our frontiers come into conflict with the Atlantic Charter?" asked Stalin.

"I never said it did," said Eden.[45]

As the records of the visit to Moscow in December 1941 show, Eden had let Stalin know that the principles of the Atlantic Charter would not be applied to the Soviet Union; he had said on record that the British government did not regard Lithuania, Latvia and Estonia as legitimate states and acknowledged that the Soviet Union had *de facto* sovereignty over them, and he had abandoned the official British policy of leaving territorial questions until the peace conference at the end of the war and promised to put the Soviet plans for territorial expansion before the British and American governments.[46] Once he returned to London, Eden submitted a memo to the War Cabinet, in which he argued against opposing the Soviet territorial claims.

The memo, dated 28th January 1942, stated that since Eden's meeting with Stalin, he had been looking at how the British government should respond to "Stalin's demand for the recognition of the Soviet Union's 1941 frontiers."[47] Eden laid out the context in which a decision would have to be made:

> Any estimate of the probable course of Soviet policy must depend upon the course of the war and its effect upon the U.S.S.R., the condition in which the Soviet Union emerges from the war and the

circumstances in which the war is terminated. If the defeat of the German armies is brought about chiefly by the action of the Soviet forces before the war potential of Great Britain and America is fully developed, Russia's position on the European continent will be unassailable. Russian prestige will be so great that the establishment of Communist Governments in the majority of European countries will be greatly facilitated, and the Soviet Government will naturally be tempted to work for this. . . . this possible development is in itself a reason for establishing close relations with the Soviet Union now while their policy is still in a fluid state, in order to exercise as much influence as possible on the moulding of their future course of action.[48]

The British government were also going to have to deal with the Americans, who they expected to protest about any territorial agreement the British might want to make with the Soviets:

> There is no gainsaying the fact that M. Stalin's demand for the Baltic States and, to a lesser degree, his demand for Finnish and Bessarabian territory can hardly be reconciled with the principles laid down in the Atlantic Charter, where it is stated that the Allies seek no aggrandisement, territorial or other; that they desire to see no territorial changes that do not accord with the freely-expressed wishes of the peoples themselves; and that they wish to see sovereign rights and self-government restored to those who have been forcibly deprived of them. By implication it also clashes with the provision of the Charter that the Allies will respect the right of all peoples to choose the form of government under which they will live.[49]
>
> It is not altogether easy to decide what real object M. Stalin has in view in insisting upon this particular demand at this juncture. Our acquiescence or refusal cannot affect Russia's post-war frontiers one way or the other: if she is in occupation of the territory involved at the end of the war, neither we nor America will turn her out. Probably, however, M. Stalin's demand is intended as an acid test to find out how far His Majesty's Government are prepared to make unpalatable concessions in order to obtain the post-war co-operation of the Soviet Union: in other words, to see what value we attach to that co-operation and what sacrifice of principle we are prepared to make in order to achieve it. If this is really M. Stalin's object, he is not likely to be prepared to accept any smaller or alternative concession in its place. Sir S. Cripps, whom I have consulted since his return from Russia, holds that his is a case of all

> or nothing, and that our refusal to satisfy M. Stalin will be the end of any prospect of fruitful co-operation with the Soviet Government in our mutual interests, and that Soviet policy will revert to the pursuit of purely selfish aims, with incalculable consequences for the post-war period. Meanwhile, I have promised M. Stalin that I would discuss the matter with the United States Government and the Dominion Governments, and I do not think we ought to delay any longer taking up the matter with President Roosevelt.[50]
>
> There is bound to be difficulty in practice in harmonising day-to-day Anglo-Russian co-operation with Anglo-American co-operation. Soviet policy is amoral; United States policy is exaggeratedly moral, at least where non-American interests are concerned. In America there is still a widely-spread feeling of distrust and dislike of Russia, which the Pact with Hitler and Russia's attack on Finland greatly augmented. As United States opinion, however, becomes more realistically minded under the stress of war, this feeling may be gradually modified . . . In practice this means that, in order successfully to reconcile American and Russian susceptibilities and to co-ordinate our policy with both of theirs, we shall have to consult the United States Government in all our discussions with the Soviet Government, and try to obtain their approval or at least their acquiescence in all Anglo-Soviet arrangements.[51]

Eden had taken a realistic view of the geopolitical situation at the beginning of 1942, and he was trying to find the best way forward for his country. Britain was fighting a long war against Germany, and as the British Chiefs of Staff had made clear in their memo of 15th February 1937, entitled "Planning for a war with Germany," and again in their May 1940 report, "British Strategy In A Certain Eventuality," Britain needed the United States and the Soviet Union as allies if she was going to end up on the winning side at the end of the war.

At this point, the Soviets were doing most of the heavy lifting, and Eden was concerned that the Soviet Union could end up being in a predominant position in the post-war era. There was nothing Britain could do after the war if the Soviets had taken control of the Baltic States, or if they had taken possession of any Finnish or Romanian territory. As Eden said, "If she is in occupation of the territory involved at the end of the war, neither we nor America will turn them out."[52] At a practical level, the Soviet position would indeed be "unassailable."[53]

The British were not able at that time to make a show of force on the battlefield, which would have demonstrated to the Soviets that they could defeat them militarily. As things stood, the British could not even get themselves on to the same theatre as the Red Army. Operation Overlord, which saw the Allies launch an invasion of the European mainland, would not take place for another two and a half years. All the British could do to try and persuade the Soviets to limit their power grab to the countries and territories they occupied at the end of the war was let Stalin know that the British government, which claimed to have gone to war to preserve the independence of another country, was now prepared to write all those territories off.

The truth of the matter was that millions of people living in the territories Stalin wanted to control after the war were being handed down a multi-generational sentence of imprisonment that would be served under the most inhumane conditions, and no one in the British government was going do anything about it.

10 Arctic Convoys

The Marquess of Lothian, Philip Kerr, who had been the British ambassador to the United States in the summer of 1940 when the government was placing massive orders for new American aeroplanes, had passed away in December that year.[1] Churchill had given the job to Halifax, and Anthony Eden had taken over the position of Foreign Secretary.[2] When Eden laid out the British government's policy towards the Soviet Union in his memorandum to the War Cabinet on 28th January 1942, he argued that American co-operation should be sought before the British reached any agreements with Stalin. On 18th February, Halifax had a meeting with Sumner Welles, who at that time was still the Under Secretary of State. The records of the meeting, which are held in the American archives, state that

> the Ambassador told me that he had come particularly to discuss recent negotiations between the British and Soviet Governments. . . . The Ambassador told me that during the time that Mr. Eden was in Moscow last autumn, Stalin had brought up the desiderata of the Soviet Government. Stalin had stated that he desired to know whether the British would guarantee that in any peace terms which might finally be settled upon, the British would support the Soviet Government in its desire to obtain as the Soviet settlement in Europe the reestablishment of the Soviet's 1941 boundaries.[3]

Halifax gave Welles a copy of a telegram he had received from the Foreign Office, which explained the problem from Eden's perspective:

> You are aware of what passed during the conversations in Moscow between Stalin and myself. . . . Since my return from Moscow we have been considering ways and means of dealing with Stalin's demand for recognition of his 1941 frontiers in Finland, the Baltic States and Roumania. . . . A simple refusal to meet him would involve the risk that Anglo-Soviet relations will deteriorate and that cooperation between Great Britain and Russia and between the United States of America and Russia both during and after the war may be seriously endangered. . . .
>
> Stalin's attitude is that before Hitler forced him into the war by an unjustified aggression he was in possession of these territories. . . . I used the Atlantic Charter as an argument against him. He pointed to 'plebiscites' in Baltic States. Our exchanges of views on this aspect of the subject would have been even less profitable than

> they were if I had suggested that those 'plebiscites' were faked. But there is another difficulty. Is it possible to comply with Stalin's demand without doing violence to the Atlantic Charter and without raising a crop of other demands from other quarters? If so that is, from the point of view of relations of our two countries with the Soviet Government, the solution we should seek.[4]

Halifax then gave Welles a second telegram from the Foreign Office, dated 15th February. Much of this telegram was copied verbatim from Eden's earlier memorandum to the War Cabinet. In a key passage, which was included in both documents, the Americans were made privy to Eden's thinking on the subject:

> The probable course of Soviet policy must depend upon the course of the war and its effect upon the U.S.S.R., condition in which the latter emerges from the war and the circumstances in which the war is terminated. We cannot be certain that Germany's defeat may not be brought about in principle by Russian action before our own and American war potentiality is fully developed. In that event Russian prestige would be enormous and the Soviet Government would be tempted to work for the establishment of Communistic Governments in the majority of European countries. Russians might moreover be in a position to denude German factories of the equipment needed to restore Russian industry and becoming in this way to considerable extent independent of British-American assistance, might no longer desire to adapt themselves to the policies which we and the United States may wish to pursue. This possible development is in itself a powerful reason for establishing close relations with Russia while her policy is still in a fluid state in order to exercise as much influence as possible on her future course of action. . . .
>
> We must therefore recognise that our refusal to satisfy Stalin's demand may be the end of any prospect of fruitful cooperation with the Soviet Government in our mutual interests and might encourage Soviet policy to revert to the pursuit of purely selfish aims with incalculable consequences for [the] post-war period. . . .
>
> Stalin would certainly not admit that his demands are in conflict with the principles of the Atlantic Charter and he may well be satisfied by nothing short of complete acceptance of his demands.[5]

According to Welles' record of the meeting, Halifax said that

> the Soviet Ambassador in London, Mr. Maisky, had asked Mr. Eden on February 12 what reply the British Government intended to make to the Soviet demand for assurances as to the restoration of its 1941 frontiers. Mr. Eden had replied that the problem had been submitted to the United States Government in a favorable manner by the British Government. Ambassador Maisky had replied that the Soviet Government required a treaty with Great Britain covering this subject but that all that the United States was asked to do was not to object to the conclusion of such a treaty between the two powers. Ambassador Maisky had emphasised his fear of the effect of any continued delay of a satisfactory reply on the policy and attitude which would be displayed by the Soviet Government.[6]

The Americans had finally come into the war on 8th December 1941, the day after the Japanese attack on Pearl Harbor. Germany had declared war on the United States on 11th December,[7] and that afternoon, Roosevelt had asked Congress to recognise that a state of war existed between the two countries.[8] One of the first things Roosevelt did as the leader of a belligerent nation was task Cordell Hull, the Secretary of State, with revising the Atlantic Charter so that all the nations that stood against Nazi Germany could sign up to it.[9] On 1st January 1942, the Declaration by United Nations, which stated that the signatories would subscribe to the principles of the Atlantic Charter, was signed by the political representatives of 26 nations, including the Soviet Union.[10]

Eden had asserted in his memorandum of 28th January that the Americans could be "exaggeratedly moral" in their dealings with other countries, and Welles' reaction to the British proposals was a point in case. The Atlantic Charter played an important part in Roosevelt's plan for the post-war world, and Welles refused to give the British government's proposals his blessing:

> I said . . . that I had no reluctance in stating that in my judgement this was the most important issue of a political character which had come up for discussion between our two Governments since the United States had entered the war or, for that matter, since Great Britain herself had entered the war. I said that it appeared to me that our two Governments were at the crossroads. We had to determine whether the Atlantic Charter meant what it said and whether we were determined to uphold in fact as well as by word the principles set forth therein. . . .

I was prepared to agree that the Soviet Government in fairness as well as a matter of policy should be entitled to ensure its own security in the future against now unforeseen contingencies, but that the obtaining of such security could not in my judgement be admitted if that implied the placing of millions of human beings under Russian domination should those human beings desire to maintain their own independence and should they be bitterly opposed to Russian overlordship. . . .

Could it be conceivable that any healthy and lasting world order could be created on a foundation which implied the utter ignoring of all of the principles of independence, liberty and self-determination which were set forth in the Atlantic Charter? If that was the kind of world we had to look forward to, I did not believe that the people of the United States would wish to be parties thereto. . . .

I said that we were face to face with a question of vital principle. I saw no hope for a stable and peaceful world in the future unless the new world order were built upon principles which could be maintained and to which adherence would be consistent. What peace could be envisaged if at this early stage in the war the British Government agreed upon selling out millions of people who looked to us as their own hope in the future and if that new world order were based upon the domination of unwilling, resentful, and potent minorities by a state to which they would never give willing allegiance?[11]

At the end of the second world war, Welles was in no position to acknowledge the Soviet Union's ignoring of all the principles set forth in the Atlantic Charter, or to lecture the British about how to create a "healthy and lasting world order." Welles, who had written disparagingly of Churchill's alcohol consumption in 1940, had been excessively drunk whilst on a train with the President in September 1940 and he had made inappropriate sexual advances towards a young man employed as a porter on the train. When the story finally came out in 1943, Welles was forced to resign.[12]

In spite of the protests of their allies across the Atlantic, the British government was trying to find a way to move forward with the Soviet Union. At a War Cabinet meeting on 6th February, Max Beaverbrook, who at that time was the Minister of War Production, argued for accepting Stalin's territorial demands and signing a formal treaty:

The Minister of War Production said that all that M. Stalin was asking for was recognition of his frontiers as they had existed in

> June, 1941, when Germany had invaded Russia. At the same date we had made a Treaty with Russia which had wiped out everything which had passed between our two countries up to that date. . . . The Minister said that our relations with Russia were deteriorating; we could not afford to wait but should hold out a hand of friendship and seal the bond with them as quickly as possible. . . . It was worth remembering that so far Russia had contributed far more to the war effort than the United States to whom we had made such frequent concessions. In a number of matters we had not acceded, or not acceded at all promptly, to Russia's requests, e.g. her requests for military aid or her request that we should declare war on Finland.[13]

Herbert Morrison, the Home Secretary and Minister of Home Security, said at the meeting on 6th February that "there must be a limit to the application of the principle of self-determination" and "it was most important that we should maintain good relations with M. Stalin, and it was worth a good deal to attain this."[14]

Archibald Sinclair, now the Secretary of State for Air, said that "provided we won the war, there was no doubt that M. Stalin's forces would be in occupation of the Baltic States and Bessarabia at the end of the war, and it would not be in our power to get them to leave. By agreeing to accept these frontiers now, we should go a long way to remove the risk of bad feeling between this country and Russia."[15]

The British government had to maintain a working relationship with the Soviet leadership, and there was nothing to be gained by making a principled stand. On 7th March, Churchill wrote directly to Roosevelt. "The increasing gravity of the war has led me to feel that the principles of the Atlantic Charter ought not to be construed to as to deny Russia the frontiers she occupied when Germany attacked her," he told the President. "I hope therefore that you will be able to give us a free hand to sign the treaty which Stalin desires as soon as possible." Churchill reminded Roosevelt who was doing most of the fighting at this point in the war: "Everything portends an immense renewal of the German invasion of Russia in the spring and there is very little we can do to help the only country that is heavily engaged with the German armies."[16]

One thing the British and American governments had done to help the Soviet Union was set up the Arctic convoys that Stalin had spoken to Hopkins about when the two met in July 1941. The first of these convoys set sail from Iceland on 21st August 1941 and reached Archangel ten days later, with no losses. As the convoy had approached the Soviet coastline, RAF pilots from the 151 Aviation Wing flew 15 Hurricane fighters ashore from the aircraft *Argus*.[17] These pilots remained in the Soviet Union until 22nd

October, flying combat missions and training Soviet pilots to use the British planes.[18]

The next convoy, codenamed PQ1, set sail on 29th August from Hvalfjödur in Iceland, carrying tanks, raw materials and more Hurricanes.[19] The Arctic convoys kept running throughout the autumn and early winter of 1941 without losing any ships, although the conditions were difficult. The ocean gales were ferocious, temperatures were so low that falling over the side would almost certainly have been fatal, and it was so dark that far north that a lookout stationed on the bridge often had difficulty seeing the bows of the ship.[20] Although only one merchant ship was sunk between December 1941 and March 1942 out of a total of 158 ships that made the journey,[21] the convoys that followed in the spring and summer of 1942 were far more dangerous affairs, and the lives of many Allied seamen were lost.

When convoy PQ15 sailed for the Soviet Union on 25th April, the Germans were waiting for them. Twenty U-boats, painted white and crewed by veteran submariners, had been allocated to the Northern Waters Flotilla, and the *Luftwaffe* now had modified Heinkel He-111s and Ju-88s, which could carry torpedoes, at their Norwegian bases.[22]

On 1st May, one of the British vessels, *Punjabi*, turned to starboard to avoid a mine and came across the path of the *King George V*, which steamed into the *Punjabi* and cut her in two. As the crew took to the ice-cold water, their anti-submarine depth charges rolled off the stern and exploded amongst the survivors.[23] This was an appalling tragedy, but things got even worse on 3rd May, when six low flying Heinkel He-111s attacked the convoy. Three of the German planes were shot down, but the others managed to drop their torpedoes and score hits on the *Botavon, Jutland* and *Cape Corso*. The *Cape Corso* was carrying a cargo of ammunition, and when the German torpedo struck, she exploded violently. Nothing was left after the explosion died away but some debris floating on the surface. A total of 73 sailors lost their lives in this attack.[24]

The *Luftwaffe* tried to attack the convoy again, but Soviet Pe-3 fighters arrived on the scene and launched their rockets at the German planes. The Soviet fighters then circled over the convoy, which acted as a deterrent to the *Luftwaffe* pilots.[25] The convoy finally reached the Kola Inlet, which gave Murmansk access to the sea, on 5th May 1942.[26]

On 16th May, the British Chiefs of Staff recognised how dangerous the Arctic convoys were becoming and recommended to Churchill that the outgoing convoy PQ16 should be postponed.[27] Churchill was now faced with a dilemma. There was an accumulation of supplies in Iceland that had not been sent through to Murmansk,[28] and Churchill knew that Molotov was about to visit Britain to sign a treaty between the two countries. The British did not have many levers of influence that could be used with the Soviets, and if Churchill had cancelled one of the convoys, it would not only have lowered his standing as a wartime leader in the eyes of both the Americans and the Soviets, it could have put the treaty in jeopardy. On the other hand, if Churchill sent out the next convoy, it would almost inevitably cost lives.

On 20th March 1942, Churchill had sent a telegram to Stalin that showed that showed just how far he was willing to go to maintain a wartime relationship with the Soviet Union. Churchill wrote,

> Ambassador Maisky lunched with me last week and mentioned some evidences that Germans may use gas upon you in their attempted spring offensive. After consulting my colleagues and the Chiefs of Staff, I wish to assure you that His Majesty's Government will treat any use of this weapon of poison gas against Russia exactly as if it was directed against ourselves. I have been building up an immense store of gas bombs for discharge from aircraft and we shall not hesitate to use these over all suitable objectives in Western Germany from the moment that your armies and people are assaulted in this way.
>
> It is a question to be considered whether at the right time we should not give a public warning that such is our resolve, as the warning might deter the Germans from adding this new horror to the many they have loosed upon the world. Please let me know what you think about this and whether the evidence of preparations warrants the warning.
>
> There is no immediate hurry, and before I take a step which may draw upon our citizens this new form of attack I must of course have ample time to bring all our anti-gas preparations to extreme readiness.[29]

If Churchill was prepared to use chemical weapons against German citizens as a display of support for the Soviet Union in the expectation that such weapons would subsequently be used upon British citizens, then he was not going to stop PQ16 from sailing at this critical moment. The relationship with the Soviet Union had to be preserved at all costs. On 17th May, Churchill wrote to the Chiefs of Staff:

> Not only Premier Stalin but President Roosevelt will object very much to our desisting from running the convoys now. The Russians are in heavy action, and will expect us to run the risk and pay the price entailed by our contribution. The United States ships are queueing up. My own feeling, mingled with much anxiety, is that the convoy ought to sail on the 18th. The operation is justified if a half

gets through. Failure on our part to make the attempt would weaken our influence with both our major Allies. There are always the uncertainties of weather and luck, which may aid us. I share your misgivings, but I feel it is a matter of duty.[30]

As Molotov was flying west in a Soviet bomber to sign the treaty between the two countries, convoy PQ16 was sailing in the other direction, towards Murmansk. The Soviet Foreign Minister arrived at Tealing Airfield just north of Dundee on 20th May, then travelled south by train to London. When discussions began the next day, Molotov pushed for Britain to recognise the Soviet territorial claims in Poland, Romania and the Baltic States.[31] The British disregarded the American position, which been explained by Welles at his meeting with Halifax, and agreed that the Baltic States would be under Soviet rule. However, the British refused to allow the Soviets to lay claim to the territory in eastern Poland that had previously been occupied by the Soviet Union under the terms of the secret protocol of the Nazi-Soviet Pact.[32] There the issue stood, until Stalin sent a telegram to Molotov and told him to forget about reaching territorial agreements with the British government. If the Soviet Union could not get what they wanted right now using political means, then the question of Soviet territorial expansion would be resolved in due course using military force.[33]

On 24th May, as these discussions with Molotov were taking place, Churchill received a "Most Secret" Naval communique which stated that

> U589, one of the six U-boats disposed to the S.E. of Jan Mayen to intercept convoy PQ16, reported engine-room defects at 1900 on 21/5, and was ordered back to Narvik.
>
> At 1035 on May 22nd, U 586 reported the wake of several ships Eastbound in 69° 45' N 04° 30' W and hydrophone contacts heard previously during the night. The five remaining U-boats were then moved at maximum speed North-Eastward to positions approximately 170 miles W.S.W. of Bear Island.[34]

The Germans had found PQ16. Churchill had let the Chiefs of Staff know that he was ready to sacrifice up to half of the boats in the convoy if it meant keeping Stalin onside until the Anglo-Soviet treaty was signed. Now the butcher's bill would have to be paid. The following day, an FW-200 Condor was seen flying over the convoy, and a U-boat was sighted on the convoy's starboard side. Just after seven o'clock that evening, the Germans began to attack, but several of the German dive bombers and torpedo planes were shot down and the attack faltered. The next morning, the Germans came back.[35]

On 26th May 1942, Britain and the Soviet Union signed the Twenty-Year Mutual Assistance Agreement Between the United Kingdom and the Union of Soviet Socialist Republics. This stated that "the high contracting parties mutually undertake to afford one another military and other assistance and support of all kinds in war against Germany and all those States which are associated with her in acts of aggression in Europe." Article 5 of the new agreement stated that upon the "re-establishment of peace" the Soviet Union and Britain would "act in accordance with the two principles of not seeking territorial aggrandizement for themselves and of non-interference in the internal affairs of other States."[36]

On the same day that the treaty was being signed in London, U-703, skippered by *Kapitänleutnant* Heinz Bielfeld, fired a torpedo into the hold of the American merchant ship *Syros*, which set off her cargo of explosives and ammunition.[37] The ship exploded and sank in a matter of minutes. Although 9 of the crew were lost, 28 men survived and were picked up by British trawlers.[38] The *Luftwaffe* carried out further attacks on convoy PQ16 that day, with Heinkel 111s dropping torpedoes and Junkers 88s executing high altitude bombing raids.[39] These attacks were ineffective but the *Luftwaffe* returned the following day, and the Allied casualties soon began to mount up. The American cargo ship *Alamar* caught fire after being hit by two bombs and was abandoned. Another American ship, the *Mormacsul,* sank after taking a direct hit from a German bomb, and five bombs hit and sank the CAM (Catapult Armed Merchantman) ship *Empire Lawrence*.[40] The British merchant ship *Lowther Castle* sank after a Heinkel scored a hit with a torpedo, and another merchant ship, the *Empire Purcell,* was hit by two bombs and abandoned.[41] The aerial attacks had begun in the early hours of the morning, and there was no respite until the *Luftwaffe* ceased operations at 2130 that night.[42] PQ16 was subjected to a total of 145 aerial attacks, and when the ships of the convoy finally began sailing into Murmansk fjord on 30th May, 11 out of the original 35 ships had been sunk.[43]

Churchill showed time and again that he would do everything in his power to keep the Red Army fighting on the Eastern Front. On 20th March 1942, he told Stalin that he would approve the use of chemical weapons against Germany, even if that meant Britain citizens would be subjected to retaliatory attacks. When Molotov was due to arrive in Britain to sign a treaty between the two countries in May, Churchill sent PQ16 out on the Murmansk run, even though he expected that up to half the ships could be lost. Churchill's actions in 1942 demonstrated that he was willing to pay almost any price to maintain the wartime relationship with the Soviet Union.

The premiership had been given to Churchill at a moment of extreme peril. Britain was already at war, the British Expeditionary Force was about to be defeated, and although many of the British troops managed to escape from France, the whole episode was a military disaster. Churchill might have been the only politician in the country who could have rallied the British people to the cause under those circumstances. However, to make sure Britain ended up on the winning side against one form of tyranny, Churchill found himself in the position where he had no option but to form an alliance with another one. And if the British government wanted to maintain that alliance with the Soviet Union throughout the war years, then they were going to have to do more than send the Arctic convoys through to Murmansk. A way would have to be found to take the war to Germany.

11 Air Power

When Chamberlain declared war on Germany on 3rd September 1939, the man who would eventually lead the bombing war against Germany was at a friend's house in Norfolk. Arthur Harris sat in front of a log fire with Jean Tresfon and their two wives and listened to Chamberlain make his announcement on the radio.[1] Tresfon asked Harris how long he thought the war against Germany would last. Harris estimated that it would last for five years, because "I knew we could not hope to reach our full effort before five years and that it would take at least our full effort to stop the Boche and considerably more to beat him."[2]

The British may have managed to create a defensive fighter force capable of fighting off the *Luftwaffe* in the summer of 1940, but to take the fight to Germany would require heavy bombers capable of reaching the German homeland. There were only 280 aircraft in the whole of Bomber Command at the end of Chamberlain's phoney war,[3] and these were not up to the task. The Vickers Wellington lacked speed and height and could only carry a limited payload.[4] The Handley Page Hampden had a top speed of 155 mph and could only carry a payload of 4,000 lbs.[5] Neither of these planes had any navigational systems worthy of the name, so pilots had to rely on educated guesswork to find their targets. After Churchill took over as Prime Minister and the RAF began to drop actual bombs on German soil instead of leaflets, the results were so bad that the German leadership found it difficult to work out what the British bombers had been aiming at.[6]

One of the men who would change that situation was Roy Chadwick, a designer at Avro, an aeronautics firm based in Manchester. Chadwick had been working on the Manchester, a twin-engined bomber that used Rolls-Royce Vulture engines, but the engines were prone to overheating, and the plane was unreliable.[7] Chadwick realised that it would be possible to produce a far better aeroplane by extending the wingspan, adding two engines, and using the new Rolls-Royce Merlin engines instead.[8] After a series of tests at the Aeroplane and Armament Experimental Establishment at Boscombe Down in Wiltshire, the design of Avro's new bomber was approved. It was officially named the Lancaster.[9] The fuselage of the new heavy bomber was 69 feet long and the wingspan was 102 feet. It could fly up to 282 mph and reach a ceiling of over 21,000 feet carrying a bombload of 14,000 lbs.[10]

When Harris took over Bomber Command on 22nd February 1942,[11] he had 44 heavy and medium bomber squadrons at his disposal, with approximately 469 night bombers, of which 54 were the new Lancaster heavies.[12] The first of the Lancasters had been delivered to 44 (Rhodesia) Squadron, which was based at Waddington in Lincolnshire, on Christmas

Eve of 1941.[13] After some initial problems, not the least of which was the tendency of the end of the wings to shear off,[14] had been addressed by the Avro engineers,[15] the bombers were deemed fit for purpose, and by March 1942, the pilots of 44 Squadron were flying the "Lancs" on active missions. Harris was a fierce, combative character who pursued his goal of destroying cities throughout Germany with a single-minded passion. "A lot of people - generally those with no qualifications to speak - are in the habit of iterating the silly phrase 'Bombing can never win a war,'" he once observed. "Well, we shall see. It hasn't been tried yet."[16]

The British air offensive against Germany had begun on 15th May 1940, five days after Churchill became Prime Minister. The Germans had surrounded the Dutch port of Rotterdam, and the *Luftwaffe* had attacked the city and set the heart of the city ablaze.[17] This attack on the Dutch city proved to be a turning point in the war. The War Cabinet authorised Bomber Command to attack oil and transport targets in the Ruhr,[18] and thirty heavy bombers flew out to attack the Blohm & Voss shipyards in Hamburg a few days later. Most of the bombers' payload landed in residential areas around the Reeperbahn, and thirty-four people lost their lives.[19]

In those early days of the bombing war, it was thought that striking German oil plants would leave the enemy in an "extremely critical" situation,[20] and Sir Charles Portal, who was Commander-in-Chief of Bomber Command at that time, was directed by the Air Staff to concentrate his attacks on German oil, aircraft and communications systems.[21] Portal believed that many of the targets were in isolated areas, so "the very high percentage of bombs which inevitably miss the actual target will hit nothing else of importance and do no damage, and the minimum amount of dislocation and disturbance will be caused by the operations as a whole."[22] The official history of the British air offensive notes that "this was a most important observation, and ultimately when carried to its logical conclusion was to have a decisive effect upon the making of bombing policy."[23]

The British targeting policy was expanded when, on 24th August 1940, German bombers veered off course during a night attack and dropped their bombs on the centre of London.[24] Churchill immediately told Sir Cyril Newall, the Chief of the Air Staff, that he wanted Bomber Command to attack Berlin.[25] It is not credible to assert that Churchill did not understand that by directing Bomber Command to attack the German capital, he would be escalating the war in a way that would inevitably result in the general population on both sides being regarded as targets.

The first British bombing attack on Berlin caused very little damage.[26] The skies over Berlin on the 25th August were cloudy and half of the British bombers could not even find their target.[27] However, the bombers returned on the night of 28th August, and they attacked the city again two nights later.[28] Hitler responded by giving a speech at the Sportpalast in Berlin on 4th September in which he promised to fight fire with fire,[29] and on the afternoon of 7th September, the *Luftwaffe* sent 625 bombers and 648 fighters over the English Channel to attack London. The first wave flew along the Thames at around 5 p.m. and dropped their bombs on various gas works, power stations and miles of docks. Just after 8 pm, a second wave of bombers arrived and resumed the attack. The following night, German bombers returned and carried out another raid. Some 842 people were killed in these first two attacks, and there was a significant amount of material damage. The bombing raids on London went on for 57 consecutive nights, as an average of 200 bombers arrived every 24 hours to drop their payloads on the capital city.[30]

On 21st September, the Air Staff issued a directive stating that German oil production facilities should still be the primary target of Bomber Command, although the city of Berlin would continue to be attacked.[31] This limited concession to area bombing did not sit well with Portal, who had told the Air Staff on 11th September that he wanted to put psychological pressure on the German public by warning twenty different towns and cities over the radio that one of them would be attacked by the RAF every time the *Luftwaffe* hit a British target. They would not know which one it would be until the first pathfinders arrived and dropped their flares. One of the targets recommended by Portal was the city of Essen.[32]

The official history of the strategic air offensive against Germany acknowledges that

> it had always been evident that any bombing attack, save against the most isolated targets such as warships at sea or troops on the battlefield, would inevitably cause damage outside the particular area of the target. . . . If there was to be any strategic bombing at all, civilians would be killed; hospitals, churches and cultural monuments would be hit. The Air Staff, as represented by its Vice-Chief, Sir Richard Peirse, believed that what was inevitable was also desirable only in so far as it remained a by-product of the primary intention to hit a military target in the sense of a power station, a marshalling yard or an oil plant. Bomber Command, as represented by its Commander-in-Chief, Sir Charles Portal, now believed that this by-product should become an end-product. He believed that the time had come to launch a direct attack on the German people themselves. He believed that this course had been justified by previous German action and that it would be justified as a strategy in the outcome.[33]

Portal became the Chief of the Air Staff on 4th October 1940, and Peirse took over as Commander-in-Chief of Bomber Command.[34] On the twenty-fifth of that month, a draft directive was sent from the Air Staff to Bomber Command, which said that since the threat of an invasion appeared to be over, the time was "particularly opportune" for Bomber Command "to make a definite attempt with our offensive to affect the morale of the German people . . ." The directive suggested that twenty or thirty German towns should be selected, and at least one of them attacked every few nights. "Thus," states the official history of the air offensive, "what had so recently been no more than a suggestion from Bomber Command, now became Air Staff policy."[35]

Peirse argued that only one in five bombers were finding their targets on longer bombing raids, and by taking on a longer target list that included twenty German cities, the frequency of raids on any one target would have to be reduced. If a larger bomber force existed, the directive may have been feasible, but attempting to carry out the directive's objectives with the bombers they had would be to invite failure.[36]

The Air Staff issued a revised directive on 30th October, and according to the official history of the British air offensive,

> The primary aim of Bomber Command remained two-fold; the attack on oil and morale. Whenever conditions were favourable, oil targets were to be the first choice. When they were not, heavy attacks were to be launched against Berlin or towns in central and western Germany. It was left to Sir Richard Peirse to decide the frequency of these attacks on towns, but he was urged to adopt the German technique of opening the raid with a fire-raising attack. 'Successive sorties', the directive continued, 'should then focus their attacks to a large extent on the fires with a view to preventing the fire fighting services from dealing with them and giving the fires every opportunity to spread.' Thus, the fiction that the bombers were attacking 'military objectives' in the towns was officially abandoned. This was the technique which was to become known as area bombing.[37]

The plan to attack military objectives such as the German oil facilities had been based on the assumption that half of the bombers would be able to find the target, and that an oil plant could be put out of action for months at a time after being hit by just four bombs.[38] Peirse had pointed out that only one in five bombers were finding their targets at the end of a long range attack inside Germany, and on 28th December, a report by the Photographic Interpretation Section on a raid on two oil plants at

Gelsenkirchen was sent to Portal and Peirse. One of the plants had been attacked by 162 aircraft, the other by 134 aircraft, and the photos taken after the raids showed that neither plant had suffered any serious damage.[39] Portal realised that there were "serious doubts about the soundness of the calculations upon which our oil policy was based" and concluded that "the next best policy to the attack on oil, if the latter is discarded, would be mass attacks on industrial areas."[40]

Harris wrote in his war memoirs that "the decision to attack large industrial areas instead of key factories was made before I became Commander-in-Chief. But whenever anyone wishes to blackguard me . . . they accuse me of being not only the executor of the bombing policy but also its author."[41] An Air Staff directive was in fact issued on 14th February 1942, which authorised Bomber Command to attack Germany "without restriction" and stated that the objective of bombing raids "should now be focused on the morale of the enemy civilian population and, in particular, of industrial workers." The targets listed in the new directive included Essen, Duisburg, Dusseldorf, Cologne, Lübeck, Rostock, Bremen and Kiel.[42] On 15th February, Portal wrote to his deputy, Norman Bottomley, and told him, "Ref the new bombing directive: I suppose it is clear that the aiming points are to be the built-up areas, not, for instance, the dockyards or aircraft factories. . . . This must be made quite clear if it is not already understood."[43]

When Harris took over at Bomber Command on 23rd February 1942, he understood what his mission was. "The general idea at this time on what civil servants always call "a high level" was that the main and almost the only purpose of bombing was to attack the morale of the industrial workers," he wrote. "This was to be achieved by destroying, mainly by incendiary bombs, the whole of the four largest cities in the Ruhr, and thereafter fourteen industrial cities elsewhere in Germany."[44]

Harris launched an attack on the German city of Essen, the second largest city in the Ruhr, on the night of 8th-9th March. Two hundred and eleven aircraft were dispatched on the raid, and seventy-four of them were equipped with a new navigational aid known as Gee.[45] This had a TR1335 cathode ray receiver installed aboard the Lancasters. Three transmitters spread out along 200 miles of the English coast sent out signals that were picked up by the receivers in the bombers. The differences in the times the three outgoing pulses were then received by the TR1335 unit in the bomber were used to calculate its position.[46] This was an improvement over what had gone before. In the early years of the war, the bombers had used a dead reckoning approach, which involved setting a course from their take-off position in England, then taking account of the prevailing winds, their speed, and the time they had been flying, and the navigator would estimate their position over Germany. If no visual markers could be identified, then an ETA (estimated time of arrival) was used to drop their bombs at where the target was supposed to be.[47]

These crude navigational techniques had not been successful, and Churchill had been made aware of how poorly Bomber Command had performed in the early years of the war. Daniel M. Butt of the War Cabinet Secretariat had been asked by Lord Cherwell, Churchill's scientific advisor, to prepare a report on the bomber offensive,[48] and the findings of the report had been presented to Churchill in August 1941.[49] The Butt Report showed that Bomber Command was not doing anything militarily significant at that stage of the war. According to the report, only two thirds of the total number of bombers that left England in June and July 1941 claimed to have attacked their designated targets in Germany,[50] and of those, less than a third had managed to drop their bombs within five miles of the target.[51] This meant that approximately one in five of the total number of bombers that had taken off from England had managed to drop their payload somewhere within the 78 square miles surrounding their designated target.[52] The problem facing the RAF in 1941 was clearly stated in the official history of the air offensive:

> Thus, for the first time in air force history the first and paramount problem of night operations was seen at the highest level to be not merely a question of bomb aiming, though that difficulty remained, but of navigation. While the bombers were still not within five miles of the aiming-point, it was a matter only of academic interest as to whether a bomb could be aimed with an error of 300, 600 or 1,000 yards.[53]

The raid on Essen ended up being a failure because the main bomber force arrived after the flares that had been dropped to mark the target had gone out. The bombers dropped their own incendiaries short of the target, and those that followed used the new fires as their targeting point.[54] Photographs taken after the raid showed that the target area had suffered minimal damage.[55] The bombers attacked again on the night of 10th March, and this time incendiaries were dropped instead of flares. The fires caused by these incendiaries would serve as a beacon for the arriving bombers.[56] The operations record for Lancaster L7566, one of the bombers from 44 Squadron that participated in the raid, reads as follows:

> 10.3.42: Target allotted and attacked Aiming point B Mosaic 437 of ESSEN. Bomb load 14 S.B.C.'s each 90 x 4 lbs. Height 15,000 feet. Time 21.56 to 22.05 hrs. Heading 270° Target identified by a pin-point on river Ruhr, final touches by vision of buildings etc. It is believed incendiaries were concentrated between two miles east of

the area and the area itself. Owing to evasion action we cannot swear to this but it is our honest opinion. Five large fires caused which were burning when target area left. 15 bundles of Nickels G.1. were dropped. Landed at Docking.[57]

Harris ordered a total of twelve attacks on Essen in the spring of 1942, but he acknowledged after the war that no serious damage had been done either to Essen, or to the Krupps factory that was based in the city.[58] As it turned out, the Gee system had only been partially effective, because there was a lot of industrial smog hanging over the area and it was difficult to visually identify the proper targets in the dark. Although Gee did help the bombers get to the general area where the targets were located, it was not unheard of for the RAF to mistake German decoy fires for the intended target, or even to drop bombs on the wrong town altogether.[59]

Harris decided to select an easier target for his bombers to attack. The city of Lübeck on the Baltic coast would be easy to identify in the dark because of its position on the river Trave, and it was not militarily significant, so it would not be heavily defended. It was also known to have a lot of wooden houses, which meant it would be more likely to burn.[60] "I wanted my crews to be well blooded, as they say in fox hunting, to have a taste of success for a change," wrote Harris.[61]

At approximately 23.15 on the night of 28th March 1942, the air raid sirens went off in Lübeck, and a few minutes later, the bombing raid began.[62] Wellington bombers equipped with the Gee navigation system dropped flares[63] to mark the centre of the old town, where the streets were so narrow there would be very little space between the wooden residential buildings.[64] A fleet of bombers then dropped high explosives to destroy the buildings and turn them into kindling, and incendiaries to set everything alight.[65] The incendiary bomb loads included standard four lb magnesium incendiaries, as well as larger incendiary bombs designed to cast benzol and rubber out in a thirty feet radius from the point of impact.[66] The operations record for 75 (New Zealand) Squadron contains the following entry:

OPERATIONS – ATTACK AGAINST TARGETS AT LUBECK.

Ten Well.III aircraft took off to attack the above target, one aircraft, Well.III.X3462, captained by Sgt.Bell failed to return to base. Bomb load consisting of 4000lb, 1000lbs, 500lbs, 250lbs and containers of incendiaries was dropped in the target area. Bombs were seen to burst on target and large fires were seen burning in the target area. Weather was clear except for light haze over west portion of the North Sea. There was very little A.A. fire and few searchlights over target. No enemy aircraft were seen. Navigation by TR1335 and D.R. was good. The whole operation was very successful.[67]

After reconnaissance photos of Lübeck were analysed, it was estimated that 190 acres, or 30 per cent of the town's built up area, had been destroyed by fire.[68] Harris sent his bombers out to attack the city of Rostock on the Baltic coast over four nights beginning on 23rd April.[69] The raids on Rostock were considered a success because the centre of the city caught fire and approximately 60 percent of the city was destroyed.[70] Bomber Command was now committed to a policy of area bombing, and the success of its raids was being measured not in the number of bombers that might have dropped their payload near a target, but in the size of the area that had been razed to the ground. There were exceptions to the area bombing rule, such as the daylight raid on the MAN Diesel plant in Augsburg, which made marine diesel engines. This operation, which took place on 17th April, was led by John Nettleton of 44 Squadron. Six planes from Nettleton's squadron and six planes from 97 Squadron, each carrying four 1000lb bombs,[71] took off in the middle of the afternoon so they would arrive at their target in time to see the MAN plant in the last of the daylight and could use the darkness of evening for cover on the return leg of their journey. The bombers flew across the Channel at low level but were intercepted by German fighters soon after they reached France, and four of the Lancasters were shot down. The remaining bombers flew on as low as they possibly could, scattering farmers and livestock in their fields as they passed by, before finally reaching Augsburg, where they flew through the German anti-aircraft fire and attacked the diesel engine plant at approximately 8 o'clock in the evening.[72] The operations record for Nettleton's Lancaster, R5508B, contains an account of the mission:

> Primary target attacked – M.A.N. Diesel Engine Factory at Augsburg. Time 19.55 hours. Height 50 feet. Bombs 4 x 1,000 lbs dropped in target area. Bombs seen to burst by rear gunner, and Captain on turning aircraft. Two of F.O. Garwell's bombs seen to fall slightly South of target and two in other section of area. Pilot states :- Set course for Selsey Bill at a low level and whole trip done at low level until it became too dark on return. After setting course from Selsey Bill it was noticed that grooves appeared in the main planes about 2 or 3 inches wide just outboard of the inboard engines on both sides. Ten minutes after crossing the coast (French) fighters were encountered and attacked the formation in the vicinity of BERNEY. On reaching the target light flak was intense and accurate, but heavy flak most inaccurate. F/O Garwell in "A" of 44 was hit and

> caught on fire. He made a successful forced landing and it is thought that all the crew would have most probably have been safe. During the fighters attack the rear guns seized after firing approx. 800 rounds. The return journey was uneventful. Three aircraft including "H" (Capt. Sgt. Rhodes) of 44 Squadron were seen to crash and another on fire. Time off 15.12. Time in 00.50 at Squires Gate.[73]

Nettleton was awarded the Victoria Cross after the Augsburg raid,[74] but in strictly military terms, the raid had not been a success. The damage to the MAN factories turned out to be negligible. The forging shop and the machine tool store had been damaged, but most of the tools inside had been untouched, and the firm had several other facilities throughout Germany to take up the slack so the impact on production was minimal.[75] Seven of the twelve Lancasters that had set out were lost, and 49 out of the 85 men who flew on the mission did not return.[76] These were unsustainable losses, and the official history of the air campaign notes that "it was becoming increasingly obvious that if Bomber Command could not fulfil the role of the rapier it would have to undertake that of the bludgeon. It was also obvious that much more force would be required to deliver effective bludgeon blows than rapier thrusts."[77] Harris took this approach as far as he could and decided that he would send a thousand bombers out against a single target.[78]

Bomber Command only had an average of 421 bombers available for any given operation in March of 1942,[79] but Harris wanted to achieve an unprecedented concentration of force over a single German city so that its defences would be unable to cope.[80] Harris sought the approval of his commanders, and both Portal and Churchill liked the idea.[81] Harris visited Chequers and sat up drinking whisky with Churchill until three in the morning, discussing his plans for what had been code-named Operation Millenium.[82] Once he had been given the green light to carry out the operation, Harris ordered his deputy, Robert Saundby, to round up the necessary planes. In theory, Saundby had 815 planes at his disposal from Bomber Command, if those flown by the two training groups were included. Coastal Command declined to co-operate and did not contribute any of their bombers to the operation, but somehow a total of 1,046 planes were found, many of them piloted by instructors and crews that had not even completed their training.[83]

Harris now had to decide which German city would be on the receiving end of this unprecedented show of destructive force. On 30th May 1942, he sat at his desk at Bomber Command HQ in the village of Walters Ash, near High Wycombe in Buckinghamshire, and studied the weather reports.[84] The cloud cover over the east coast of England was predicted to break up that night, and Harris pondered his maps for a moment before drawing his finger from England, across to western Europe, then into Germany. Only one of the possible targets was likely to have reasonable weather through the night, so Harris made his decision. It was to be Cologne.[85]

The city had already been subjected to several bombing raids, the most recent one being in March of that year, when 135 aircraft had caused a significant amount of damage and ended up killing sixty-two people.[86] Now, seven times that number of planes were going to be involved in an attack on the same target. The Operations Record of 10 Squadron, which flew Wellington bombers out of RAF Leeming in Yorkshire, provides an account of the devastation wreaked by the first thousand bomber raid. "The target was one mass of flames and bursts could not be picked out against the general conflagration," said one account. "Attacked primary target at 0219hrs from 13,000 ft. and bomb bursts were observed. The whole Cologne area appeared to be in flames," said another. "Attacked primary target at 0115hrs from 14,000 ft," said the report of the Halifax bomber W7695. "The glow of fires which raged throughout the target area could be seen 125 miles away."[87]

44 Squadron was also in action over Cologne. "There was a solid area of fire about 3 miles long by 2 miles wide covering the town. I saw the fires on the return journey from 100 miles distance," wrote the pilot of Lancaster L7568, "and at this range I could see what appeared to be large explosions occurring in the town." The operations record for Lancaster R5516, piloted by Flight Lieutenant Halls, reads as follows: "Weather was perfect from English Coast and we were able to map-read to target which was visible roughly 60 miles away burning fiercely. . . . Large fires burning in town – in fact all of centre seemed alight." Squadron Leader Herring, who was flying in one of the older Manchester bombers, L7480, during this operation, wrote, "Target was identified easily as visibility was good but it was impossible to see results because of the number of fires. . . . I have never seen a target burn so well before."[88]

A total of 915 tons of incendiaries and 840 tons of high explosives were dropped on Cologne during the operation, and it was estimated later that more damage had been done to the city on the night of 30th May than in all the previous raids put together. Approximately 13,000 buildings were destroyed, some 45,000 people were de-housed by explosive bombs or fire, and 469 people lost their lives.[89] It is impossible to say how many of the dead had ever voted for Hitler's NSDAP (National Socialist German Workers Party) or had been working in a plant producing weapons or supplies for the *Wehrmacht*. It might be argued that industrial plants within Germany, and by extension the people who worked at those plants, could be considered legitimate military targets, but their families did not have to die for them to stop producing goods for the German war machine, nor did anyone else have to be de-housed or killed. Those civilian fatalities, together with the destruction of so much privately owned property, would today be classified as collateral damage.

Harris wrote after the war that "the bomber offensive, or what could be made of it, was the only means we had of actively helping the Russians, who, though the German offensive in Russia had been halted, had every appearance of being *in extremis*."[90] In his book, *The Storm of War*, the British historian Andrew Roberts wrote that "rather like the Arctic Convoys to Murmansk, the bombing offensive was conceived almost as a kind of displacement therapy. In the end, helping Russia was indeed to be its chief value to the war effort."[91]

The area bombing campaign against Germany certainly helped Churchill to keep the Soviet Union onside throughout 1942. After convoy PQ17 had turned into one of the worst naval disasters in British history, with 24 out of 39 ships destroyed and much of its cargo sent to the bottom of the sea,[92] it became clear that it was too dangerous to send any more of the Arctic convoys through to Murmansk. When Churchill wrote to Stalin and advised him that this decision had been made, he "got a rough and surly answer."[93] The new British ambassador to the Soviet Union, Sir Archibald Clark Kerr, wrote to London warning that the Soviet leadership did not believe "that we are yet taking the war seriously. They set up their own enormous losses against our (by comparison) trifling losses in men and material since the close of 1939."[94] Kerr suggested that Churchill should visit Moscow to speak with Stalin face-to-face.[95]

Churchill duly flew out to Moscow via Cairo in early August in an unheated and unpressurised bomber.[96] He wrote later that as he made what must have been a rather uncomfortable journey, in more ways than one, "I pondered on my mission to this sullen, sinister Bolshevik State I had once tried so hard to strangle at its birth, and which, until Hitler appeared, I had regarded as the mortal foe of civilised freedom. What was it my duty to say to them now?"[97]

The records of Churchill's first meeting with Stalin on 12th August show that Stalin was not pleased when he was told that there would be no second front in France that year, but when Churchill began to describe the area bombing campaign against Germany, his words fell on fertile soil. When Stalin spoke about driving the Germans back from Belgium and France so they would be deprived of the industrial capacities of those nations, Churchill told him, "This was why we were bombing the German centres of industry." Churchill assured Stalin that "the present bombing was nothing to what would be done in six months, or even in three months' time."[98]

"M. Stalin agreed that this bombing was of tremendous importance," according to the records of the meeting. "Some military experts were inclined to underrate its effects, but he was not. It was not only German industry that should be bombed, but its population too. This was the only way of breaking German morale."[99]

Churchill warmed to the subject. "As regards the civil population, we looked upon its morale as a military target," he said. "We sought no mercy and we would show no mercy."[100]

Stalin responded by saying, "That was the only way."[101]

The record of the meeting goes on: "The Prime Minister said that we hoped to shatter twenty German cities, as we had shattered Cologne, Lübeck, Dusseldorf and so on. More and more aeroplanes and bigger and bigger bombs. M. Stalin had heard of 2-ton bombs. We had now begun to use 4-ton bombs, and this would be continued throughout the winter. If need be, as the war went on, we hoped to shatter every German dwelling in every German city."[102]

Churchill's commitment to send Bomber Command to inflict an unprecedented level of death and destruction upon the German homeland made an impression on the Soviet leader. "These words had a very stimulating effect upon the meeting," the records state, "and thenceforward the atmosphere became progressively more cordial."[103]

Churchill went on to describe the Anglo-American project codenamed Operation Torch. This would involve the Americans finally entering the war in a fighting capacity by joining their available forces with the British to invade North Africa.[104] According to Churchill's account, the Soviets liked the sound of "Torch," and the meeting ended on a more positive note altogether.[105]

When Churchill became Prime Minister in May 1940, war had already been declared against Germany, and Churchill had to fight against the enemy in the only way possible. As the Chiefs of Staff had recognised back in 1937, the only feasible strategy was to try and fight a long war, and to rely on help from the United States and the Soviet Union. It is to Churchill's credit that he managed to work at a personal level with both Roosevelt and Stalin for the duration of the war. As Eden had observed, those relationships could not be maintained without making "unpalatable concessions."[106] Machiavelli has been criticised for advising political leaders that they will have to do things that are "not good," but *The Prince* is essentially a descriptive work, which provides real-life examples to illustrate each point the author makes. As the Prime Minister in a time of war, Churchill had to do whatever it took to make sure Britain would end up on the winning side at the end of the war. Soon after he had become Prime Minister, Churchill had to prevent the French fleet from falling into German hands, so he did something he would never have considered in a time of peace and authorised the British naval attack on their former allies at Mers-el-Kébir. Once the Soviet Union entered the war in June 1941, Churchill agreed to divert massive amounts of sorely needed British supplies to the Soviet Union. In May 1942, Churchill sent the Arctic Convoy PQ16 out to Murmansk against the advice of the British Chiefs of Staff because Molotov was due to arrive in the UK to sign the Anglo-Soviet Treaty. Churchill said that he was willing to sacrifice half of the ships in the convoy to preserve Britain's relationship with the other members of the Grand Alliance. On 20th March 1942, Churchill offered to carry out gas attacks on Germany on behalf of the Soviet Union, in the expectation that the British public would then be subjected to retaliatory attacks. The British government gave up on the Baltic States and allowed them to be taken over by the Soviet Union, knowing full well that this violated the principles of the Atlantic Charter, and they even declared war on Finland in December 1941, for no other reason than to please Stalin. In the course of their meeting on 12th August 1942, Churchill told Stalin, while they were discussing the possibility of opening a second front in France, that "if by throwing in 150,000 to 200,000 men we could render him aid by drawing away from the Russian front appreciable German forces, we would not shrink away from this course on the grounds of loss."[107] The number of casualties did not cause the British government to shrink away from conducting a bombing offensive on Germany either. The area bombing campaign would eventually claim the lives of 55,573 members of Bomber Command, almost 15 per cent of all the British military personnel who died during the war.[108]

The British government needed the Soviet Union to keep fighting the *Wehrmacht* on the Eastern Front until an invasion of Europe by American, British and Commonwealth forces became possible. In the meantime, Britain would concentrate much of her industrial power on creating a force of heavy bombers that could bring the war to Germany. The British government had warned the Americans in February 1942 that if the Soviets managed to defeat Germany before the Americans and the British landed their own land forces in Europe, then "Russian prestige would be enormous and the Soviet Government would be tempted to work for the establishment of Communistic governments in the majority of European countries" and "might no longer desire to adapt themselves to the policies which we and the United States may wish to pursue." Soviet foreign policy could then "revert to the pursuit of purely selfish aims with incalculable consequences for the post-war period."[109] The area bombing of Germany may have demonstrated to Stalin that his allies meant business and wanted to see their common enemy defeated, but the British warning to the Americans had been well founded. The Soviets had been pursuing their own agenda since before the war began, and that was never going to change.

12 Barbarossa

When the Soviet Union signed a non-aggression pact with Germany in August 1939, it allowed them to take possession of the Baltic States and the eastern half of Poland, then sit back and watch as Germany fought against Britain and France.[1] If the second world war had been anything like the first, then that conflict could have dragged on for years. However, the French generals failed to anticipate Germany's advance through the Ardennes, and the French and British forces crumbled before the *Wehrmacht* in a matter of weeks. This left the Nazis in control of western Europe, a situation which the British were powerless to change until June 1944, when Operation Overlord was launched. The Soviets had no reason to think they would be attacked so long as Hitler was fighting in western Europe, but the failure of the British and the French to stand up to the *Wehrmacht* changed everything. Since the Nazi-Soviet pact meant there was no longer a territorial buffer between the two nations, the Soviets could now be attacked without any warning.[2] In July 1940, following the Anglo-French collapse in western Europe, the Red Army began to draw up war plans that identified Germany as the enemy.[3]

The Soviet Union had several natural advantages that would make it difficult for any invasion to succeed. The *Wehrmacht* may have been able to take control of France and the Low Countries in 1940, but as the historian Chris Bellamy has pointed out, the European mainland widens out in the shape of a "funnel" the farther east one goes. As the German forces advanced into Soviet territory, the length of their front lines would steadily increase, and they would have to try and control more and more territory with the same number of tanks and troops.[4] There was also no natural backstop for the Germans to use to trap the soldiers of the Red Army. They could keep on retreating into the almost endless spaces of the Soviet Union, crossing any rivers in their path then taking up defensive positions on the far bank, making the enemy pay dearly for reaching the other side before retreating again. This would leave the German forces with no option but to keep advancing and try to control more and more physical territory, all the while extending their supply lines as they got farther away from Germany. At the same time, the Red Army would be getting closer to their own supply centres inside the Soviet Union. The danger here had been recognised by the military theorist Carl von Clausewitz, who warned that an offensive force will inevitably grow weaker as it advances because it is moving farther away from its supply centres, whereas a defending force is falling back towards the sources of its strength. According to Clausewitz, every military attack has a culminating point, where an attacking army will reach its limits and be forced to go on the defensive.[5] If this ever happened on the Eastern Front, then it would be disastrous for Germany. The *Wehrmacht* had been created to engage in a *Bewegungskrieg* (war of movement), not to engage in a positional war of attrition deep inside enemy territory.

The Nazis believed that it was the primary function of a state to take from the earth whatever its own people needed to survive, with no regard for the man-made concept of national borders.[6] Hitler's goal had always been to conquer sufficient *Lebensraum* in the east for the German state to achieve a condition of *autarky* (economic self-sufficiency) so the German people would have the resources they needed to survive in a hostile world.[7] Operation Barbarossa therefore had two initial military objectives. The enemy's military forces would have to be destroyed so that the Soviet regime would have to stop fighting and surrender, and the natural resources that Germany needed to achieve *autarky* would have to be taken from the territory captured by the army as it headed east. If the German forces were victorious, then a blockade-proof economic system could be set up at the expense of the people who had been living in the occupied territories so that the British would be unable to threaten Germany, either directly or through a naval blockade.[8]

It remained to be seen whether an invasion of the Soviet Union was feasible. On 29th July 1940, Major General Erich Marcks, the Chief of Staff of the 18th Army, was briefed by General Franz Halder at Army High Command headquarters and tasked with preparing a military analysis of the proposed operation.[9]

Marcks initially argued that the focus of the attack should be made south of the Pripet marshes, with a secondary advance being made to the north, but Halder rejected this idea and insisted that Moscow should be the primary target of the invasion.[10] The final version of the Marcks plan, which was submitted to Halder on 5th August 1940, broke the invasion into four stages.[11]

The first stage of the Marcks plan was to drive the Red Army back to its original defensive positions on the other side of what used to be the Polish border. If the Soviet forces could be destroyed before they retreated that far, then in Marcks' estimation, the outcome of the campaign could be decided there and then.[12] If a decisive blow had not been struck by that time, then the second stage of the Marcks plan would come into play. The Soviet defensive lines would have to be breached, and the remaining Soviet forces would have to be pursued for up to 200 km (approximately 125 miles) and encircled so that they could be destroyed in *Kesselschlachten* (cauldron battles).[13]

Marcks recognised that by the time the German forces had advanced to the Polish border with the Soviet Union, then made a second push to the east to encircle and destroy the surviving Soviet armies, they would probably have to pause operations so they could carry out essential maintenance to their vehicles and establish new supply lines to the front.[14] A third advance to the east would then be required before the German forces could capture Moscow, Leningrad and eastern Ukraine.[15]

The fourth and final phase of the Marcks plan had the German forces occupying Soviet territory up to the Don, middle Volga and the upper Dvina rivers.[16] Marcks completed his analysis in the first week of August, but he continued to think about what could happen following an invasion of the Soviet Union. Marcks eventually wrote a second report, which he called "Evaluation of Situation Red," in which he argued that if the Soviets could withstand the initial German attack, then they could end up forming an alliance with the British. That would leave Germany fighting a war on two fronts, and if Britain joined forces with the United States as well, then Germany would no longer be in a tenable position.[17] No record has been found of this report ever reaching Halder's desk, let alone being shown to Hitler.[18]

A second invasion plan was drawn up for the OKW (*Oberkommando der Wehrmacht*) by Lieutenant-Colonel Bernhard von Lossberg. This was completed on 15th September.[19] Lossberg's plan called for two army groups to advance north of the Pripet marshes and one to invade from the south,[20] using Romania as a staging ground.[21] Lossberg did take into consideration some of the difficulties involved in supplying the invasion force as it advanced, and he planned for the army group in the centre to wheel north towards Leningrad so the Baltic States could be captured and their ports used to supply the German forces.[22] Lossberg also argued that it would be necessary to capture and make use of the local trains, which would be able to run on the different sized railway lines in the Soviet Union.[23]

The Army Quartermaster-General, Major General Eduard Wagner, met with Halder in November 1940 and warned him about the limitations of the German army's power. As quartermaster, Wagner was concerned with keeping the troops fed and making sure the army's vehicles kept running. Wagner told Halder that, given the necessity of keeping over three million men and six hundred thousand horses fed and watered each day, and taking into account the projected fuel consumption as the panzers and other motorised vehicles headed east, the army would only be able to sustain its initial drive into Soviet territory for approximately 500 miles.[24] This is significant because, according to the terms of the Friendship and Boundaries Treaty, the new German border crossing with the Soviet Union was at Czyzew, approximately 67 miles north-east of Warsaw, halfway between the old Polish capital and Bailystock.[25] From there, it was approximately 650 miles to Moscow. If Wagner's estimate was correct, then the German army would run out of fuel and food before they got there.[26]

N
FINLAND
Helsinki
Leningrad
ESTONIA
LATVIA
LITHUANIA
Vilnius
Dvina
Volga
SOVIET
UNION
Moscow
Smolensk
Dnepr
Minsk
Brest
Warsaw
POLAND
Pripet
Marshes
Voronezh
Don
Kiev
Kharkov
Dnepr
SLOVAKIA
HUNGARY
Odessa
Rostov
Sea of Azov
ROMANIA
Sevastapol
Black Sea
BULGARIA
22nd June 1941
Front line 22nd June
National border
0
200 miles
0
200Km

The German army was going to have to fight its way across what used to be Poland for over 220 miles just to reach Minsk. Once they reached the capital of the Byelorussian Soviet Socialist Republic, they would have to fight their way through Soviet territory for approximately 190 miles to reach Smolensk, and once that goal was reached, they would have to keep going for another 230 miles to reach Moscow. Marcks had recognised that the army would probably have to stop after its second movement to carry out essential repairs on their vehicles and let their supply systems stabilise. Lossberg had realised that the roads in the Soviet Union would not be good enough to keep the army's supplies moving to the front lines, and the Quartermaster-General was saying they would run out of fuel and supplies anyway. The writing may have been on the wall, but there was no Daniel there to interpret the letters for the German military leadership, and once Hitler issued a formal directive for the invasion of the Soviet Union on 18th December 1940, there was no turning back.[27]

The Soviet forces facing Army Group Centre in June 1941 had been deployed in two echelons. The first consisted of three operational belts of 57, 52 and 62 divisions respectively. The five armies in the second echelon contained a total of 57 divisions. These second echelon armies, which were under *Stavka* (Soviet High Command) control, had assembled along the Dnepr and Dvina rivers.[28] In the Polish territory still being occupied by the Soviet Union, the 10th Army under Lieutenant General K.D. Golubev, with the 3rd Army under Lieutenant General V.I. Kuznetsov on its right flank, and the 4th Army under Major General A.A. Korobkov on its left flank,[29] were stationed in the Bailystock salient.[30] The geography of the Nazi-Soviet Pact had left these armies in an exposed position, and the German commanders intended to take advantage of that.[31]

In May 1940, there had been ten panzer divisions available for the campaign in France, and only six other divisions were fully mechanized.[32] Many of the German soldiers at that time had not been active-duty troops, but reservists and *Landwehr* units, which were made up mostly of veterans of the First World War.[33] The German army had been expanded significantly since then,[34] and Hitler had increased the number of panzer divisions by taking a regiment from each of the existing divisions to form the core of a new division, which then had a regiment of motorized infantry added to it.[35] The German tanks would fight in four panzer groups, operating between the Baltic Sea and the Black Sea. Army Group North and Army Group South would have one panzer group apiece, and Army Group Centre, under Field Marshal Fedor von Bock, would have two panzer groups, led by Colonel General Heinz Guderian and Colonel General Herman Hoth.[36]

When Operation Barbarossa finally began on 22nd June, the panzer groups of Army Group Centre advanced into Soviet occupied territory.

Before the end of the day, Hoth's 3rd panzer group had cut through the Soviet defences on the northern flank of the Bailystock salient and reached the river Neman, which flows south-east to north through Hrodna (Grodno).[37] By 24th June, the 3rd panzer group had managed to capture Vilnius, the capital of Lithuania.[38] On the southern side of the Bailystock salient, Guderian's 2nd panzer group had a difficult time crossing the Bug River. One of Guderian's commanders, General Joachim Lemelsen, reported that his tanks were sinking into the ground on the approach roads to the captured bridges,[39] and once over the river, the roads were even worse.[40] The German commanders soon discovered that many of the roads marked on their maps were little more than rough, unmaintained tracks that turned to mud when it rained.[41] In fact, the Soviet Union only had 40 thousand miles of hard surfaced roads in the entire country.[42]

General Adolf von Schell, the General Plenipotentiary for Motor Vehicles at the OKW, had been trying to make the German army more mechanised since 1938. However, the German car industry consisted of several relatively small independent companies and Germany was short of raw materials to begin with, so it had not been possible to mass-produce motor vehicles for the army.[43]

Instead of trying to find a way to increase vehicle production, Halder had decided in 1940 to embark on a de-motorisation scheme. This would reduce the total overall number of vehicles used by the army, and if less vehicles were used to begin with, then the number that had to be taken off the road every month would match the number of replacements that could be produced. This may have appeared to Halder to be the only way he could create a sustainable supply of motor vehicles, but as the war progressed, the increased demand for transport would have to be met somehow. To make up for the discrepancy between the limited German capacity to supply motor vehicles and the inevitable increase in demand during a war, Halder had orders drawn up for the procurement of more horses, harnesses and carriages.[44]

When the war began, the German state commandeered approximately sixteen thousand civilian trucks for use by the military, but many of these vehicles were only two wheel drive and had been designed to drive on roads in normal conditions, so they were not fit for purpose and many of them broke down during the Polish campaign.[45] Some of the vehicles that ended up being used in Operation Barbarossa had been taken from Czechoslovakia and France,[46] and still more had been brought in from Switzerland.[47] When Operation Barbarossa was launched in June 1941, the German army was using approximately two thousand different types of motor vehicle.[48] They were going to be operating in difficult terrain, so it was inevitable that some of these vehicles would break down. Instead of having standardised plants in Germany providing spare parts that could be sent in single deliveries to any military unit, where they could be used to repair any vehicle in their unit that had broken down, the spares for these different vehicles would have to be supplied from factories all over Europe. Individual military units on the Eastern Front that were using several types of vehicle would need multiple deliveries of spare parts, because the parts for a French truck, for example, would be no use if the mechanics were trying to repair Czech or Swiss machinery.

The method of attack being used by the German military in Operation Barbarossa was a hybrid technique based partially on the *Blitzkrieg* concept, which required tanks to break through the enemy's defences and thrust forward into the enemy's rear, acting independently to break down the enemy's command structure and thereby paralyse the enemy forces so they would be unable to continue fighting. The more traditional method of fighting involved making coordinated flanking movements then encircling the enemy, before physically destroying their forces in *Kesselschlachten* (cauldron battles).[49]

As the German tanks pushed forward into the Soviet interior, they would be travelling faster than the Germany infantry. Many of the soldiers were on foot, and approximately 625,000 horses were being used to haul heavy weapons and supplies.[50] The difference in speed between these two ground forces meant they would get farther and farther apart as the tanks moved deeper into enemy territory. If the tank commanders pushed forward too far, then the two components of the German army would eventually separate. If that happened, then an effective encirclement would no longer be possible, because the enemy's forces could escape through the gaps between the tanks and the infantry. It follows that there was a limit to the distance the tanks could advance before they had to turn inwards and close the trap on the enemy forces.

As the German tanks advanced, the German commanders disagreed on how to proceed. Bock had tried to persuade Halder and Field Marshal Walter von Brauchitsch, the Commander-in-Chief of the army, that the German tanks should push forward as quickly as possible,[51] to prevent the Red Army troops from being able to withdraw and set up defensive positions east of the Dvina and Dnepr rivers. However, Hitler's adjutant, Colonel Rudolf Schmundt, paid a visit to Bock's headquarters on 25th June and told him that Hitler was worried that the army was operating too deep inside Soviet territory and even an encirclement at Minsk might be attempting too much, so he was considering closing the ring at Novogrudock, which was 73 miles closer. Bock realised that he was going to have to adopt a "lesser of two evils" policy, and he ordered his forces to make for Minsk as quickly as possible. If Hitler could see that the Minsk encirclement was already under way, then at least Bock's forces would be able to leave what had once been Polish territory and enter Soviet Belorussia.[52]

General Rudolf Schmidt's XXXIX Panzer Corps and General Adolf Kuntzen's LVII Panzer Corps, which formed part of Hoth's 3rd Panzer Group, headed south east towards Minsk, where they were met by a determined enemy in fixed defensive positions.[53] On the left flank of Schmidt's 20th Panzer Division, the 7th Panzer Division managed to fight its way to within twenty kilometres of Minsk, but fifty per cent of its obsolete Mk II tanks were now gone, and its more advanced Mk IV tanks had suffered 75 per cent losses.[54] Guderian's 2nd Panzer Group was also heading towards Minsk, but the 29th Motorised Division, which was part of General Joachim Lemelsen's XLVII Panzer Corps,[55] was ordered back to help the 4th Army, which was commanded by Field Marshal Hans Günther von Kluge, to seal the southern border of what would be Army Group Centre's first major encirclement on the Eastern Front.[56] Bock also sent in his reserve tanks, and put them under Kluge's command in an effort to complete the encirclement.

With Guderian and Hoth's tanks converging on Minsk, General Dmitry Pavlov, the commander of the Red Army's Western Front,[57] ordered his forces to retreat and form a new defensive position behind the Shchara river, but when they got there they found that the *Luftwaffe* had destroyed most of the bridges, so they had to abandon much of their heavy equipment, and the only course of action open to them was to try and escape on foot.[58] The German tanks reached Minsk on 29th June, but the ring was not completely secure,[59] and many of the Soviet troops broke out of the encirclement and were able to fight on against the invaders.[60]

On 29th June, a directive was issued from Moscow stating that as the Red Army retreated, everything that the Germans could use should be removed or destroyed, so that there would be no food, no transport and no fuel left for the enemy.[61] On 16th August, Stalin issued Order 270, which let the soldiers fighting in the Red Army know what to expect if they were captured on the field of battle. Anyone unfortunate enough to be trapped in a German encirclement had to be ready to fight to the death rather than surrender. If anyone did wave the white flag in the face of the enemy, then they would be treated as a deserter and executed at the earliest opportunity, and their families would be arrested.[62] Political prisoners held by the NKVD in territory overrun by the German forces were treated with typical Soviet brutality. Rather than allowing anyone to be rescued by the advancing Germans, Beria's men shot thousands of these prisoners, often burying them in mass graves.[63] General Pavlov, who had been in command of the Soviet forces opposing Army Group Centre, would soon meet a similar fate.

In the eighteenth century, the British had executed Admiral John Byng after he had been charged with "failing to do his utmost."[64] Shot to death by a squad of marines aboard the *Monarch* on 14th March 1757, the scene was replicated by Voltaire in his book *Candide*: "Talking thus they arrived at Portsmouth. The coast was lined with crowds of people, whose eyes were fixed on a fine man kneeling, with his eyes bandaged, on board on of the men of war in the harbour. Four soldiers stood opposite to this man; each of them fired three balls at his head, with all the calmness in the world; and the whole assembly went away very well satisfied."[65] When Voltaire's character asks why the Admiral has been killed, he is told, "In this country it is found good, from time to time, to kill one Admiral to encourage the others."[66]

In the years before the war, Stalin had purged the military of anyone he thought could possibly be a threat to his authority.[67] Now that Stalin's partners in crime had turned on him and his country was at war, he could not execute everyone who was left. As a purely practical matter, Stalin needed his remaining generals to fight, so the unfortunate Pavlov was removed from the field of battle, charged with "criminal behaviour in the face of the enemy," then swiftly tried and executed – *pour encourager les autres*.[68]

The German forces no longer had the element of surprise, and the second advance by Army Group Centre, from Minsk to Smolensk, was always going to be more difficult than the initial attack had been. Marshal Georgy Zhukov had begun to establish two new defensive lines, the first along the Dvina and Dnepr rivers and the land bridge between them from Vitebsk to Orsha. Zhukov's second defensive line ran from Selizharovo in the north to Smolensk, then went south to Roslavl and Gomel.[69] Pavlov had been replaced by Marshal Seymon Timoshenko, who used the forces in the Red Army's second echelon to defend the Dnepr river line.[70] The Red Army was also beginning to show more tactical awareness. Instead of launching head-on attacks, the Soviets fought organised rear-guard actions, which gained them the time they needed to withdraw to the defensive positions on the Dvina and Dnepr rivers.[71]

The Germans would not be able to destroy the Soviets' industrial capacity west of the rivers either. On 23rd June, an Evacuation Council was set up in Moscow which organised the immediate dismantling of more than 1,500 industrial plants, including armament factories, located in the west of the country. In an incredible effort by everyone involved in the project, these plants were uplifted and physically moved hundreds of miles east to new sites in Siberia and Kazakhstan, where they were reassembled and began operating again.[72] Approximately 16.5 million Soviet workers began working in what were extremely difficult conditions so that their country would continue to function, no matter what was happening west of Moscow.[73]

As the Soviets fell back across the Dvina and Dnepr rivers, their production centres and supply lines were secure, but as the German forces advanced, their supply lines grew ever longer. Once inside the Soviet Union, the railway lines could not be used by the German trains, because the lines were set at a different gauge from those used in Europe. Only 40,000 of the total 850,000 miles of road in the Soviet Union had been laid with a hard surface,[74] and the rest turned out to be rough tracks that turned to mud whenever it rained. As Hoth and Guderian headed towards Smolensk, the vehicles being used by Army Group Centre began to break down under the pressure of operating in such primitive conditions. The civilian vehicles that had been appropriated by the military did not have enough clearance to cope with being driven on the Russian tracks, so they would often bottom out and damage the engine's sump. When these vehicles broke down and could not be repaired in the field, they were left at the side of the road as the advance continued.[75] The conditions on the Russian roads were so bad that more tanks and trucks were taken out of service due to breakdowns than were destroyed in combat.[76]

When the rain stopped and the roads dried out, the German forces had to contend with another hazard that their vehicles' engines could not cope with. The columns travelling on the Russian roads threw up great clouds of dust which covered everything and everyone,[77] and the air filters in the German vehicles were soon clogged with dust. If an engine's air filter is clogged, then air cannot be sucked into the combustion chamber, and the engine will not run properly. Take the filter out so the engine will run, and the dust will enter directly into the engine, which will ruin it in short order. This affected tanks and trucks alike, and as the number of breakdowns increased,[78] one problem bled into another. There had been no need for the German military to have a system in place to repair broken down tanks during their earlier campaigns because these were all concluded swiftly, and the tanks could then be returned to Germany for major overhauls if it was necessary.[79] Now there were not enough maintenance facilities in the field, so many of the tanks that broke down in the extreme conditions on the Eastern Front could not be repaired and returned to combat readiness.[80]

Hoth's 3rd Panzer Group managed to cross the Dvina on 7th July,[81] and Guderian soon forced his way across the Dnepr, but these advances had come at a cost. The tanks were vital to the German method of fighting, but the farther the German forces advanced, the more their tanks were being degraded, by the prevailing conditions as much as the enemy. As Guderian continued his advance to the south of Smolensk, XXIV Panzer Corps was protecting his southern flank and XLVII Corps was trying to secure the southern side of the encirclement. Rather than use his remaining XLVI Panzer Corps to help close the ring on Smolensk, Guderian sent them farther east towards Yel'nya.[82] A gap therefore remained in the Smolensk encirclement, which allowed more than 100,000 Red Army soldiers to escape.[83] Guderian may have been trying to push farther east with the ultimate goal of the campaign in mind, which was not to capture Minsk or Smolensk, but to actually bring about the defeat of the Soviet Union. The fact that one strategic goal had to be forsaken to pursue another indicated that the *Wehrmacht* did not have the resources necessary to be victorious in this theatre of war, no matter which strategy the commanders of Army Group Centre adopted.

If Chamberlain had not given a war guarantee to Poland, then the Polish leaders would have been left in the unfortunate position where they had to choose a side from between their two neighbours. If Germany had managed to reach an agreement with Poland that allowed them to launch Operation Barbarossa from Poland's eastern border, then it may have been possible for the *Wehrmacht* to reach Moscow in two strategic movements. Instead, the invasion had to start from halfway through what had been Polish territory, and the German military only had the resources to advance as far as Smolensk before reaching a culminating point.[84]

On 22nd June, Guderian had 953 tanks available in Panzer Group 2, but by 29th July, only 286 remained. There were 132 obsolete Mark I and Mark II tanks and 19 armoured command vehicles included in that number. Only 97 Mark III tanks and 38 Mark IVs were left in Panzer Group 2 at that point, after only five weeks of combat.[85] Hoth's tanks had also been degraded significantly, with XXXIX Panzer Corps only having 23 Mark IVs in service, and LVII Panzer Corps having only 14 Mark IVs and 76 Czech Kpfw models left available for combat.[86] The situation had become so bad that by the end of July, Halder recognised that the tanks would have to be withdrawn from the front lines to be refitted. It was estimated that a break of ten days would be necessary for the panzer divisions to be brought back up to sixty to seventy percent of their original fighting strength.[87] However, the German supply system could not transport sufficient replacement engines and spare parts to the front.[88] The Soviet railway lines were set at a different gauge from the German carriages and only some of the lines had been replaced,[89] so most of the German supplies had to be transported in by truck. This meant driving all the way to the supply depots at the front, which the trucks available to the German military could not do without suffering their own breakdowns.[90] The German supply system was beginning to fail, and the units at the front could no longer employ the aggressive battlefield tactics that had brought them success in the past. Instead of using their tanks to cut through an enemy's defences at a *Schwerpunkt* of their choosing then driving into the enemy's rear, the German forces stationed along the front were being shelled relentlessly by Soviet artillery units that were closer than ever to their supply centres, which meant they had access to plenty ammunition. One German unit at Yel'nya reported that 156 artillery shells had landed on them in just five minutes.[91] The Soviets had also achieved air superiority, and their bombers launched attacks on the Germans all along the front. On the ground, the German anti-tank guns were proving to be useless against the Soviet T-34 tanks. At Yel'nya, the soldiers of the SS *Das Reich* division had no option but let the Soviet tanks pass through their own lines, then either use Molotov cocktails against them, or climb aboard and use fuel cans to set them alight.[92] Germany had created a military force capable of using *Blitzkrieg* tactics to drive into the enemy's rear, before turning inward and destroying the enemy forces in cauldron battles. If the German leaders had managed to reach an understanding with the Poles about which flag would fly over the city of Danzig, then they may have been able to recruit the Poles, whose distrust of their neighbours in the east ran deep, to their cause. If Germany had been able to launch the invasion of the Soviet Union from Poland's eastern border, then the *Wehrmacht* may then have been able to reach Moscow in two movements, instead of only advancing as far as Smolensk and stalling, some two hundred miles short of the capital. In the event, the successes of the *Wehrmacht* in the summer of 1941 may very well have been significant military achievements, but they did not, and could not, deliver an ultimate victory. It did not matter how far inside the Soviet Union the front lines were if the German forces came to a halt, and the conflict changed from a war of movement into a positional war of attrition. Hitler may have undermined the British government's attempt to reach an agreement with the Soviet Union in the summer of 1939, and signing the Nazi-Soviet Pact in August that year may have ensured that Chamberlain's guarantee would be worthless, but cutting Poland in two and handing the eastern part of the country to the Soviets meant that when Operation Barbarossa was finally launched in June 1941, Army Group Centre would be too far away from Moscow to reach it before their supply system began to break down, and a culminating point was reached.

13 Typhoon

On 20th July 1941, Stalin sent Churchill a telegram that read:

> Let me express my gratitude for the two personal messages which you have addressed to me.
>
> Your messages were the starting point of developments which subsequently resulted in agreement between our two governments. Now, as you said with full justification, the Soviet Union and Great Britain have become fighting allies in the struggle against Hitlerite Germany. I have no doubt that in spite of the difficulties our two States will be strong enough to crush our common enemy.
>
> Perhaps it is not out of place to mention that the position of the Soviet forces at the front remains tense. The consequences of the unexpected breach of the Non-Aggression Pact by Hitler, as well as of the sudden attack against the Soviet Union – both attacks bringing advantages to the German troops – still remain to be felt by the Soviet armies.
>
> It is easy to imagine that the position of the German forces would have been many times more favourable had the Soviet troops had to face the attack of the German forces not in the regions of Kishinev, Lwow, Brest, Kaunas, and Viborg, but in the regions of Odessa, Kemenets Podolski, Minsk, and the environs of Leningrad.[1]

Churchill responded the next day:

> I am very glad to get your message, and to learn from many sources of the valiant fight and the many vigorous counter-attacks with which the Russian armies are defending their native soil. I fully realise the military advantage you have gained by forcing the enemy to deploy and engage on a forward westerly front, thus exhausting some of the force of his initial effort.[2]

There was no mention in either telegram of the way the Polish people had been treated by the occupying Soviet forces. That had been conveniently forgotten, as the leaders of both countries recognised that the division of Poland between Germany and the Soviet Union, which had been agreed to as part of the Nazi-Soviet Pact, had given the Soviets a buffer zone beyond their border, which the Germans had to fight their way through before they could reach Soviet Belorussia. Stalin was surely correct when he argued that "the position of the German forces would have been many times more favourable" if they had launched Operation Barbarossa from Poland's eastern border, instead of having to fight the Red Army for over two hundred miles just to reach Minsk. And Churchill was not wrong when he said there was a military advantage to be had by allowing the Germans to exhaust some of the force of their initial military effort on what used to be Polish territory.

Marcks had understood that if the Soviets could weather the initial storm of a German invasion, then they could end up forming an alliance with Britain. The United States would probably join this alliance at some point, which would make an Anglo-American invasion of Europe possible.[3] The scenario laid out by Marcks in "Evaluation of Situation Red" was similar to the one envisioned by the British Chiefs of Staff in their memorandum of 15th February 1937, which argued that if Britain could withstand an initial German attack and the Soviet Union ended up joining the war as a co-belligerent and American industry provided the necessary materiel, then it would be possible to launch an Allied (not exclusively British) counterattack at some point.[4] The British government had always understood that using this strategy to fight a long war was the only way to prevail against Germany.

Churchill had spoken about forming a "Grand Alliance" with the Soviet Union as early as 3rd April 1939,[5] but more than two years would pass before the Soviet Union ended up fighting on the side of Great Britain. The government's attempt to recruit the Soviet Union in the summer of 1939 had been a failure, and the Anglo-Polish Agreement of 25th August that year committed Britain to a course of action that would almost inevitably end in a war against Germany that would have to be waged without the military assistance of the Red Army. However, that agreement did not oblige the British to assist Poland in the event of an invasion if the Soviet Union was the aggressor, so the door to future military cooperation with the Soviets had been left open. The German invasion of the Soviet Union in June 1941 had given Churchill the opportunity to begin forming the "Grand Alliance" that would eventually win the war against Germany, but it would not be complete until Hitler took it upon himself to declare war against the United States on 11th December of that year. If the German forces had reached at least one of their primary targets on the Eastern Front before America became a belligerent party, then the entire course of the war could have been quite different. However, the German supply system could not keep their drive to the east going after Guderian's tanks had reached Yel'nya. From their starting point in the middle of what used to be Poland, the German forces could not advance far enough into the ever-widening "funnel" of Soviet-controlled territory to take down its capital.

The Germans made a final effort to drive east and take Moscow before the Russian winter arrived. Hitler had decided on 21st August to try and seize the Soviet industrial and coal-mining region in the south, and Guderian's tanks had been ordered to head south into Ukraine.[6] There were nearly a million troops in the area around Kiev, and these Soviet forces would have presented a threat to the right flank of Army Group Centre if the advance had continued east towards Moscow.[7] As the infantry dug in on the front lines of Army Group Centre's advance, which had halted altogether,[8] Guderian's tanks helped to complete a massive encirclement of the Soviet forces around Kiev.[9] This may have been a significant military success, but it was dangerously late in the year by the time the advance to Moscow, codenamed Operation Typhoon, finally resumed.

Colonel General Erich Hoepner's IV Panzer Group had been brought in from Army Group North to carry out the central assault of the operation.[10] The intention was for Hoepner's tanks to drive into the Soviet defences and force them to first break apart, then coalesce around Vyazma and Bryansk, where they would then be encircled. Hoth would come in from the north around Vyazma, and Guderian would close the second trap by coming in from the south of Bryansk.[11] These two encirclements did end up being successful,[12] but Hoepner had wanted to make the encirclements deeper to make sure the Soviet reserves were captured as well. If the Red Army could use its reserves to replace the soldiers they lost in these cauldron battles, then these successes on the battlefield would not bring about a decisive victory over the enemy.[13] The problems that had affected the German invasion from the start remained. If the tanks drove forward in classic *Blitzkrieg* fashion, then the enemy forces the tanks had bypassed would keep on fighting and they would be a threat both to the infantry and to the flanks of the panzers' supply columns. The tanks had to swing inwards and work with the infantry to eliminate the enemy forces in cauldron battles. However, if the tanks moved inwards early enough to complete the encirclement, then they would not be able to advance far enough to capture a significant military target that could bring about the enemy's defeat.

As the German advance continued, Kluge's 4th Army seized Kaluga and Guderian's tanks captured Mtensk, north east of Orel, which put them in a position to threaten Moscow from the south.[14] In the north, Hoth's 3rd Panzer Group had reached Kalinin,[15] which left Moscow susceptible to a pincer movement. In the Soviet capital, the situation was being taken seriously enough for Stalin to order the evacuation of the top military and Party officials to Kuibyshev, the city on the Volga that was to serve as a command centre if the capital fell.[16] As the officials were leaving the city, many of the people started to panic. There was looting in the streets, and people were trying to get out of the city by train or by road with whatever personal belongings they could take with them.[17] Many people who could not leave took down pictures of Stalin and Lenin and burned any Communist literature in their homes, in case the Germans came into the city and found them in their possession.[18]

As Stalin was preparing to leave Moscow, he went to the station where his own train was waiting to take him to Kuibyshev. One railway worker who claimed to have been present recalled later that Stalin paced up and down the platform for a moment but did not board the train.[19] Stalin decided that he was going to stay and fight, and with the decision made, he declared martial law and ordered NKVD agents out on to the streets of Moscow to maintain order. These NKVD units were given the authority to use lethal force.[20] Emergency tribunals were set up to deal with anyone breaking the law, with offenders often receiving a death sentence.[21]

Stalin also sent for reinforcements to shore up the capital's defences. Siberian troops stationed in the remote east of the U.S.S.R. were ordered to board trains immediately and travel west to help defend Moscow.[22] These Siberian units would have no problem operating in the conditions west of Moscow, unlike the German soldiers, who were discovering that the Russian weather could be just as deadly as any man-made weapon. The German advance had stalled in the middle of October when the autumn rains began to fall, which turned the roads to mud and made them impassable.[23] As the Germans were bogged down in these extreme conditions, Zhukov was using every soldier he could find, from raw recruits and former military rejects to the reinforcements that were arriving from Siberia, to mount a defence of Moscow.[24] By 15th November the Russian winter had arrived, and the ground froze enough for Bock to resume his advance. The tanks rolled forward again until they were within 20 miles of the Moscow suburbs.[25] It soon began to snow, and the temperature kept on falling. On 4th December, it reached minus 34 degrees Celsius, and the next night it fell even further, reaching minus 40 in some places.[26] No strong defensive fortifications had been prepared for the German soldiers to take shelter in, because the German high command wanted to keep the advance going and reach Moscow.[27] The soldiers existed in primitive dug-outs, wearing layers of lice-ridden clothes that could not protect them against the savage cold of a Russian winter.[28] If hot food was prepared in the field kitchens, it often froze before it reached the front lines.[29] The misery of the German soldiers' existence on the Eastern Front intensified once the Siberian troops arrived and began raiding the German lines, often during whiteout snowstorms. As German sentries braved the eastern winds that drove the snow at them horizontally, the Siberian ski troops, camouflaged in white, would appear from nowhere and shoot at the German sentries with machine guns, or throw grenades into the German trenches, before disappearing back into the snow.[30]

The fighting became more desperate as the Soviets dug in and fought to the death. “Moscow is behind us!” became the rallying cry of the city’s defenders, meaning that there was nowhere to retreat to, and that the German soldiers must not be allowed to reach the capital.[31] The Germans managed to gather enough resources for one final push towards Moscow, but they were now at the extreme limits of their strength. At the same time, the Soviets had managed to bring more military equipment and reinforcements into Moscow to make sure the city would not be taken.[32] The situation deteriorated on 6th December when the Red Army launched a counterattack,[33] just as the German forces expended the last of their energy on their failed assault.[34] The assertion made repeatedly by the German high command, that no matter how bad the conditions may have been for the German soldiers, the Red Army was in even worse shape and had to be close to collapse, was exposed as wishful thinking.[35] On 8th December, Hitler issued Directive No. 39, which stated that the difficulties presented by the winter conditions, together with the problems the Germans were having bringing supplies to the front lines, meant that Army Group Centre would have to abandon any plans to take Moscow, and go over to the defensive.[36]

The German military system was starting to break down, and their commanders could not take the strain of fighting a losing battle on the Eastern Front any more than their vehicles could. Field Marshal Gerd von Rundstedt, the commander of Army Group South, had been dismissed by Hitler and replaced by Walter von Reichenau on 1st December,[37] but Reichenau only lasted on the Eastern Front until 17th January 1942, when he died of a heart attack.[38] Rundstedt also suffered a heart attack in early December, although he survived the event.[39] Bock, the commander of Army Group Centre, was suffering from ill health and in the middle of December, he asked Hitler if he could go on sick leave.[40] Brauchitsch, the Commander-in-Chief of the army, had also had a heart attack in mid-November, and he resigned from his command on 16th December.[41] Hitler decided that he would take the position on himself, so that he could direct German military operations personally.[42] Once he had authority over the German forces, Hitler insisted that the soldiers on the front line were not to retreat voluntarily, and that they must fight for every inch of ground.[43] The Red Army was attacking along the front line between Kalinin (Tver), which lay 100 miles north-west of Moscow, and Yelets, which lay 200 miles to the south.[44] The German forces could not hold their positions after the Soviets went on the offensive, and with their bodies breaking down after five months of combat and small arms that no longer worked in the extreme cold,[45] the Germans began to retreat.

There was no disguising the fact that the invasion of the Soviet Union had been a failure. The Germans had failed to take any of their primary targets, and instead of making it impossible for Britain to form an alliance with the Soviet Union, the German invasion had helped to bring that alliance about. When Hitler decided to declare war on the United States on 11th December 1941, that set against him a tripartite military alliance that he would never be able to defeat. In the third volume of his history of the war, Churchill wrote that

> I could not foretell the course of events. I do not pretend to have measured accurately the martial might of Japan, but now at this moment I knew the United States was in the war, up to the neck and in to the death. So we had won after all! . . . England would live; Britain would live; the Commonwealth of Nations and the Empire would live. How long the war would last or in what fashion it would end no man could tell, nor did I at this moment care. Once again in our long Island history we should emerge, however mauled or mutilated, safe and victorious. We should not be wiped out. Our history would not come to an end. We might not even have to die as individuals. Hitler's fate was sealed. Mussolini's fate was sealed. As for the Japanese, they would be ground to powder. All the rest was merely the proper application of overwhelming force.[46]

14 Stalingrad

In the autumn of 1942, the city of Stalingrad, known today as Volgograd, stretched out along the right bank of the Volga as the river flowed south towards the Caspian Sea. The Dzerhizinsky Tractor Works, which had been converted to produce T-34 tanks, the Barrikady Gun Factory and the Red October plant, which produced various metal components and small arms, were all situated in the northern part of the city.[1] Housing blocks up to six stories high had been built nearby for the people who worked at these plants.[2] In the south of the city, the Dar Gova district housed still more workers in mainly wooden houses.[3]

On the afternoon of 23rd August, the *Luftwaffe* launched the first of a series of air raids on the city, targeting the residential areas in a deliberate terror attack. The German bombers carried incendiaries as well as high explosive bombs.[4] There had been a heatwave in the city, with temperatures reaching over 37 degrees, so all the wooden buildings had been completely dried out and were highly flammable.[5] The results of the attack were devastating. The telephone exchange collapsed, trapping the people who worked there beneath the broken ruins. The city's hospital collapsed after it was hit by German bombs. Almost all the wooden buildings, many of which housed workers at the city's industrial plants, were destroyed. William Craig asserts in his book, *Enemy at the Gates*, that there were many civilian casualties throughout the city.[6] The New Zealand-born academic Joel Hayward has argued that at least as many people died in these air raids on Stalingrad as had lost their lives in similar Allied raids on German cities.[7]

The German forces had crossed the Don at Vertyachiy, 32 miles from Stalingrad, on 21st August. General Friedrich Paulus, the commander of 6th Army, had sent 14th Panzer Corps, under the command of General Gustav von Wietersheim, across the Don into this bridgehead during the night of 22nd August 1942. With Lieutenant General Hans-Valentin Hube's 16th Panzer Division in the vanguard, supported by 3rd Motorised Division and 60th Motorised Division, the German forces headed east towards Stalingrad. *Fliegerkorps VIII* provided aerial support for Hube's tanks by bombing and strafing the Soviet positions in their path.[8] The *Luftwaffe* was not being used to simply bomb cities. In accordance with German military doctrine, air power had an important role to play on the battlefield. Before any major attack, the *Luftwaffe* commanders would consult with their counterparts in the army to establish the location of the *Schwerpunkt* (the exact point where the ground forces would attack the enemy) and to coordinate the efforts of the different forces involved, which would see tanks in the vanguard, mobile artillery supporting the infantry, and air power being used to attack the enemy directly in front of the German advance.[9] This was the proper application of military force as the *Wehrmacht* saw it, and these battlefield tactics were extremely successful. Throughout the day of 23rd August, the tanks of 16th Panzer made good progress. As they approached the Volga to the north of Stalingrad, a unit of female citizen soldiers operating 37 anti-aircraft gun emplacements, who had previously worked at the Barrikady Gun Factory, lowered their weapons to bring them to bear on the approaching enemy and although they did everything in their power to defend their city, their efforts came to naught.[10] Stukas from *Fliegerkorps VIII* bombed their positions, and the tanks of 16th Panzer soon overran the unit. Some of the German tankers dismounted at the scene and found female clothing and body parts amongst the wreckage.[11]

At 23:10 on 23rd August, Paulus received a message at 6th Army H.Q. at Ossinovskoy informing him that 16th Panzer had reached the Volga that afternoon. Although these tanks had reached their objective, the three components of 14th Panzer Corps had become separated as they travelled east. The 3rd Motorised Division was still twelve miles to the rear, cut off by the Soviet 35th Guards Division and 169th Tank Brigade, and 60th Motorised Division was ten miles farther back, trying to fight its way through against the Soviet 214th Rifle Division.[12] The three Germans divisions were therefore compelled to adopt defensive "hedgehog" positions.[13]

As night fell, the *Luftwaffe* launched another attack on Stalingrad. As the German incendiaries fell upon the city, many of the remaining wooden buildings were set ablaze. In the north of the city, oil tanks on the banks of the river had been destroyed, and the waters of the Volga were covered in burning oil.[14] As the city burned along its entire length, the flames were visible up to forty miles away. The air raids continued for another two days.[15] On 25th August, Colonel General Wolfram von Richthofen, who had taken over as fleet commander of *Luftflotte 4* on 21st July[16] and handed command of *Fleigerkorps VIII* over to Lieutenant General Martin Flieberg,[17] flew over Stalingrad and watched the latest air raid in real time. He wrote later that the city had been destroyed and there were no more worthwhile targets for his bombers to attack.[18]

That same day, the Soviet Regional Party Committee declared a state of siege and proclaimed that Stalingrad would never be surrendered to the German invaders. According to this declaration, the city was to be turned into an impregnable fortress and its inhabitants, both military personnel and civilians, were to do everything in their power to defend Stalingrad.[19] The German army, which had been created to engage in a war of movement where speed and space was paramount, would now have to fight a war of attrition in an urban environment.

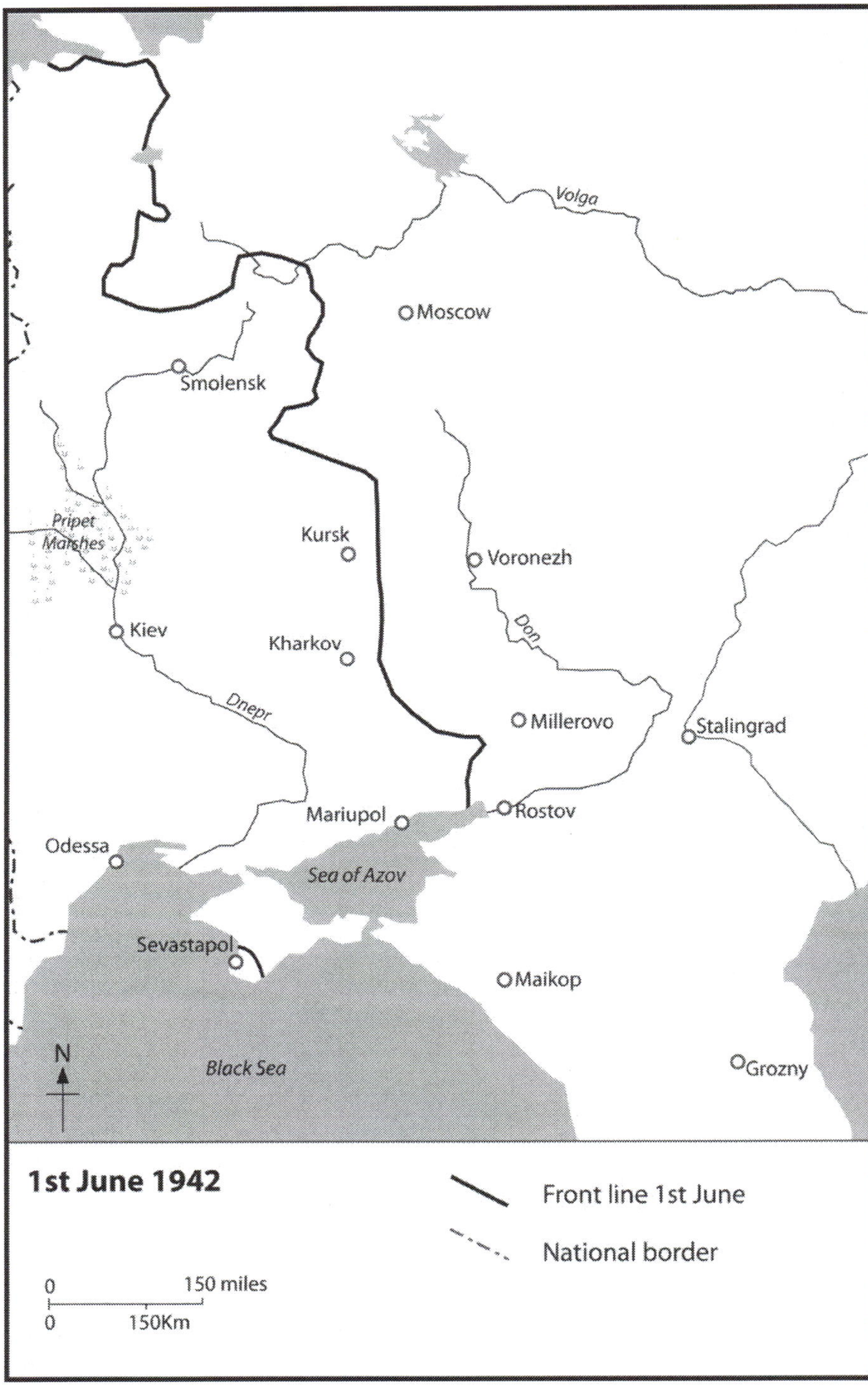
Volga
Moscow
Smolensk
Pripet Marshes
Kursk
Voronezh
Don
Kiev
Kharkov
Dnepr
Millerovo
Stalingrad
Mariupol
Rostov
Odessa
Sea of Azov
Sevastapol
Maikop
N
Black Sea
Grozny
1st June 1942
Front line 1st June
National border
0
150 miles
0
150Km

Stalingrad had not been one of the main targets in Hitler's Directive 41, which was issued on 5th April 1942. This stated that

> as soon as weather and terrain conditions are favorable, the superior German command and German forces must take the initiative once again to force the enemy to do our bidding.
>
> The objective is to wipe out the entire defense potential remaining to the Soviets and to cut them off as far as possible from their most important sources of supply.
>
> For this purpose all available forces of Germany and our allies will be brought up. At the same time, however, the occupied territories in western and northern Europe, particularly the coasts, must remain adequately protected under all circumstances.[20]

The opening paragraphs of Directive 41 are significant, because the goals of the 1942 campaign are clearly laid out. The Germans were trying to physically destroy the Soviet armed forces in front of them, and to cut off the oil fields in the south from the rest of the country. It is noteworthy that Hitler acknowledged here that Germany's allies would have to take part in the campaign if it was to have a chance of succeeding. The directive went on to outline the "general plan" for the campaign:

> In keeping with the original plans for the eastern campaign, it is intended to hold the central part of the front, in the north, to bring about the fall of Leningrad and effect a juncture with the Finns by land, and on the southern wing of the Army front to force a breakthrough into the Caucasus area.
>
> Considering the situation at the end of the winter campaign, the forces available, and the transport conditions, this objective can be attained only in several stages.
>
> Therefore to begin with all available forces are to be combined for the main operation in the southern sector, the objective being to destroy the enemy before the Don in order to gain the oil region in the Caucasian area and to cross the Caucasus mountains.[21]

The problems the under-mechanised Germany army had the year before as the tanks and infantry advanced at different speeds had been recognised. There were to be no *Blitzkrieg* tactics employed in this campaign and encircling the enemy and trying to annihilate their forces in cauldron battles would only be attempted on a smaller scale:

> Considering that, as often enough demonstrated, the Russians are not very vulnerable to large encirclements, we should strive particularly to carry out the individual breakthroughs as separate pincer operations, similar to the battle of Vyazma-Bryansk.
>
> We must avoid closing the pincers too late, thus giving the enemy the possibility of escaping destruction.
>
> It must not happen that by advancing too swiftly and too far the tanks and motorized forces lose connection with the infantry following them, or that they lose the possibility of assisting the infantry forces of the Army pressing ahead, by direct attacks on the rear of the encircled Russian Armies.[22]

The directive went on to say that "the objective is, as already stated, to take the Caucasus front, destroying the Russian forces from Voronezh to the south and west and north of the Don." This was to be the main operation on the Eastern Front in 1942. "Because of the manner in which the available forces must be brought up, this operation can be carried out only in a series of successive attacks, which, however, are in connection with each other or supplement each other."[23] The campaign would begin with an attack from the front lines east of Kursk towards Voronezh, on the far side of the Don. As this was taking place, another thrust towards Voronezh would begin from a starting point just north of Belgorod.[24] "The aim of this breakthrough is to capture Voronezh," the directive stated.[25]

The second phase of the operation would see the armoured and motorised units at Voronezh continue south-east along the right bank of the Don, where they would act as a backstop to another attack that would head east towards Millerovo from a starting point just south of Kharkov.[26] The stated goal here was "not to break the Russian front as such, but rather, in cooperation with the motorized forces advancing down the Don, to destroy the Russian forces."[27]

In the third phase of the operation, another attack would be launched from the area north of Taganrog, the port city on the shore of the Sea of Azov. These forces would head east and meet up with second phase units that were to keep advancing along the right bank of the Don towards Stalingrad.[28] The directive stated that "we must try to reach Stalingrad or at least to subject this city to bombardment of our heavy weapons to such an extent that it is eliminated as an armament and traffic center in the future."[29] Stalingrad did not need to be captured to fulfil the directive's operational goals. The river traffic could be interrupted at any point along the Volga, and the factories could be attacked and destroyed by artillery and from the air.[30] German bombing raids could also de-house workers from the Soviet factories by using incendiaries to set the residential areas alight. If the city could no longer function as an industrial centre, regardless of how that was brought about, then the fourth phase of the operation could be undertaken, and the German forces could head south to capture the oil fields in the Caucasus.[31]

The necessity of capturing the oil fields in the south of the Soviet Union so that Germany would be able to fight a long war had already been discussed at the highest level. On 19th November 1941, Hitler had told Halder that he intended to launch an offensive towards the Caucasus the following year,[32] and on 30th November, Hitler spoke with Goebbels about the war lasting at least into 1943.[33] At a meeting with the Japanese ambassador on 3rd January 1942, Hitler said that he intended to launch an offensive in the direction of the Caucasus as soon as the weather permitted.[34] On 19th March, Hitler told Goebbels that he planned to have the army establish winter quarters in the east at the end of that year's campaign season, and that Germany might even establish a permanent defensive line and accept the continued existence of a Soviet state.[35]

The fact of the matter was that Germany needed more oil than she could produce. Only approximately twenty percent of the amount of oil that Germany was using came from domestic sources. Synthetic oil production had been increased significantly during the war years, but Germany still relied primarily on the Romanian oil fields for her supplies.[36] The yield from these oil fields was decreasing, and the Romanians were burning through their oil reserves as they attempted to keep the level of their deliveries to Germany as high as possible.[37] At a meeting on 12th February 1942, Ribbentrop was advised by Ion Antonescu, the Prime Minister of Romania, that the only long-term solution to this problem was for Germany to use her military to seize territory that was rich in oil.[38]

If Germany was going to fight a long war against Britain and the United States, then she not only needed to secure a supply of oil that would keep her military forces operational. The resources the Soviet Union needed to function would have to be taken away from her so she would not be able to actively fight a war. Germany might still be able to change her fortunes in what had become a global conflict by launching an attack in the south of the Soviet Union and capturing the oilfields around Maikop and Grozny, then advancing through the Caucasus mountains to seize the oilfields beside Baku, on the coast of the Caspian Sea.

On 29th April 1942, a meeting was arranged with the Italians at Klessheim Castle in Salzburg. Ribbentrop talked with the Italian Foreign Minister, Count Galeazzo Ciano. "An offensive against the Russians in the south with the oil wells is a politico-military objective," Ciano was informed.[39] "When Russia's sources of oil are exhausted she will be brought to her knees. Then the British Conservatives, and even Churchill himself, who, after all, is a sensible man, will bow in order to save what remains of their mauled empire."[40]

If the campaign in the south was successful, then the Germans could make it impossible for the Red Army to keep fighting against the *Wehrmacht*. If the fighting on the Eastern Front died down, then most of the German forces could be transferred elsewhere, and any Anglo-American invasion of Europe would not face a weakened opponent that was fighting a war on two fronts. The coastal defences in France would be staffed by a battle-hardened enemy who had forced the BEF back into the sea once before. This would make any invasion of France much more difficult. Hitler had said before launching Operation Barbarossa that one of the reasons for the German invasion was to deprive the British of their only means of taking on the *Wehrmacht*. Now that the Americans were actively involved in the war as a belligerent party, the window of opportunity to strike a decisive blow in the east was closing. Whether Germany could still do this was another question altogether. Of the 162 divisions deployed on the Eastern Front at the end of March 1942, only 8 were fully operational, and 47 more could only carry out limited offensive manoeuvres. The 16 armoured divisions had 140 serviceable tanks between them, which was less than the number usually assigned to a single division.[41] Vehicles were taken from the other army groups to allow the forces stationed in the south to regain some of their mobility on the battlefield, and most of the tanks and weapons being produced that year were given to Army Group South.[42] By the middle of June, Army Group South had 68 German combat divisions ready to take part in Operation *Blau*.[43] The German leadership recognised that they also needed more soldiers on the Eastern Front, and since they could not replace their losses from the previous year themselves, they turned to other countries for assistance. Goering visited Rome at the end of January[44] and was promised two divisions of Italian troops for the Eastern Front. At the meeting with the Italians in Salzburg that April, still more troops were promised.[45] When Operation *Blau* finally began on 28th June 1942, there were ten divisions from Hungary, six from Italy and five from Romania fighting in the southern theatre.[46] These foreign divisions would be used primarily to guard the flanks as German units headed east towards the Volga.

Army Group South was now commanded by Field Marshal Fedor von Bock, who had recovered from his health scare the year before. Colonel General Maximillian von Weichs commanded 2nd Army, and 4th Panzer Army was commanded by Colonel General Hermann Hoth.[47] The 2nd Hungarian Army, under the command of Lieutenant General Gustav Vitez Jany, also formed part of Army Group South.[48] On the morning of 28th June, after the enemy's defences were softened up by an artillery bombardment and air raids carried out by *Fleigerkorps VIII*, Weichs sent 48th Panzer

Corps and 24th Panzer Corps forward. Both tank units made good progress and reached the Kshen river, approximately halfway between Kursk and Voronezh, on the first day of combat.[49] Although the rain began falling the next day, which turned the terrain to mud and slowed the German advance, the forces from 2nd Army kept moving forward and reached the Olym river on the afternoon of 1st July.[50]

The 6th Army launched a second drive towards Voronezh on 30th July, south of and parallel to the northern arm of the pincer.[51] They broke through the Soviet defences, and by the end of the following day, 6th Army units were establishing a bridgehead on the far bank of the Oskol river.[52] The 100th Light Infantry Division, which was part of 8th Corps,[53] was detached from the inner flank of the advance and ordered to head north, along the banks of the Oskol.[54] Bock also sent the 16th Motorised Infantry Division, which was part of the 2nd Hungarian Army,[55] south from the northern arm of the pincer to meet the advancing 6th Army troops east of the city of Stary Oskol.[56] This attempt to carry out an encirclement under the new operational guidelines in Directive 41 proved to be a failure. The 16th Motorised Division claimed to have encountered stiff resistance on their route south, and they requested air support.[57] Richthofen was highly critical of the ground troops, arguing that there were not many enemy forces in the area, and they should do whatever was necessary to close the pocket.[58] By the time the Hungarians reached their assigned position east of Stary Oskol, the 100th Light Infantry still had not advanced far enough to meet them.[59] Richthofen sent his bombers to attack the enemy forces that were trying to escape to the east, but the air raids alone were not sufficient to seal the pocket. When the German ground troops finally reached their assigned positions, most of the Soviet units had already escaped, taking their heavy weapons and other equipment with them.[60]

After the failure of this encirclement, the overall success of Operation *Blau* hung in the balance. If the Soviets managed to withdraw their forces across the Don before the Germans could take Voronezh and send their armoured units south, where those forces were supposed to prevent the Soviet forces from escaping and meet up with the next attack farther south, then there would be no decisive cauldron battle and the operation would have failed in one of its primary objectives - to destroy the enemy forces west of the Don. Hitler flew out to Bock's headquarters in Poltava and tried to salvage the situation. According to the available records, Hitler gave Bock permission to decide whether Voronezh should be bypassed or attacked. On 4th July, a regiment of the 24th Panzer Division captured a bridge across the Don and established a bridgehead on the far side. Bock decided to cross the river and take the city, although Hitler insisted the following day that a tank unit should be withdrawn from the operation and sent south along the Don.[61] Bock sent the 40th Panzer Corps from the 6th Army south-east along the river, but the Soviets had sent reinforcements in to help defend Voronezh, which meant Bock could not send another two units, the 24th Panzer Division and the *Grossdeutschland* Division from the 4th Panzer Army, south-east until the morning of 8th July.[62]

The Soviet tactics had directly affected the outcome of the first phase of Operation *Blau*. Rather than stand fast and be captured or annihilated in a cauldron battle, the Soviets had withdrawn, and the attempted German encirclement at Stary Oskol had been unsuccessful. The fighting at Voronezh had forced Bock to send three German units south-east in piecemeal fashion as and when they became available, instead of immediately sending armoured divisions out in strength to establish an effective backstop along the Don. Instead of accepting that the Soviets had learned from their experiences the year before and now knew how to evade an attempted encirclement, which meant the troops that would have been captured or eliminated in a cauldron battle would still have to be fought at a later date, and that the German forces that were still available in the summer of 1942 simply could not take full control of even this limited area of the vast territory of the Soviet Union, Hitler decided to divide his forces and send 4th Panzer Army south to assist Kleist's 1st Panzer Army, which left 6th Army to advance along the Don on its own.[63] Paulus' troops did not face much resistance until they reached the Chir river, but they were strung out and significantly weaker than they would have been with 4th Panzer Army leading the way along the banks of the river and into the Don bend.[64]

The fundamental problem facing the German commanders on the Eastern Front was that they did not have the forces necessary to take control of the vast spaces they found themselves operating in. This problem was only exacerbated following the fighting at Voronezh, when Army Group South was disbanded and replaced by a new command structure. The new Army Group A, which was placed under the command of Field Marshal Wilhelm List, consisted of 1st Panzer Army, 11th Army, 17th Army and the Hungarian 3rd Army. Army Group B consisted of 2nd and 6th Armies, 4th Panzer Army, the Hungarian 2nd Army and the Italian 8th Army. Command of Army Group B was given to Weichs,[65] who had previously been in command of 2nd Army.[66] The different phases of Operation *Blau* were supposed to have taken place sequentially, with the drive to the oil fields in the south being the final stage of the whole operation. Hitler now decided that the two new army groups would go after different targets at the same time.

Führer Directive No. 45, which was issued on 23rd July, stated that Army Group A would "encircle and annihilate the enemy forces south and southeast of Rostov which escaped across the Don. . . . After destroying the enemy forces south of the Don, it will be the most important task of Army

Group A to capture the entire coast of the Black Sea, and thus to eliminate the Black Sea harbors and the enemy Black Sea fleet."[67] This meant advancing as far as the port of Sochi, which was 250 miles south of Rostov, then to Batumi, some 180 miles farther along the coast. Army Group A was also tasked with crossing the river Kuban and "occupying the plateau of Maikop and Armavir" then heading south-east to capture the oil producing area beside the city of Grozny, which lay another 250 miles from Armavir.[68] The directive then stated that the Baku region, which lay almost 300 miles south-east of Grozny, was to be captured "by an advance along the Caspian Sea."[69]

Army Group B was tasked with advancing on Stalingrad "to smash the enemy forces being assembled there, occupy the city itself, and block the land bridge between the Don and the Volga as well as the river itself." Weichs was then to send "fast units" along the Volga to Astrakhan, which was 230 miles away. These units were then supposed to block the main branch of the Volga, which ran through the city.[70]

Field Marshal Ewald von Kleist, the commander of 1st Panzer Army, had been told by Hitler back in April that once the campaign began, his tanks would be going after the Soviet oilfields in the south.[71] Kleist's 1st Panzer Army managed to cross the Don on 25th July. Hoth's 4th Panzer Army crossed the river on 29th July, although Hoth was ordered to send only the 16th Motorised Division south-east. The rest of 4th Panzer Army was sent back north to assist Paulus in the attack on Stalingrad.[72] Kleist's tanks advanced rapidly once they had crossed the river, and they reached the city of Maikop on 9th August.[73] However, the Soviets had sabotaged the nearby oil fields, which meant the Germans were not going to be able to develop an alternative source of oil in the territory they had just captured. As they tried to advance farther, the German commanders discovered that the terrain was so rough and the surrounding forests to impenetrable that only mountain troops and mules could make any headway. Soviet counterattacks made the situation even more difficult, and the German advance soon stalled in the Caucasus mountains.[74]

Hoth's 4th Panzer Army had made good progress initially as it headed towards Stalingrad, thanks to the assistance of Fiebig's *Fliegerkorps VIII*, whose dive bombers attacked the Soviet units in their path. However, as Wietersheim's 14th Panzer Corps was heading across the land bridge between the Don and the Volga on 23rd August, Hoth's advance slowed due to a shortage of fuel and ammunition.[75] On 27th August, it began to rain, which made the terrain more difficult for Hoth's tanks, and as they attempted to advance north-east towards Lake Sarpa and north towards Stalingrad itself, they met stiff Soviet resistance.[76] To the north of the city, the Soviets were attacking the "hedgehog" formation established by 16th

Panzer Division.[77] Hube moved his headquarters into a ravine close to the river, which offered some protection against air attacks, and took to sleeping in a straw lined pit underneath one of his tanks.[78] The beleaguered 16th Panzer managed to hold on until 30th August, when 103rd Panzer Battalion from 3rd Motorised Division fought their way through into the pocket. 103rd Panzer had captured a Soviet freight train loaded with American jeeps and lorries being unloaded west of Kuzmichi. These vehicles, which had come ashore at Murmansk, were now being used by 3rd Motorised Division.[79] Two days later, 60th Motorised Division and the six infantry divisions of 51st and 8th Corps also fought their way through to the pocket, and the corridor to the Volga was finally secured.[80]

On 30th August, 4th Panzer reached the Karpovka river south of the city and formed a bridgehead at Gavriolovka, approximately twenty miles from Stalingrad.[81] Weichs sent a message to Paulus instructing him to launch an attack southward and destroy the enemy forces west of Stalingrad, with the assistance of Hoth's 4th Panzer Army. However, Paulus could not spare any armoured units for such an attack, because he could not afford to weaken the corridor to the Volga, which was still being attacked by the Soviets.[82] Weichs understood that there was an opportunity to attack the Soviet armies defending Stalingrad in a pincer movement, but by the time 6th Army managed to head south and link up with the advancing 4th Panzer units, the Soviet forces had moved beyond their reach.[83] On 3rd September, Richthofen ordered *Fliegerkorps VIII* to launch another bombing raid on the wrecked city that destroyed the command centre of the Soviet 62nd Army and almost killed its commander, General Vasily Chuikov.[84] Richthofen and Paulus met at a forward command post and studied the ruins of the city through field glasses. The Soviet 62nd and 64th Armies had withdrawn into the city itself, so there was still some fighting to be done, but the German commanders believed that a victory in Stalingrad was inevitable.[85] The *Wehrmacht* may have been victorious against all the opponents they faced in the early years of the war, but what could have been seen by some as an unstoppable military force was now going to be confronted by an immovable object. This apparent paradox was about to be resolved on the banks of the Volga, in the city that bore Stalin's name.

The Germans launched a concerted effort to take Stalingrad in the early hours of the morning on 13th September. An artillery barrage had been laid down upon the city for the preceding twenty-four hours, and at 06:30, the 71st, 76th and 295th Infantry Divisions attacked from their positions north of the Tsaritsa river, which flowed through the centre of Stalingrad and into the Volga. Just south of the Tsaritsa, the 94th Infantry Division and the 29th Motorised Division, supported by the 14th and 24th Panzer Divisions, headed into the Dar Gova district. The two attacks were to meet at the main landing area on the banks of the Volga, which would cut the city in half and deprive its defenders of that facility, so they could not receive supplies or reinforcements from the far bank.[86]

The German tactics as they advanced into the city were to send three or four tanks along with each company of infantry. When the enemy opened fire, that would give their position away to the panzer commanders. The German tanks would then shell the building the enemy was in at almost point-blank range. However, the tanks could not elevate their guns sufficiently to target the upper floors, so most of the buildings would remain untouched.[87] The Germans did try to recruit soldiers to carry flamethrowers so these buildings could be burnt down, but very few people wanted to volunteer for this hazardous duty, not least because the Soviets would burn these soldiers to death if they were ever captured.[88]

Whenever the Germans thought they had cleared a particular building, they found that the enemy would soon reappear and open fire on them again. It took some time before they figured out that the Soviets had knocked holes through the attic walls of adjoining buildings and were moving through these passageways during the night, back into what the Germans thought were empty buildings.[89] The German army had been created between the wars to fight a *Bewegungskrieg* - a war of movement in open terrain - but the battle for Stalingrad soon became a static war of attrition where movement was impossible and German soldiers were forced to fight amongst the rubble of the bombed city, often in hand-to-hand combat, against a ruthless and determined enemy who would never give in.

By 21st September, the Germans had cleared the banks of the Tsaritsa all the way to the Volga and set their guns up by the city's main landing area. The Soviets now had to rely on the factory ferries in the northern part of the city for the delivery of supplies and reinforcements.[90] Still the defenders of the city refused to give up. As the fighting dragged on and the victory foreseen by the German commanders failed to materialise, the strategy employed by the Soviets was to send just enough reinforcements into the city to allow Chuikov to keep on fighting. Between 1st September and 1st November, only five infantry divisions were sent across the Volga. This was just enough reinforcements to replace the soldiers who had been killed in what the Germans were now calling the *Rattenkrieg* – the rats' war.[91] There was no expectation of a breakout. Chuikov's 62nd Army had to hold fast and let the German forces exhaust themselves by continually attacking a dead *Schwerpunkt*, while twenty-seven new infantry divisions and nineteen armoured brigades were formed up in the rear, and preparations were made for a counterattack along the German flanks.[92]

Paulus made another attempt to overcome the Soviet defences when, on the morning of 27th September, an offensive was launched in the north of the city. German dive bombers laid waste to the factory district north of the Tsaritsa,[93] and the 24th Panzer Division, together with most of the 389th Infantry Division and the 100th Jaeger Division, advanced towards the Barrikady Gun Factory and the Red October plant. Paulus also ordered the 14th Panzer Division and the 94th Infantry Division to move up from the southern part of the city and join in the attack.[94] On 2nd October, the Germans bombed oil storage tanks on the banks of the river just above where Chuikov had established his headquarters. Burning oil poured down the slopes, around Chuikov's headquarters and into the river.[95] As the days passed, the Germans did everything in their power to break the Soviets and take control of the city, but they could not take that final step and claim victory. Chuikov's 62nd Army held on, using the ruins of the city to their advantage and forcing the German soldiers to fight a battle of attrition, and relying on artillery from the far side of the Volga, together with the devastating *Katyusha* rocket launchers that reversed out of their hiding places on the western banks of the river to let their payloads go before heading back under cover,[96] to further degrade the attacking German forces.

The Soviet counterattack had been proposed to Stalin by General Georgi Zhukov, the Deputy Supreme Commander of the Red Army,[97] and Alexandr Vasilevky, the Chief of the General Staff, on 13th September.[98] The plan, codenamed Operation Uranus, was to attack the 3rd Romanian Army, which was holding the German lines west of Stalingrad, from the bridgehead at Serafimovich. Another assault would be made from the Kletskaya bridgehead to the east, and these forces would then drive south-east and head for Kalach, which lay south of the Don bend. The Romanian 4th Army, which had been tasked with defending the lines south of Stalingrad, was also to be attacked, and the Soviet forces were then to head north-west and meet up with the main assault at Kalach.[99]

The German commanders were not unaware of the dangers involved in what they were doing. By leaving their allies to guard their flanks and concentrating most of their own forces on driving forward, they were inviting a counterattack that could potentially cut off 6th Army and leave Paulus and his men stranded in Stalingrad. General Kurt Zeitzler, who replaced Halder at the OKH in late September, presented Hitler with an official report warning that the forces available on the ground could not take control of the amount of territory that Hitler wanted to occupy in the east, and that the weakest section of the German lines, which was held by Hungarian, Italian and Romanian troops, lay between the right flank of Army Group Centre and Stalingrad.[100] Hitler would not accept that these assertions were true, and he refused to allow the German troops to withdraw to a more defensible front line, or to make plans to do so in the event of a Soviet attack.[101]

At 07:20 on the morning of 19th November, the Soviet artillery began to lay down fire on the positions of the Romanian 3rd Army, which had been tasked with defending the northern flank of the German advance. The territory around the Soviet bridgeheads on the right bank of the Don, which had not been dealt with during the advance to Stalingrad, now became the base for a Soviet attack. Once the artillery ceased at 08:50, the Soviet 5th Tank Army and 21st Army attacked the Romanian positions. The Romanian troops around Kletskaya fought back desperately, but they could not hold the line. When the Soviets sent in their tanks, the Romanian troops gave up their defensive positions altogether and began to retreat.[102] The 4th Tank Corps and 3rd Guards Calvary Corps from 21st Army were sent into this breach in the lines. Thirty miles farther west, the 1st and 26th Tank Corps and the 8th Cavalry Corps of 5th Tank Army broke through the Romanian lines and started heading south-east towards Perelazovsky, Ostrov and ultimately, Kalach.[103]

The German commanders responded by sending 48th Panzer Corps, under Lieutenant General Ferdinand Heim, to intercept the Kletskaya attack. This unit had been held in reserve by Zeitzler, to be activated in the event of an attack from the Soviet bridgeheads on the Don.[104] Less than an hour after the tanks had set off, Heim was ordered to change course and head north-west to intercept the other Soviet attack. The weather conditions were so bad, and visibility was so poor, that contact was lost with 1st Romanian Panzer Division, which stayed on its original course.[105] The Romanian tanks could not stop the Soviet forces that were heading south from Kletskaya, and when 22nd Panzer Division, the other armoured component of 48th Panzer Corps, encountered the advancing Soviet tank units at Peschany, they fought as best they could against the Soviet T-34s but were quickly forced to retreat to avoid annihilation.[106] Zeitzler spoke with Hitler and tried to persuade him that it would now be prudent to pull back from Stalingrad, but Hitler refused to allow a major withdrawal.[107]

When Weichs, who was in command of Army Group B, saw what was happening on his northern flank, he signalled Paulus and ordered him to send some of his armoured units west to try and block the Soviet counterattack. Paulus duly ordered the 14th, 16th and 24th Panzer divisions to withdraw from the fighting around Stalingrad, but Chuikov's 62nd Army were fighting harder than ever, which made it difficult for these German units to disengage, and in any event, there was barely enough fuel for these tanks to travel far enough west to intercept the Soviet forces.[108] The German tanks finally arrived on the battlefield in scattered, piecemeal fashion. All they could do was slow the Soviets down by twenty-four hours or so.[109] When the Soviets arrived at Kalach on 23rd November, the German soldiers stationed at the bridge there, which had been used as a main conduit for

German supplies being transported to Stalingrad, mistakenly believed that the armoured personnel carriers approaching at the head of the advancing column were carrying German soldiers. When they allowed the vehicles on to the bridge, these personnel carriers stopped halfway across. Approximately sixty Soviet soldiers got out and began shooting at the German engineers who had made the bridge ready for demolition. The explosives were quickly removed, the bridge was made safe, and twenty-five of the Soviet tanks crossed over and headed south-east.[110]

At 10:00 on the morning of 20th November, the Soviet artillery opened fire on the 4th Romanian Army, which was defending the southern flank of the attack on Stalingrad. After approximately seventy-five minutes, the Soviet 57th Army attacked the sectors being held by the 2nd and 18th Romanian Infantry Divisions. The Romanian defences collapsed in a matter of hours. When the second echelon attacked, the 13th Mechanised Corps broke through the line and headed north. Between Lake Tsatsa and Lake Barmantsak, the Soviet 51st Army attacked the section of the front line that was being held by the 1st and 4th Romanian Infantry Divisions. Panic broke out among the Romanians, and officers and troops alike abandoned their posts and tried to escape using whatever vehicles were available. When the second Soviet echelon attacked at 14:00, the three mechanised brigades and two tank regiments of the 4th Mechanised Corps tore through the decimated Romanian defences and headed north-west, towards Kalach.[111]

On 23rd November, units from the 4th Mechanised Corps reached the town of Sovetsky, some ten miles south-east of Kalach. That afternoon, soldiers from the 36th Brigade sighted a column of tanks heading towards their position from the north-west. The oncoming tanks, which belonged to the 45th Tank Brigade, from the 4th Tank Corps, sent up a green flare as a recognition signal.[112] This was a significant event, because it showed that the Soviets were now using the enemy's own battlefield tactics against them, and unlike the German encirclements in 1941, the Red Army had enough assets on the ground to make sure the cauldron they had created was sealed tightly shut.

Hitler had travelled to Munich to give a speech at the *Loewenbräukeller* on the evening of 8th November to mark the anniversary of the failed *putsch* of 1923.[113] He had decided to stay at the Berghof, his home in the Bavarian mountains, instead of returning to the Wolf's Lair, the fortified military complex that had been built for him in the forest near Rastenburg, in East Prussia. When Zeitzler telephoned him with the news that the Soviets had launched a counterattack and argued that the 6th Army should be allowed to withdraw from Stalingrad and fall back to the Don bend, Hitler said that he was not going to leave the Volga, and that the 6th Army should stand fast.[114]

Hitler boarded his personal train at Berchtesgaden on the evening of 22nd November and returned to the Wolf's Lair,[115] where he was given confirmation that the 6th Army had been surrounded. Paulus and his men were now facing the possibility of being annihilated in a *Kesselschlacht*. Hitler spoke with Paulus over the radio and ordered him to move his headquarters into the city and adopt a "hedgehog" defence.[116] The *Luftwaffe* was given the job of resupplying the German soldiers trapped in the pocket, but this proved to be an impossible task. The *Luftwaffe* did not have enough transport planes to carry out the mission,[117] and without the food and supplies they needed, the only hope left for the trapped soldiers of the 6th Army was a rescue attempt that would be led by Field Marshal Erich von Manstein. This was codenamed Operation Winter Gale.[118] Although the objective was to break into the pocket and open a channel to the west, Hitler refused to allow the 6th Army to fight their way out of the pocket at the same time.[119] When one of the panzer units involved in the rescue was redeployed to counter a Soviet attack farther north, the rescue attempt stalled, leaving Paulus and his men stranded.[120] Zeitzler realised that the German units currently in the Caucasus were likely to be cut off if the Soviet forces kept advancing, and he somehow managed to convince Hitler that 1st Panzer and 17th Army would have to retreat.[121]

Operation *Blau* had proven to be a failure. In the south, the Germans had not captured the oil fields they had gone after, and in the ruins of Stalingrad, Paulus had been left to watch his men die in a freezing cauldron, surrounded by the enemy. On 18th December, Ciano visited the Wolf's Lair, and explained the Italian perspective to their partners in the Pact of Steel: "Mussolini is especially anxious to have Hitler know (and he has already spoken of it to Goering) that he considers it extremely advisable to come to an agreement with Russia, or at least to fix upon a defensive line that can be held by small forces."[122] The Germans he spoke to appeared to understand the gravity of the situation on the Eastern Front, although they were reluctant to take the advice of their allies and even tried to blame them for what had happened. "When I arrived, no one tried to conceal from me or from my collaborators the unhappiness over the news of the breakthrough on the Russian front," Ciano wrote in his diary. "[Walther] Hewel, who is very close to Hitler, had the following conversation (in English) with Pansa. Pansa: "Had our Army many losses?" Hewel: "No losses at all; they are running." Pansa: "As you did in Moscow last year?" Hewel: "Exactly."[123]

In 1941, the *Wehrmacht* had fought its way across Soviet territory until it reached a culminating point. A year later, the German forces had reached the banks of the Volga, but they had faced an enemy with seemingly inexhaustible resources, and they had been forced to fight a type of war they could not win. Trapped in the city of Stalingrad, Paulus and his men fought on as best they could until, on 8th January 1943, the Soviets formally offered terms of surrender. Prisoners of war were to be given normal rations, the wounded would receive medical treatment and all prisoners would have their rank recognised by their captors. Paulus radioed the terms of the proposal back to Hitler, only to have his request for freedom of action refused. The 6th Army had to fight on.[124]

Hitler's blind insistence that the German troops who had fought their way into Stalingrad should not retreat from the banks of the Volga, together with the positioning of their allies on the flanks of the German advance, had given the Soviets an opportunity to strike a decisive blow on the battlefield. Paulus was now expected to offer himself up as a sacrifice on the altar of Hitler's flawed leadership. To prevent Paulus and the other officers in the 6th Army from surrendering to the Soviets, Hitler issued a series of field promotions. Paulus was given the rank of Field Marshal, and 117 other senior officers were promoted.[125] None of this made any difference to the situation on the ground.

The Soviets steadily worked to reduce the size of the pocket in Stalingrad, splitting it in two and then into three smaller pockets. Eventually, on the last day of January, the Soviets made their way to the headquarters of 6th Army, and when another offer of surrender was made, it was accepted. Approximately 20,000 Romanian troops had already been evacuated by air, along with 29,000 wounded. All that Paulus could do now was lead approximately 91,000 of his men into captivity. Broken and defeated, these survivors of the failed German campaign of 1942 were transported to prisoner of war camps in Siberia.[126]

Instead of securing the resources he needed to fight a long war against Britain and the United States, Hitler now had to face the inevitability of defeat. The Red Army would now be able to go over on to the offensive and push the *Wehrmacht* back. Once that happened, there would be no turning the tide. An Anglo-American invasion in the west would force Germany to fight a war on two fronts and weaken them still further. It would only be a matter of time till Germany was defeated and the hammer and sickle flew over Berlin.

The significance of the Soviet contribution to the second world war was acknowledged by Churchill when he delivered a long speech in the House of Commons on 2nd August 1944:

> I must say that in talking about all these various campaigns that are going on at once all over the world, I have left the obvious, essential fact till this point, namely, that it is the Russian Armies who have done the main work in tearing the guts out of the German army. In the air and on the oceans we could maintain our place, but there was

no force in the world which could have been called into being, except after several more years, that would have been able to maul and break the German army unless it had been subjected to the terrible slaughter and manhandling that has fallen to it through the strength of the Russian Soviet Armies.

I salute Marshal Stalin, the great champion, and I firmly believe that our 20 years' treaty with Russia will prove to be one of the most lasting and durable factors in preserving the peace and the good order and the progress of Europe.[127]

15 Heavy Bombers

The air offensive against Germany was at the centre of British strategic thinking at the end of 1941, but it was going to take an enormous industrial effort to fight this new kind of war. On 30th June of that year, Bomber Command only had 532 serviceable aircraft, and by November, a total of 526 aircraft had been lost on operations. This "wastage" of aircraft would have to be continually replaced to maintain Bomber Command as an effective fighting force, and more bombers would have to be added to that if the area bombing campaign was ever going to work. It was not a case of simply ramping up production at existing facilities within the UK, because the RAF were also determined to replace their older bombers with the new heavies such as the Lancaster.[1]

The first Lancaster bombers would only be delivered to 44 Squadron just before Christmas in 1941, and it would take time for the inevitable engineering problems with the new aircraft to be addressed and for enough of these heavy bombers to be produced to make a significant difference to Bomber Command. In the meantime, the British government tried to persuade the Americans to build more heavy bombers.[2] As Churchill sailed across the Atlantic to visit Roosevelt that December following the German declaration of war on the United States, he prepared a series of papers for the President to read, in which he tried to get the United States to join in the air offensive against Germany:

> It may be mentioned here that we greatly desire American bomber squadrons to come into action from the British Isles against Germany. Our own bomber programme has fallen short of our hopes. It is formidable and is increasing, but its full development has been delayed. It must be remembered that we place great hopes of affecting German production and German morale by ever more severe and more accurate bombing of their cities and harbours, and that this, combined with their Russian defeats, may produce important effects upon the will to fight of the German people, with consequential internal reactions upon the German government. The arrival in the United Kingdom of say, twenty American bomber squadrons would emphasise and accelerate this process, and would be the most direct and effective reply to the declaration of war by Germany upon the United States. Arrangements will be made in Great Britain to increase this process and develop the Anglo-American bombing of Germany without any top limit from now on till the end of the war.[3]

Churchill had read the Butt report in August of that year, so the assertions that Bomber Command would be targeting German morale as well as production facilities and that the area bombing campaign "may produce important effects upon the will to fight of the German people, with consequential internal reactions upon the German government"[4] are significant. As early as December 1940, the Ministry of Information had stated that "all the evidence goes to prove that the Germans, for all their present confidence and cockiness will not stand a quarter of the bombing that the British have shown they can take." The first volume of the official history of the strategic air offensive against Germany states that "there emerged a picture of the German people, exhausted by the rearmament programme, unelated by Germany's military victories, being driven forward to further unendurable efforts, short of food and the comforts of life, fearful of bombing, eager to spring into revolt against the Nazi regime and, perhaps above all, in desperate need of a peaceful rest each night."[5]

One prominent and influential figure who had always been in favour of bombing German civilians was Hugh Trenchard, later to become Lord Trenchard, who was head of the Royal Air Force during the first world war, and who was regarded as an authority on fighting a war in the air.[6] Trenchard wrote to Churchill on 19th May 1941, and argued that

> to him [Trenchard], the experience of two wars suggested that the Germans were peculiarly susceptible to bombing and it was against Germany that the Royal Air Force should strike again and again. If ships at sea were attacked, Lord Trenchard argued, then ninety-nine per cent of the effort would be wasted because ninety-nine per cent of the bombs would fall in the sea. If targets in occupied territory were bombed, then ninety-nine per cent of the effort would be more than wasted, for the bombs would kill and disturb old friends and allies. If, however, targets in German cities were attacked, then ninety-nine per cent of the bombs would contribute directly to the destruction of German morale. This form of attack should, Lord Trenchard believed, be mounted every night, even if on occasions it was only possible to send one bomber. The offensive should be carried to Munich, Stuttgart and eventually Vienna in the East. To achieve this, Lord Trenchard admitted, would be a costly adventure and would require an ultimately enormous force.[7]

Roosevelt had spoken to the American people in one of his fireside chats on 26th May 1940, as the BEF (British Expeditionary Force) was being driven out of France and across the English Channel by the advancing

Wehrmacht. "At this moment of sadness throughout most of the world, I want to talk with you about a number of subjects that directly affect the future of the United States," said Roosevelt. "We are shocked by the almost incredible eyewitness stories that come to us, stories of what is happening at this moment to the civilian populations of Norway and Holland and Luxembourg and Belgium and France." Roosevelt continued: "I think it is right on this Sabbath evening that I should say a word on behalf of women and children and old men who need help – immediate help in their present distress – help from us across the seas, help from us who are still free to give it."

Roosevelt assured his audience that the American Red Cross was "rushing food and clothing and medical supplies" to civilians in these countries, and he asked everyone to "please give according to your means to your nearest Red Cross chapter, give as generously as you can. I ask this in the name of our common humanity."

Roosevelt then argued that the American people could not safely ignore the threat on the other side of the Atlantic. "On this Sabbath evening, in our homes in the midst of our American families," he said, "let us calmly consider what we have done and what we must do." Roosevelt proceeded to lay out how much money the government had spent on the American armed forces since he took over from Herbert Hoover in 1933:

> Between 1933 and 1940 – these past seven fiscal years – your government will have spent $1,292,000,000 more than it spent on the Army the previous seven years.
>
> What did we get for this money?
>
> The personnel of the Army, as I have said, has been almost doubled. And by the end of this year every existing unit of the present regular Army will be equipped with its complete requirements of modern weapons. Existing units of the National Guard will also be largely equipped with similar items.
>
> Here are some striking examples taken from a large number of them:
>
> Since 1933 we have actually purchased 5,640 airplanes, including the most modern type of long-range bombers and fast pursuit planes, though, of course, many of these which were delivered four and five and six and seven years ago have worn out through use and been scrapped.
>
> We must remember that these planes cost money – a lot of it. For example, one modern four-engine long-range bombing plane costs $350,000; one modern interceptor pursuit plane costs $135,000; one medium bomber costs $160,000. . . .

Within the past year the productive capacity of the aviation industry to produce military planes has been tremendously increased. In the past year the capacity more than doubled, but that capacity is still inadequate. But the government, working with industry, is determined to increase that capacity to meet our needs. We intend to harness the efficient machinery of these manufacturers to the Government's program of being able to get 50,000 planes a year. . . .

Yes, we are calling upon the resources, the efficiency and the ingenuity of the American manufacturers of war materiel of all kinds – airplanes and tanks and guns and ships, and all the hundreds of products that go into this materiel. The government of the United States itself manufactures few of the implements of war. Private industry will continue to be the source of most of this materiel; and private industry will have to be speeded up to produce it at the rate and efficiency called for by the needs of the times. . . .

We are calling on men now engaged in private industry to help us in carrying out this program and you will hear more of this in detail in the next few days.

This does not mean that the men we call upon will be engaged in the actual production of this materiel. That will still have to be carried on in the plants and factories throughout the land. Private industry will have the responsibility of providing the best, speediest and most efficient mass production of which it is capable. The functions of the business men whose assistance we are calling upon will be to coordinate this program – to see to it that all of the plants continue to operate at maximum speed and efficiency.

Patriotic Americans of proven merit and unquestioned ability in their special fields are coming to Washington to help the government with their training, their experience and their capability.

It is our purpose not only to speed up production but to increase the total facilities of the nation in such a way that they can be further enlarged to meet emergencies of the future.[8]

On Tuesday 28th May, Roosevelt telephoned Bill Knudsen, who was then the President of General Motors, and asked him to visit Washington and meet with him.[9] Knudsen had arrived in America in 1900 as an immigrant from Denmark, and had started working in the shipyards in the Bronx before getting a job with Keim Mills in Buffalo in 1902. Before long, the firm had obtained a contract to make axle housings for Ford, who were starting to produce their Model T cars.[10] The American car industry was beginning to take off and in 1911, Ford bought over Keim Mills. Knudsen became one of the new engineers who could also manage large operations successfully. He was given the responsibility of organising Ford plants all around the United States so that they ran more efficiently.[11] Knudsen understood that the key to efficiency in any engineering business was not speed but accuracy. Files and hammers were banned as workers were forced to rely on the machining processes that were put in place.[12] Instead of buying a building then figuring out how to fit machinery into it, new factories were designed around the machinery that would be needed to make the final product, and each machine was placed where it needed to be on what would be the factory floor so that one process could lead into the next without delay. By designing plants so that large, complex engineering tasks were broken down into smaller, more manageable processes that were carried out in a deliberately planned sequence, Knudsen was helping to create a system of production that would revolutionise the car industry throughout America.[13]

Knudsen left Ford in April 1921 and went to work for General Motors.[14] He was able to turn around the fortunes of Chevrolet and make them profitable again,[15] then he had an idea that would change the car industry forever. Knudsen decided that Chevrolet would build new models every year. Feedback from their own customers would guide what the firm's designers and engineers were doing, so that the new models would end up being what people wanted to buy. This meant that the firm would have to practice "flexible mass production" and constantly change what they were doing inside their plants so that they could produce the new cars.[16] The idea of using flexible mass production to produce new products was a success, and by the late thirties, General Motors had become the largest industrial corporation in the world.[17]

When Knudsen travelled to Washington on 30th May, he was met by Harry Hopkins, who invited him to accept an unpaid position as part of the Council of National Defense Advisory Commission.[18] Knudsen accepted the government's offer, and working together with people like Edward Stettinius Jr., the president of U.S. Steel, Knudsen began to prepare the United States for a war in which she would be acting as the "arsenal of democracy."[19]

Knudsen understood that this would not happen overnight. A lead time of approximately eighteen months would be required before the industrial potential of America became a reality.[20] Knudsen travelled to New York on 13th October for the annual Automobile Show at Madison Square Garden. At a dinner held by the Automobile Manufacturers Association, Knudsen gave a speech and told his audience that American industry would have to find a way to build more heavy bombers.[21] When Knudsen attended a follow-up meeting on 29th October, he brought with him a team from the

Air Corps and several aviation executives. One of the pilots at the meeting was Major Jimmy Doolittle, who went on to lead a bombing raid on Tokyo in April 1942. Doolittle explained to the car manufacturers what would be needed to build modern bombers, laid out displays of different components for them to examine, and asked them to figure out which of the parts their companies could produce.[22]

The car executives agreed to form the Automotive Committee for Air Defence, with Clarence Carleton of Motor Wheel as chairman, and arranged for different engineering firms to operate as subcontractors and make aircraft parts for major firms such as Douglas and Boeing.[23]

The top aeronautical companies in America also came together to form the Aircraft War Production Council, which was led initially by J.H. Kindelberger of North American.[24] This organisation eliminated the traditional competition between these companies. Throughout the war, they shared their technical knowledge, specialist machinery and raw materials with one another.[25] It may have taken some time for American production to come online, but the sheer scale of the industrial effort in the United States can be contrasted with the inadequate supply system that was available to the Germans. Halder had been forced to embark on a de-motorisation scheme before the war began because he could see no way to maintain a large fleet of motorised vehicles, and the army was still relying on the horse and cart to transport weapons and supplies to the front lines when Operation Barbarossa was launched in June 1941.

In December 1940, Doolittle had approached Edsel Ford and Charlie Sorenson, one of the top executives at Ford at the time, and asked if the company could build the new four-engined B-24 bomber.[26] Sorensen had already told Knudsen at the meeting in Detroit that he did not want to make parts for other businesses to assemble and he had insisted that Ford would be able to build fully assembled planes.[27] Following Doolittle's request, Sorenson toured the Consolidated Aircraft plant in San Diego, where the bombers were currently being constructed. Sorenson was confident that Ford could do better, and he negotiated a contract with Washington on 25th February 1941 to build more of the heavy bombers. Sorensen intended to construct a new plant on a green field site that would allow Ford to build planes using the same mass production principles they used to make motor cars.[28]

In March 1941, the Ford company began construction of the largest factory anywhere in the world at Willow Run, to the west of Detroit.[29] Sorenson had envisaged an assembly line a mile long,[30] but Henry Ford decided that the plant would have to be L-shaped, with massive turntables fitted at the junction to turn the bombers around by ninety degrees. Ford did not want the building to keep going in a straight line because it would cross into Wayne County, which was controlled by Democrats.[31] The new plant, which ended up being 3,200 feet long and was 1,279 feet across at its widest point,[32] was not initially successful. As the USAAF was starting to send personnel across the Atlantic in the spring of 1942 to establish 8th Bomber Command on British soil,[33] Willow Run still was not producing any aeroplanes. Bill Knudsen, who had been given the rank of Lieutenant General and was now working as the Head of Production for the War Department, arrived at Willow Run on 27th July to troubleshoot the problem.[34]

Knudsen had seen a similar situation arise a year earlier, when Glenn Martin was struggling to get B-26 Marauders built. Knudsen had spoken to Robert Patterson, the Undersecretary of War, and told him that the people at Glenn Martin were trapped in a cycle of re-tooling again and again to incorporate a never-ending stream of new design adaptations, and they needed to be left alone to concentrate on building aeroplanes to a fixed design. Knudsen proposed building a series of field modification centres around the country. The new planes could be flown to these centres, and any modifications carried out there to make them combat ready.[35] Knudsen realised that this approach would allow the Ford plant at Willow Run to get moving as well.[36] The plant had other problems to overcome, not the least of which was the lack of accommodation for the thousands of people who came there looking for work, but once the plant was able to operate using a static design, instead of continually having to re-tool to accommodate design modifications, the bombers eventually started rolling off the end of the production line on to the tarmac. The bombers were then flown to a modification centre operated by Bechtel-McCone, which was spread out over 285 acres of land near the municipal airport at Birmingham, Alabama.[37] This centre employed approximately 14,000 people, many of whom had never worked on aeroplanes before, but using the same production and engineering practices that had worked on other projects, they carried out the modifications that were required.[38]

By the end of 1942, American industry had produced 24,754 tanks, 2,300,000 small arms and 663,000 machine guns. A total of 47,873 aeroplanes, including 2,618 bombers, came off the assembly line that year, which was just short of the target Roosevelt had set following the attack at Pearl Harbour.[39] In 1943, the numbers were greater still. 18,434 battleships, cruisers, carriers, subs and destroyers came out of American shipyards, tank production rose to 29,495 and the number of heavy bombers produced increased to 9,616, an increase of 267 per cent from the year before.[40] Willow Run finally came good, and when the plant was running at peak efficiency in March 1944, it was able to produce a completely assembled B-24 heavy bomber every 63 minutes.[41]

Churchill had said that once the United States became a belligerent nation, the war would be won through "the proper application of overwhelming force."[42] As the British were developing their own heavy bombers and using Bomber Command to attack the German homeland in darkness, the Americans had their own ideas about how Germany could be brought down. The USAAF (United States Army Air Forces) was under the command of Lieutenant General "Hap" Arnold, who had attended the ATCS (Air Corps Tactical School) at Maxwell Field in Alabama, as had other prominent American airmen such as Carl "Tooey" Spaatz and Ira C. Eaker. One of the ATCS lecturers, Lieutenant Colonel Harold George, had studied American industry and developed the idea of an "industrial web." Every industrial process needed things like steel, ball bearings and electricity for it to work. If the facilities producing these could be attacked in some way, this would prevent the whole "industrial web" from operating properly.[43] The Americans believed they had the technological means to pursue this goal. The brilliant engineer Carl Norden had arrived the United States in 1904, having served an apprenticeship in a Swiss machine shop as a young man before graduating as a qualified mechanical engineer from the Zurich Federal Polytechnic School. Norden worked for several American firms before finally setting up his own company in the 1920s. Norden and his partner, Theodore H. Barth, spent several years designing and developing a new bombsight that used a plane's airspeed and altitude to calculate the trajectory of its bombs, and to figure out when they should be released in order to hit their target.[44] The U.S. Navy had been using the NBS (Norden bombsight) to help defend the coastline of the United States, but when the ATCS learned about Norden's bomb-aiming technology, it was thought that the NBS would allow an offensive bombing campaign to be undertaken in daylight hours against an enemy's "industrial web."[45]

Ira Eaker, who had been put in charge of VIII Bomber Command, arrived in Britain on 21st February 1942, just as Arthur Harris was about to take over at Bomber Command.[46] Harris immediately invited Eaker to stay with him at Springfield, his home at High Wycombe, and by all accounts, the two men got on very well.[47] Permanent accommodation for Eaker and his staff was arranged by turfing out the residents of the Wycombe Abbey School for girls,[48] and several air bases in East Anglia were handed over to the Americans for their own use. British Spitfires were assigned to act as fighter escorts for the B-17 Superfortress bombers, the Americans were given access to the British radar and communications systems, and British resources were used to build and equip more air bases for VIII Bomber Command to use.[49] With this British assistance, the Americans managed to carry out a total of 27 operations against targets in France and the Low Countries by the end of

1942. They were still operating within the range of their fighter escorts at this time, and they only lost approximately 2 per cent of their planes.[50]

The Americans were committed to bombing through the day, but they had yet to cross the German border or go beyond the range of their fighter escorts. Churchill wrote to Roosevelt on 16th September and said that although the initial American operations were "very encouraging" they had not struck "very deep."[51] Portal wrote to Archibald Sinclair on 27th September and argued that the American formations would not be able to defend themselves effectively on long range operations. "The Ruhr is 300 miles away and assuming that the American fighters can go in 200 miles the Fortresses would have 200 miles to fly unescorted," he wrote. "Berlin is 550 miles and would involve 700 miles unescorted flying. . . . I do not think that they will ever be able regularly to penetrate further than the Ruhr and perhaps Hamburg without absolutely prohibitive losses resulting from being run out of ammunition by constant attack or from gunners being killed or wounded."[52]

Nevertheless, Archibald Sinclair wrote to Churchill on 23rd October and with an eye on the situation on the other side of the Atlantic, he argued that there were some people in the United States who wanted to concentrate the American air forces in the Pacific, and some who wanted the air force to support the army in land operations. "It is in your power to crystallise American opinion and to unite it behind those schools of thought which want to attack Germany and want to do it by building up an overwhelming force of bombers in this country," he wrote. "Instead, however, of uniting those schools of thought which want to build up a big bomber force and want to use American power for a decisive attack upon Germany in 1943 and 1944, you will throw these forces into confusion and impotency if you set yourself against their cherished policy of daylight penetration."[53] Sinclair acknowledged that it was the Americans' "firm intention to drop bombs on Germany in daylight next month. It would be a tragedy if we were to frustrate them on the eve of this great experiment."[54]

Sinclair argued that if the American policy was practicable, then it would be possible "in the earliest months of next year for us to send a thousand bombers over Hamburg one night, for the Americans to follow up with 5 or 600 bombers the following day and, if the weather is kind, for us to follow up with a large force of heavy bombers the next night – and then to go on bombing one city after another in Germany on that scale."[55]

The British Chiefs of Staff released a memorandum on 30th October[56] which made it clear that air power alone was not going to bring about the defeat of Germany. The British and American heavy bombers were to be used to "undermine Germany's military power by the destruction of the German industrial and economic war machine before we attempt invasion."[57] In order to create the conditions where a land invasion was possible, the general aim of the air offensive was defined as "the progressive destruction and dislocation of the enemy's war industrial and economic system and the undermining of his morale to a point where his capacity for armed resistance is fatally weakened."[58]

The Chiefs of Staff believed that it would be possible to drop 10,000 tons of bombs on Germany each month by the end of the year. "We should aim at dropping at least 20,000 tons a month on Germany by June 1943," they stated, "and at attaining a target force of the order of 4,000 – 6,000 heavy bombers by April 1944 with a monthly bomb delivery of 60,000 – 90,000 tons. With American co-operation," they concluded, "we believe this can be achieved."[59]

A second memorandum was released by the Chiefs of Staff on 24th November 1942, which redefined the offensive policy of Britain as being firstly, providing material assistance to the Soviet Union, secondly, preparing for a land invasion of Europe and thirdly, bombing north-western Germany.[60] The findings in the earlier memorandum were now being questioned by both Sir Dudley Pound, the First Sea Lord, and Sir Alan Brooke, who was now the Chief of the Imperial General Staff. Brooke believed that prioritising the bomber construction programme would leave the army short of resources, and he was not convinced that the proposed air offensive against the German homeland would reduce the *Wehrmacht's* ability to fight to any significant extent.[61] Pound estimated that putting the bomber force that had been proposed into the air would mean importing an extra five million tons of aviation fuel, and he did not think this could not be done unless the American merchant fleet was "immensely increased."[62] Although the Chiefs of Staff had all signed off on the earlier memorandum, their thinking now was that building a bomber force that might possibly bring Germany to its knees by the middle of 1944 would consume so much of Britain's resources in the meantime that it could slow down or even prevent the development of the land forces that would inevitably be required to take western Europe back from the *Wehrmacht*.

According to the official history of the air offensive against Germany, Churchill "had always placed a high value upon the bombing offensive and he had done much to nourish it" but "he was concerned to preserve a balance between the various possibilities and, perhaps, above all, he was anxious to preserve a freedom of choice." Churchill "had to examine many sides of many questions and more often than not his rulings and advice were addressed to subordinates who were often and necessarily considering only one side of one question."[63] In the memo Halifax handed over to Sumner Welles on 18th February 1942, the Foreign Office had acknowledged that it was not impossible that the Soviet Union could defeat their common enemy before the Americans, together with the British and the Commonwealth countries, had gathered sufficient forces to participate in the final land battle for Germany. If that ever happened, and all that Britain and America had done in the meantime was bomb the living daylights out of Germany, then the RAF may as well have replaced the roundels on their bombers with a red star, because all that Bomber Command would have done was soften up Germany so that in the end, the Soviet Union could take over most of Europe.[64]

Portal accepted that it was going to be necessary for allied armies to advance into Germany, and for his part, Brooke agreed that "the bombing offensive was the necessary, or at least the expedient, preliminary to this operation."[65] In a further memorandum dated 31st December 1942, the Chiefs of Staff defined the aim of the bombing offensive as "the progressive destruction and dislocation of the enemy's war industrial and economic system, and the undermining of his morale to a point where his capacity for armed resistance is fatally weakened."[66] However, instead of arguing for a force of four to six thousand bombers by the middle of 1944, this new memorandum only referred to three thousand bombers by the end of 1943. The official history of the air offensive recognises that the different memoranda produced by the Chiefs of Staff "showed the difficulties which were experienced in trying to reach agreement even on the general strategy which ought to govern the bombing offensive. Still more they showed the much greater difficulty which was encountered as soon as the debate touched any detailed considerations."[67] The official history of the air offensive states that an "agreement could only be reached by a compromise stated in such general terms that it could later be interpreted by those taking part in it according to their particular and generally conflicting predilections."[68]

This left the door open for Harris to join forces with VIII Bomber Command to attack a target that both Portal and Sinclair had suggested would be at the limits of the Americans' operational possibility. On the night of 24th July 1943, a total of 791 British bombers left their airfields in England and flew across the North Sea. The heavy bombers came together eighty miles from the German coast, then formed into a single bomber stream that stretched back across the sky for approximately two hundred miles. Their target for the night was the city of Hamburg.[69]

16 Katyn and Gomorrah

When Churchill took over as Prime Minister, some eight months after his predecessor had declared war on Germany,[1] he was faced with a military disaster in France and the prospect of a German invasion of the British Isles. Churchill made the decision to fight on. In the years that followed, Churchill fought the only war he could, given the circumstances he found himself in at the time. Machiavelli wrote in *The Prince* that a political leader who wanted to maintain his state would have to "learn how not to be good, and to use that whenever he needs to."[2] Churchill demonstrated the truth of this assertion on several occasions. He sanctioned an attack on the French fleet, declared war on Finland to keep the Soviets onside, and ordered PQ16 to sail out to Murmansk when Molotov was due to arrive in Britain to sign a treaty between the two countries. Churchill also told Stalin that he would order gas attacks to be carried out on German civilians, in the expectation that British citizens would be subjected to retaliatory attacks.[3]

Chamberlain's intentions may have been for his guarantee to Poland to serve as a deterrent, and it may be possible to justify the war against Germany retrospectively by noting the evil actions committed by the enemy during the war and arguing that the world is a better place without the Nazi regime in it. Since the second world war ended, it has been perceived by many as a mythical event that saw the forces of light in the world pitted against a dark, destructive force that threatened to undo us all.[4] If there are supernatural forces operating in the world, then that perception of the war may very well turn out to be correct, but even if every positive assertion that could possibly be made about the second world war regarding the intentions of the people involved, the nature of the enemy that was defeated and the consequences after it was over are all granted, it does not follow that it was a good war. As the spring of 1943 turned to summer, two more events demonstrated that, as Machiavelli observed, the leader of a country needed to "have a mind disposed to turn however the winds and variations of fortune command him" and he should "not leave the good if he can, but he should know how to enter into evil when it is necessary."[5]

In April that year, the Germans discovered a series of mass graves in the Katyn forest, and they did not hesitate to make their findings public. Radio Berlin immediately announced the news to the world,[6] and Goebbels had neutral journalists stationed in Berlin taken to the scene of the crime.[7] The British government's response to the discovery of these bodies was recorded by Sir Owen O'Malley, the British ambassador to the Polish government in exile in London, who sent a report on the matter to Anthony Eden on 24th May of that year. Churchill passed the report along to

Roosevelt, advising him in a covering letter that "the first of these two papers is a grim, well-written story, but perhaps a little too well written. Nevertheless if you have time to read it, it would repay the trouble. I should like to have it back when you have finished with it as we are not circulating it officially in any way."[8]

"We do not know for certain who murdered a lot of Polish officers in the forest of Katyn in April and May 1940," O'Malley wrote in his report. "But this at least is already clear, that it was the scene of terrible events which will live long in the memory of the Polish nation."[9] O'Malley's report, which was declassified in December 1972, contained the following account of events:

> The number of Polish prisoners taken by the Russian armies when they invaded Poland, in September 1939, was about 180,000, including police and gendarmerie and a certain number of civilian officials. . . . At the beginning of 1940 there were in the three camps named above round about 9,000 or 10,000 officers and 6,000 other ranks, policemen and civil officials. . . . Of the 10,000 officers, only some 3,000 or 4,000 were regular officers. The remainder were reserve officers who in peace time earned their living, many with distinction, in the professions, in business and so on.
>
> In March of 1940 word went round the camps at Kozielsk, Starobielsk and Ostashkov that, under orders from Moscow, the prisoners were to be moved to camps where conditions would be more agreeable and that they might look forward to eventual release. All were cheered by the prospect of a change from the rigours which prisoners must endure to the hazards and vicissitudes of relative freedom in Soviet or German territory. . . . Anticipations of a better future were clouded only by the fact that 400 or 500 Poles had been listed for further detention, first at Pavlishchev Bor and eventually at Griazovetz. These were, as it turned out later, to be the only known survivors of the lost legion. . . .
>
> Entrainment of the 10,000 officers from the three camps went on all through April and the first half of May, and the lorries, lined with cheerful faces, which took them from camp to station, were, in fact, the last that was ever seen of them alive by any witness to whom we have access. Until the revelations made by the German broadcast of the 12th April, 1943, and apart from a few words let drop at the time by the prison guards, only the testimony of scribblings on the railway wagons in which they were transported affords any indication of their destination. The same wagons seem to have done a shuttle service between Kozielsk and the detraining

station; and on these some of the first parties to be transported had scratched the words "Don't believe that we are going home."[10]

O'Malley then presented a series of arguments in support of the conclusion that "there is now a good deal of negative evidence, the cumulative effect of which is to throw serious doubt on Russian disclaimers of responsibility for the massacre."[11]

First, he argued that

> there is the evidence to be derived from the prisoners' correspondence, in respect to which information has been furnished by officers' families in Poland, by officers now with the Polish army in the Middle East, and by the Polish Red Cross Society. Up till the end of March 1940 large numbers of letters had been despatched, which were later received by their relatives, from the officers confined at Kozielsk, Starobielsk and Ostashkov; whereas no letters from any of them (excepting from the 400 moved to Griazovtez) have been received by anybody which had been despatched subsequent to that date. The Germans overran Smolensk in July 1941, and there is no easy answer to the question why, if any of the 10,000 had been alive between the end of May 1940 and July 1941, none of them ever succeeded in getting any word through to their families.[12]

Churchill clearly appreciated the power of this argument, for he used it himself when he wrote his own history of the war. "Until the spring of 1940 there had been intermittent news of the existence of these prisoners," he asserted. "From April 1940 silence descended upon the three camps. Not a single sign or trace of their occupants ever appeared for thirteen or fourteen months. They were certainly in Soviet power, but no letter, message, escapee, or scrap of information ever came from them."[13] O'Malley noted in his report that several written requests for information about the missing Polish officers had been presented to the Soviet government. "To none of all these enquiries extending over a period of two and a half years was a single positive answer of any kind ever returned,"[14] he wrote. The Soviets had claimed that the officers must have been released, or that they were already in Germany, or that there was no information about their whereabouts.[15] In O'Malley's view, these were not tenable positions:

> It is incredible that if any of the 10,000 were released, not one of them has ever appeared again anywhere, and it is almost equally incredible, if they were not released, that not one of them should

> have escaped subsequent to May 1940 and reported himself to the Polish authorities in Russia or Persia. That the Russian authorities should have said of any Polish officer in Soviet jurisdiction that they had "no information" also provokes incredulity; for it is notorious that the N.K.V.D. collect and record the movements of individuals with the most meticulous care.[16]

O'Malley then noted that the grave sites had been visited by two Polish commissions which had included doctors, priests, journalists and representatives of the Red Cross, and that "it is deposed by all that several hundred identifications have been established."[17] Although O'Malley conceded that "all this evidence would normally be highly suspect since the inspections took place under German auspices," he concluded that "there are fair grounds for presuming that the German broadcasts accurately represented the findings of the commissions, that the commissions' findings were at any rate in some respect well founded, and that the grounds were sound on which at any rate some of the identifications were made."[18]

Next, O'Malley argued that "there is the fact that a mass execution of officer prisoners would be inconsistent with what we know of the German army."[19] The German army may indeed have "committed innumerable brutalities" in the past, but if they had ever been in charge of 10,000 Polish officers, "we can be sure that they would have placed some or all of them in the camps in Germany already allotted to Polish prisoners, while the 6,000 other ranks, policemen and civil officials would have been put to forced labour."[20] It is not unreasonable to think that the Polish authorities would have been in contact with at least some of these prisoners at some point between May 1941 and April 1943 "but, in fact, none of the men from Kozielsk, Starobielsk or Ostashkov have ever been heard of from Germany."[21]

O'Malley then argued that "the confusion which characterises explanations elicited from or volunteered by the Soviet Government between August 1941 and the 12th April, 1943, when the Germans announced the discovery of the grave at Katyn," such as the assertion that all the Polish officers captured in 1939 had already been released, or the acknowledgement made to the Polish Ambassador by "a Russian official who had drunk more than was good for him" that "a tragic error" had been made, or the note Molotov sent to the Polish Ambassador saying that "the bodies at Katyn were those of Poles who had at one time been prisoners of the Russians but had subsequently been captured by the Germans in their advance at Smolensk in July 1941" had evidentiary value, because "this confusion cannot easily be understood except on the assumption that the Russian Government had something to hide."[22]

The overall conclusion was restated: "The cumulative effect of this evidence is, as I said earlier, to throw serious doubt on Russian disclaimers of responsibility for a massacre."[23]

O'Malley then provided his own reconstruction of events. This was the "grim, well written story" that Churchill sent to Roosevelt on 13th August. Although Roosevelt never acknowledged that he had read O'Malley's report, a copy of this document can still be found in the American archives today:

> With all that precedes in mind it is comprehensible that the relatives and fellow-officers of the men who disappeared should have concluded that these had in fact been murdered by their Russian captors and should picture their last hours – somewhat as follows – with bitter distress. The picture is a composite one to which knowledge of the district, the German broadcasts, experience of Russian methods and the reports of visitors to the grave have all contributed, but it is not so much an evidentially established description of events as a reconstruction in the light of the evidence – sometimes partial and obviously defective – of what may have happened. But it – or something like it – is what most Poles believe to have happened, and what I myself, in the light of all the evidence, such as it is, incline to think happened. . . .
>
> Smolensk lies some 20 kilom. from the spot where the common graves were discovered. It has two stations and in or near the town the main lines from Moscow to Warsaw and from Riga to Orel cross and recross each other. Some 15 kilom. to the west of Smolensk stands the unimportant station of Gniezdowo, and it is but a short mile from Gniezdowo to a place known locally as Kozlinaya Gora or "The Hill of Goats." The district of Katyn, in which this little hill stands, is covered with a primeval forest which has been allowed to go to rack and ruin. The forest is mostly coniferous, but the pine trees are interspersed here and there with hardwoods and scrub. . . . At Gniezdowo the prison vans from Kozielsk, Starobielsk and Ostashkov discharged their passengers into a barbed-wire cage surrounded by a strong force of Russian soldiers, and the preparations made here for their reception must have filled most of the Polish officers with disquiet, and some indeed with dismay who remembered that the forest of Katyn had been used by the Bolsheviks in 1919 as a convenient place for the killing of many Czarist officers. . . . From the cage the prisoners were taken in lorries along a country road to the Hill of Goats, and it must have been when they were unloaded from the lorries that their hands were bound and that dismay gave way to despair. If a man struggled, it seems that the

executioner threw his coat over his head, tying it round his back and leading him hooded to the pit's edge, for in many cases a body was found to be thus hooded and the coat to have been pierced by a bullet where it covered the base of the skull. But those who went quietly to their death must have seen a monstrous sight. In the broad deep pit their comrades lay, packed closely round the edge, head to feet, like sardines in a tin, but in the middle of the grave disposed less orderly. Up and down on the bodies the executioners tramped, hauling the dead bodies about and treading in the blood like butchers in a stockyard. When it was all over and the last shot had been fired and the last Polish head been punctured, the butchers – perhaps trained in youth to husbandry – seem to have turned their hands to one of the most innocent of occupations: smoothing the clods and planting little conifers all over what had been a shambles. It was, of course, rather late in the year for transplanting young trees, but not too late; for the sap was beginning to run in the young Scots pines when, three years later, the Polish representatives visited the site. . . .

The political background against which the events described in paragraph 15 are viewed by Poles is by contrast a matter of undisputed history, including as it does all the long story of partitions, rebellions and repressions, the Russo-Polish war of 1919-20, the mutual suspicions which this left behind it, the unannounced invasion of Poland by Russia in September 1939, the subsequent occupation of half Poland by Russia and the carrying into captivity of some million and a half of its inhabitants. More recently comes the virtual annexation of the occupied eastern parts of Poland, the refusal of the Russian Government to recognise as Polish citizens the inhabitants of the occupied districts, the suppression of relief organisations for Poles in Russia and the persecution of Poles refusing to change their own for Russian nationality. When Poles learned that, in addition to all these misfortunes, round about 10,000 men of the best breeding stock in Poland had (according to Russian accounts) been either dispersed and "lost" somewhere in the Soviet Union or else abandoned to the advancing German armies, or had (according to German accounts) been found to have been murdered by the Russians, many of them naturally concluded (though I do not here give it as my own conclusion) that the Soviet Government's intention had been to destroy the very foundations upon which their own Poland could be rebuilt. This sinister political intention imputed by Poles to Russia poisoned the wound and enhanced the suffering of a nation already outraged and dismayed by the conduct of the Soviet Government. Some Poles, remembering

> Lenin's attitude to the holocausts of 1917 and subsequent years, and probing the dark recesses of Stalin's mind when he took (if take he did) the dreadful decision, compare disciple with master. Lenin would have broken apart the heads of ten thousand Polish officers with the insouciance of a monkey cracking walnuts. Did corpses pitching into a common grave with the precision of machines coming off a production-belt similarly satisfy a nature habituated to manipulate blood and lives with uncompassionate detachment? Some at any rate so interpret Stalin's mind. "These men are no use to us," they imagine him as saying; "in fact they are a nuisance and a danger. Here is an *elite* of talent, here is valour and a hostile purpose. These stallions must not live to sire a whole herd of hostile Christian thoroughbreds. Many of the brood-mares have already been sold to Siberian peasants and the camel-pullers of Kazakstan. Their foals and yearlings can be broken to Communist harness. Rid me of this stud farm altogether and send all this turbulent bloodstock to the knackers."[24]

In this section of his report to the Foreign Office, O'Malley forces his readers to confront the horror of the crimes that had been committed in the Katyn forest. When news of the discovery of the mass graves was broadcast, General Wladyslaw Sikorski and Count Edward Raczynski were invited to attend a meeting at 10 Downing Street.[25] According to Sir Alexander Cadogan, the Permanent Under Secretary at the Foreign Office,[26] Churchill advised Sikorski not to respond to the discovery of the graves at Katyn by doing anything that might provoke Stalin.[27] The Poles had intended to ask the Red Cross to carry out an official investigation into the fate of the missing Polish officers. Churchill acknowledged that what the Germans were saying was probably true,[28] but told his guests that nothing they could do now would bring the Polish officers back to life.[29] Churchill could not afford to take a principled stand here, because he was responsible for charting a course towards the best possible outcome for the Polish people, one where Sikorski and Raczynski remained in power and Poland and the U.S.S.R. were not at loggerheads over something that had happened years ago. By writing off the Polish prisoners who died at Katyn, as he had been willing to write off half of the ships in convoy PQ16,[30] Churchill showed one again that he was able to do what Machiavelli advised, and act in ways that were "against his faith, against charity, against humanity, and against religion"[31] when it was necessary for him to do so.

After reading O'Malley's report, Cadogan wrote that:

> This is very disturbing. I confess that in cowardly fashion, I had rather turned my head away from the scene at Katyn – for fear or what I should find there.
>
> There may be evidence that we do not know of, that may point in another direction. But on the evidence that we have, it is difficult to escape from the presumption of Russian guilt.
>
> This of course raises terrible problems, but I think no one has pointed out that on the purely moral plane, these are not new. How many thousands of its own citizens has the Soviet regime butchered? And I don't know that the blood of a Pole cries louder to Heaven than that of a Russian. But we have perforce welcomed the Russians as Allies and have set ourselves to work with them in war and peace.
>
> The ominous thing about this incident is the ultimate political repercussion. How, if Russian crime is established, can we expect Poles to live amicably, side by side with Russians for generations to come? I fear there is no answer to that question. The other disturbing thought is that we may eventually, by agreement and in collaboration with Russians, proceed to the trial and perhaps execution of Axis 'war criminals' while condemning this atrocity. I confess I shall find that extremely difficult to swallow.
>
> However, quite clearly for the moment, there is nothing to be done. As to what circulation we give to this explosive material, I find it difficult to make up my mind. Of course it would be only honest to circulate it. But as we know (all admit) that the knowledge of this evidence cannot affect our course of action or policy, is there any advantage in exposing more individuals than necessary to the spiritual conflict that a reading of this despatch excites.[32]

The Poles disregarded Churchill's advice and asked the International Red Cross to investigate,[33] but Stalin responded by saying that it was the Germans who were guilty of the crime, then he told Churchill that the Poles were collaborating with the Nazis to make the Soviets look bad in the eyes of the other members of the "Grand Alliance."[34] Churchill had no option but to go along with Stalin's lies. He even promised Stalin that he would censor the Polish press so that nothing would be said publicly in Britain that might make the Soviet Union look bad.[35]

O'Malley acknowledged in his report that

> in handling the publicity side of the Katyn affair we have been constrained by the urgent need for cordial relations with the Soviet Government to appear to appraise the evidence with more hesitation

> and lenience than we should do in forming a common sense judgement on events occurring in normal times or in the ordinary course of our private lives; we have been obliged to appear to distort the normal and healthy operation of our intellectual and moral judgements; we have been obliged to give undue prominence to the tactlessness or impulsiveness of the Poles, to restrain the Poles from putting their case clearly before the public, to discourage any attempt by the public and the press to probe the ugly story to the bottom. In general we have been obliged to deflect attention from possibilities which in the ordinary affairs of life would cry to high heaven for elucidation, and to withhold the full measure of solicitude which, in other circumstances, would be shown to acquaintances situated as a large number of Poles now are. We have in fact perforce used the good name of England like the murderers used the little conifers to cover up a massacre; and in view of the immense importance of an appearance of Allied unity and of the heroic resistance of Russia to Germany, few will think that any other course would have been wise or right.[36]

Under normal circumstances, if murder victims were found buried in a forest, then no one would help the killer to cover up what they had done. Everyone would want the crimes to be investigated so that the guilty party could be identified and prosecuted to the full extent of the law. However, groups of people can adopt an entirely new set of values when they find themselves in a radically different set of circumstances. O'Malley marked this change in many of his colleagues. The leaders of the British government were in a situation where their natural sense of morality was "constrained by the urgent need for cordial relations with the Soviet Government" so they had "perforce used the good name of England like the murderers used the little conifers to cover up a massacre."[37]

Maisky visited Churchill's home at Chartwell on the evening of 23rd April and assured him that the Soviet Union was innocent of the mass murder of the Polish prisoners-of-war. Churchill explained Britain's policy towards the Soviet Union in a nutshell: "We have got to beat Hitler, and this is no time for quarrels and charges."[38] Churchill acknowledged after the war had ended that "in the trials of Germans at Nuremberg for war crimes the murder of the Poles at Katyn was mentioned in the indictment of Goering and others, who laid the White Book of the German investigation before the court. It was decided by the victorious Governments concerned that the issue should be avoided, and the crime of Katyn was never probed in detail."[39]

The British government had looked the other way when the Soviet Union invaded Poland on 17th September 1939. After the Soviets took over the Baltic States, Eden let Stalin know that the British government had written those countries off. When the British and American governments set up a massive arms deal with the Soviet Union, they applied pressure to the Finns so they would not cut the railway line out of Murmansk. The British government even declared war on Finland on 6th December 1941 to keep the Soviets onside. When the Katyn massacre came to light in April 1943, the British government looked the other way once again. They were never going to do anything else, because they still needed the Red Army to do the heavy lifting against the *Wehrmacht* on the Eastern Front.

On his visit to Moscow in August 1942, Churchill had promised that Bomber Command would attack Germany's cities.[40] The Bombing Operations Directorate in the British Air Ministry had selected Hamburg from a list of potential targets in November 1941, three months before Arthur Harris was given control of Bomber Command, and it had been decided that the most efficient way to destroy the city would be to use a mixture of incendiaries and high explosives. Some of the British HE bombs were to be fitted with delayed action fuses so they would injure or kill members of the emergency services who responded to the initial blaze.[41] A method had also been developed to counter the German radar. There had been some opposition to the use of this new anti-radar system, which had been code-named Window, because it was feared that the other side would be able to figure out how it worked and start using themselves when they attacked British cities.[42]

On 15th July 1943, Churchill and Herbert Morrison, the Minister for Home Security, attended a meeting with the Chiefs of Staff. Morrison was worried about the public being on the receiving end of a bombing raid that the British defences would not be able to see coming, but Churchill believed that minimising Bomber Command's losses had to take priority over everything else, so he gave the go-ahead for the new technique to be used in a series of bombing raids scheduled to begin in the last week of July 1943.[43] This joint Anglo-American attack on Hamburg had been code-named Operation Gomorrah, after the destruction of two cities recorded in the nineteenth chapter of Genesis.

The first of these bombing raids began just before 1 a.m. on 25th July 1943, when pathfinders flew across Hamburg and dropped marker flares to guide the rest of the planes to the centre of the city.[44] The new Window system proved to be successful, and with their Freya and Würzburg radars unable to guide them to their targets, the German fighters and anti-aircraft guns had failed to locate the bomber stream.[45] The Operations Record for 83 Squadron reads as follows:

Lancaster "H" J.A. 686: Bombed 0057½ hrs. 20,000' 210° M. 140 knots. No cloud, hazy. Being first aircraft on target nothing had happened. When aircraft was on homeward journey about 20 miles saw large explosion in Hamburg area with a smaller explosion 2/3 secs later. Bombed on "Y". Small flak hole in bomb door received over Hamburg at 00.51½ hrs. 20,000'.

Lancaster "A" E.D. 984: Bombed 00.59 hrs. 20,000' 126° M. IAS 140 knots. No cloud with fair vis. Bombed by special equipment T.Is seen to fall and 4,000lb seem to burst. Two lots flares seen 00.57, 01.01 hrs 2 lots reds T.I close together followed by greens 0107.5 vivid red explosion and smoke bellowed up.

Lancaster "B" J.A. 712: Bombed 0112,2 hrs. 20,000' 160° M. IAS 140 knots. Clear with slight haze. T.I green in bombsight which was in position of red which had burned out previously. Markers were generally well placed and concentrated with many large fires. One red approximately 5 m. N.E. of Hamburg. Collision with another Lanc. from Warboys which was doing wrong circuit. Starboard rudder missing. Top of fin damaged but made good landing.

Lancaster "X" W.4959: Bombed 0103.5 hrs. 18,000' 137° M. 165 knots. Clear but ground haze. Saw dock area and streets by light of flares. T.I red in bombsight. On leaving, target large fire orange flame shot up and continued to burn approx. S end of town. Camera u/s.[46]

The British bombers flew over the city in six waves, and the entire attack lasted for almost exactly one hour.[47] A total of 2,400 tons of bombs, including 350,412 incendiaries, were dropped on the city.[48] The summary of events in the Operations Record Book for 44 Squadron reads:

> Twelve aircraft were detailed for an attack on Hamburg. . . . Weather over the target was clear and visibility good. The target was identified by Red and Green tracking flares and T.Is. Window was used on this raid and according to pilots' remarks, worked successfully against searchlights. Sgt. Rollin observed a terrific explosion which was seen 4-5 minutes from target and lasted about one minute; this lit up the whole sky; glow from fires could be seen 60 miles away.[49]

With Churchill as Prime Minister, the British government had come a long way since September 1939, when the War Cabinet decided to drop propaganda leaflets over Germany because "it was believed that these leaflets would have an important effect on German public opinion."[50] Now the British were totally committed to an area bombing campaign that needed thousands of bombers to be built so it would be possible to drop tens of thousands of tons of high explosives and incendiaries on German cities every month. Once the commitment to build a heavy bomber force had been made at the highest levels and the industrial machinery of Britain and America was set in motion to that end, the bombing war had inevitably escalated. The bombers were being built at the expense of developing any alternatives, so they had to be used, and they would be used.

The British historian Max Hastings asserts in his book *Bomber Command* that "the attack on Hamburg was the most perfectly orchestrated since the war began."[51] Huge areas of the city were set ablaze that first night, and the success of the Window anti-radar system meant that only twelve British bombers were lost.[52] The USAAF arrived over the skies of Hamburg the next day, with the intention of using their Norden bombsight to attack the Blohm & Voss shipyards in the south of the city and the Klöckner aero-engine factory in the south-east.[53] The Blohm & Voss shipyards had been targeted by the British when they began their bombing campaign against Germany in May 1940. More than three years later, the shipyards were still standing. This attack would take place in daylight, and with the NBS on board, the American bombers would at least have a chance of hitting the target.

The Americans were flying B-17F bombers, nicknamed "Flying Fortresses," on this raid. These aeroplanes were armour plated, and they had fourteen .50 calibre machine guns fitted from front to rear - four machine guns in the nose, four on the roof, two in the belly of the plane, two on either side and two in the tail.[54] The bombers were flown in three groups of twenty planes, with a second group higher and to one side of the lead group, and a third group flying lower on the other side. If a German fighter came within range of the bomber formation, they could have up to a hundred guns firing at them at any one time.[55]

When the USAAF bombers reached the German coast, there were *Luftwaffe* fighters waiting for them, but they maintained their defensive formations and the German pilots failed to shoot down any of the bombers before they reached their target.[56] However, the tactics adopted by the heavily armed bombers also made them more vulnerable to anti-aircraft fire, because it was easier for the German anti-aircraft gunners to see the bombers at high altitudes when they were flying in groups. When they reached their target and began their bombing run, the American pilots had to fly as straight and level as possible, which also made the anti-aircraft gunners' jobs easier.[57] Of the 123 bombers that had started out from their bases in England, 14 had aborted their mission early on due to mechanical failures, and by the time they reached Hamburg, almost half of the remaining planes had been damaged by anti-aircraft fire, and several had been hit by the ever-present German fighters.[58] In the lead group of planes assigned to bomb the Blohm and Voss shipyard, the pilot of the *Judy B* had been killed after a German fighter had fired into the side of the plane's cockpit. The co-pilot, a 19 year old named Charles Bigler, held the pilot's body up with one hand so he did not fall on to the controls, and made the bombing run one-handed. The young Lieutenant only called for help once the bombs were away.[59]

When the bombers had taken off from England and climbed to their operational altitude, they had enjoyed flying conditions known as CAVU – ceiling and visibility unlimited.[60] Once they reached Hamburg, they discovered that the British raid the night before had set the city upwind alight, and now a westerly breeze was blowing black smoke across their target area.[61] The 91st and 351st Bombardment Groups, which had been ordered to attack the Klöckner factory, decided that it would be impossible to see their assigned target through the smoke, so they joined the 379th, the 303rd and 384th BGs as they tried to find the Blohm and Voss shipyard.[62] A gap appeared in the smoke as the bombers flew overhead, and although the Blohm and Voss shipyard was still obscured, the buildings owned by Howaldstwerke, another of the city's shipbuilders, were visible long enough for the Americans to identify them. The 384th BG immediately dropped their payload on the newly acquired target. The 379th, 303rd, 351st and 91st BGs followed suit at approximately one minute intervals, dropping a mixture of HE and incendiaries on to what the Americans considered a legitimate military target.[63]

On the return leg of their journey, the German fighters waited for any of the damaged bombers to develop mechanical problems that would slow them down. If any individual bombers fell behind the group, they would lose the protection of the guns on the planes around them and become easier targets, and the German flyers were determined to shoot down as many of the returning bombers as possible.[64] The *Luftwaffe* fighters first went after these slow-flying stragglers, then they concentrated their attacks on the bombers at the lowest rear point of the formation, which was known as "Purple Heart Corner" or "Coffin Corner" because these bombers did not have the guns of the other planes around them.[65] Once these lower formations had been degraded so they had fewer planes to defend each other with supportive fire, the German fighters concentrated on them all the more.[66] The fighters followed the bombers halfway back across the North Sea, returning to their bases to refuel and flying multiple sorties. By the time the Americans reached their bases back in England, fifteen of their planes had been shot down. When the survivors assembled in the mess hall at RAF Grafton Underwood in Northamptonshire that evening to eat, there were seventy empty chairs around them.[67] Some of the surviving flyers were issued sleeping pills, and some took a dram or two of whisky before retiring to bed, hoping to have few hours of sleep.[68] These young men needed whatever rest they could get, because the next day, the Americans were going back.[69]

It had been the Americans' intention to attempt precision bombing in daylight hours using the Norden bombsight and to attack legitimate military targets only, but the cost in their own lives and equipment was to prove too great. Fifteen of the American planes were shot down on the first Hamburg raid - twelve per cent of the total number that had set off from England. This attrition rate was clearly not sustainable. Sixty seven of the bombers – almost exactly half the original force – had been shot up during the mission, and only seventy three bombers – approximately sixty per cent of the original force – had managed to drop their bombs anywhere near the designated targets.[70]

On the morning of 26th July, the USAAF crews were told that they were returning to Hamburg to attack the same targets - the Blohm and Voss shipyards and the Klöckner factory.[71] Three other combat wings were going to attack a rubber factory in Hanover, and there would be a series of diversionary flights over French territory, which would hopefully pull the German fighters in different directions.[72] After the planes had taken off, the 379th BG and the 384th BG could not find the rest of the Klöckner wing as they flew out across the North Sea, and both groups eventually aborted their mission and returned to base.[73] Only four Bombardment Groups were left to fly on to Germany, and when they arrived at Hamburg, they found that their targets were once again obscured by black smoke. This time the Germans had deliberately created a defensive smokescreen, so that the Blohm and Voss shipyards would not be visible from the air. As they had the day before, the Americans went after the Howaldtswerke shipyard instead, and all three of the groups in the combat wing dropped their bombs on this secondary target in less than a minute.[74] The 303rd BG, which was all that remained of the Klöckner wing, decided not to go after their assigned target, and instead, attacked the Neuhof power station south-east of the Howaldtswerke premises. They managed to score a direct hit that shut the plant down for over two weeks, which if nothing else showed that the Norden bombsight was accurate and could be used in combat conditions.[75]

The American bombers managed to escape from German airspace and get back across the North Sea with only two losses, but the wings that had attacked Hanover were not so fortunate. Sixteen of their planes had been shot down, and six more were lost from a wing that had attacked

Wilhelmshaven, which once again meant an overall attrition rate of twelve per cent of all effective planes.[76] On Wednesday 28th July, another twenty two planes were shot down over Kassel and Oschersleben, ten more were shot down on the Thursday, and another twelve on Friday.[77] The Americans had launched attacks on twenty three towns and cities across northern Europe in what they were calling "Blitz Week"[78] but the cost in men and machines was prohibitive. In all, a total of eighty-eight of their Flying Fortresses had been lost and almost 900 American flyers were dead or MIA.[79] The British had been unable to persuade their allies to abandon the idea of daylight raids and could only watch as the American drama played out in the skies over Germany.

On 27th July, Bomber Command launched another raid on Hamburg. The bombers approached from the north-east this time, having approached from the north-west on the previous occasion, so that any creep-back from the initial bombing point would end up destroying a different part of the city.[80] The bombing loads had also been changed so that approximately 240 tons more of incendiaries were being carried.[81] The British had realised that HE bombs were most effective when they were used to blow the roofs off buildings and smash windows and doors in, so that fires started by the incendiaries could get inside. It was now understood that it was fire that did the most damage when urban areas were being bombed, and the objective was now to keep dropping incendiaries in the same area until the fire services were overwhelmed, so that the fires that were started by the incendiaries could not be stopped.

Britain's financial and industrial resources could have been used differently during the war years. An air force could have been created with the primary function of providing tactical support to the army during a land war. However, the decision had been made at the highest level to create a heavy bomber force capable of attacking German cities, and on 27th July 1943, the full destructive potential of the British heavies was fully realised. The natural conditions around Hamburg on that night contributed to what turned out to be an unprecedented level of destruction, although the science behind the Hamburg firestorm was not understood well enough at the time for this to have played any part in the British planning. The exceptionally warm weather meant that the heat generated throughout the day had already risen to form a ceiling of hot air above the city. When the bombers arrived and set the buildings on the ground on fire, the heat generated by these fires rose into and through the hot air above the city. The vacuum this created on the ground was filled by cooler air that was sucked into the city at ever increasing speeds. The incoming air acted as fuel and the fires burned ever hotter, which sent even more hot air into the sky directly above the city.[82] As the German historian Jörg Friedrich has argued, the British were not simply killing people on the streets of Hamburg on this raid, they had altered the fundamental conditions of reality so that their target area no longer supported human life.[83]

As the firestorm continued to rage, the vicious circle of conditions that had created it began to accelerate. The cooler air being sucked into the city reached speeds of over 120 mph, and the temperatures inside the inferno became high enough to melt the glass in car windows.[84] Trees were uprooted by the winds, and people trying desperately to escape were picked up and thrown through the air. According to Leo McKinstry's account, "It was the most savage firestorm in history, not so much Gomorrah as the Apocalypse. People burned to death in the streets from sheer intensity of the heat. Trams and trains buckled and collapsed. The asphalt of roadways turned to boiling liquid."[85]

Thousands of people died in their bunkers when the oxygen was sucked out to feed the firestorm, or when the buildings above collapsed and blocked the air vents and exits.[86] Some people realised that they could not remain inside the bomb shelters, but where could they go? Some tried to find their way into the local parks and sports stadiums, fighting their way through the flying debris so they were not pulled by the howling winds into the centre of the inferno,[87] but even with those open spaces around them acting as a firebreak, many people still died from the incredible heat.[88] In desperation, some people tried to make their way to one of the canals that ran through the city, in the hope that they could shelter in the water, but many of the boats that were on fire after being hit by incendiaries became floating hazards, debris still flew the air and the dirty, oily water could catch fire in these extreme conditions.[89]

From the air, it soon became clear that the scale of the destruction in their target area was unprecedented. The Operations Record for Lancaster JA675 of 467 Squadron records that as they were about to make their bombing run: "Explosions seen 0104½. 0105. Huge column of smoke seen up to 18/19000 ft. Navigation excellent."[90]

The Operations Record for Lancaster JA702 of 156 Squadron for 27th July reads:

> Task HAMBURG. Target identified by Green TIs and attacked at 0130 hrs from 20000 ft. Own bombs burst in centre of TI Greens, which covered an area of about 2 miles across. A mass of flames covered the whole target area and a large black cloud of smoke was rising up to more than 20000 ft. Special equipment was U/S. Some rocket type heavy flak over target with some 70 S/Ls attempting to cone. "Windows" carried and dropped. One photo attempted. Bomb load as above.[91]

The Operations Record for Lancaster EE173, piloted by Flight Sergeant W.H. Rose, reads:

> Task HAMBURG. Target attacked after being identified by TI Greens, at 01.01.3 hrs. from 19000 ft. Our bombs seen to burst on TI Greens, and while we were over the target the attack was quite concentrated and fires had a good hold. The glow of the fires could be seen 150 miles away on return journey. Moderate heavy flak, not so much as before, but S/L activity was more than on previous trip. "Windows" carried and dropped. One photo attempted. Bomb load as above.[92]

At the beginning of the war in September 1939, there was a commonly held belief that "the bomber will always get through"[93] and civilian casualties would be high in any future war. By the middle of 1943, the British had created a heavy bomber force that had made that prediction come true. They had studied the effects of the German bombing of their own cities, and while this provides an answer to the technical question of how the British had figured out how to be so good at this, it does not tell us why a heavy bomber force had been created in the first place, or why it was being used to carry out a policy of area bombing on German cities.

Lord Salisbury, the Leader of the House of Lords, wrote to Archibald Sinclair on 23rd November and asked whether Britain ought to be deliberately targeting cities rather than attempting to hit legitimate military targets. "There is a great deal of evidence that makes some of us afraid that we are losing some of our moral superiority to the Germans," he wrote. "Of course the Germans began it, but we do not take the devil as an example."[94]

The unpalatable truth is that any war can develop into an entirely different form of reality, where moral questions are no longer even asked when significant decisions are being made because the answers no longer matter. When Churchill took over as Prime Minister on 10th May 1940, it was understood that he was the only political candidate who would be able to operate effectively in that environment. Churchill may have been the best person for the job and Nazi Germany may have been defeated in the end, but it does not follow that the second world war should now be thought of as a good war. If you are leader of a nation state that has declared war on another country, then sooner or later, you are going to find yourself in a position where you have no option but to do things that are "not good." You may end up attacking your allies, as Britain did to France, or declaring war on countries that have done you no wrong, as Britain did to Finland, or forming an alliance with a regime that, in some ways, is no better than your enemy.

You may send a convoy through the Norwegian Sea expecting half of your ships to be sunk just so you can sign a political treaty. You may find yourself helping to cover up a mass murder, or you may find yourself promising to use chemical weapons against the enemy, knowing all the while that your own citizens could be subjected to retaliatory attacks. The second world war was so horrific that many of the people who lived through it could only describe the experience by saying that "all hell broke loose."[95] In the hours between midnight and morning on 28th July, the firestorm that raced through the streets of Hamburg created a facsimile of hell on earth.

After this second British attack, Karl Kaufmann, the *Gauleiter* of Hamburg, decided that the city would have to be evacuated.[96] This would not be a straightforward operation, because the railway lines had been damaged and many of the roads in the area that had been bombed were impassable.[97] In the end, many of the survivors had to walk to the perimeter of the area that had been devastated by the firestorm. Refugee camps were set up to process the survivors, and the authorities commandeered as many vehicles as they could find to transport everyone out of the city. More than three quarters of a million people were taken to the nearest railway stations, and from there to towns and cities throughout Germany.[98] Some of the refugees were heard yelling at people wearing a Nazi uniform, saying that what had happened was their fault, and some of the survivors were overheard saying that Hitler ought to be hanged.[99] It could be argued that the morale of some of these refugees had been affected by the bombing of Hamburg to the extent that they now felt able to criticise the Nazis openly, but the notion that these dispossessed and psychologically damaged individuals would have the resources necessary to overpower the SS units stationed at the refugee collection points throughout their city,[100] travel 160 miles to Berlin, then somehow force the National Socialists from the seat of power in Germany was clearly an absurdity. The survivors of the firestorm had been left with nothing but the clothes on their backs and whatever they had managed to take with them out of the destruction zone.[101]

The Soviets broadcast the news of what had happened at Hamburg through loudspeakers aimed at the German lines so that the enemy would know that their home cities were under attack. Many of the soldiers did not believe what they had heard until they travelled back home on leave from the front.[102] However, there were thousands of people throughout Germany who understood exactly what had happened when the British attacked Hamburg in the closing days of July 1943, because they had seen for themselves some of the people who had been trapped in the centre of the firestorm.

As civilians were leaving Hamburg, the emergency services were sending more personnel into the city, more searchlights and anti-aircraft guns were arriving, and the fire brigades were trying to put out any remaining fires before the bombers returned.[103] Harris stated in his war memoirs that the decision to carry out an area bombing campaign had been taken before he took over Bomber Command, but he was personally committed to the campaign. Harris had no qualms about what his bombers were doing, and there was no upper limit to the suffering and destruction he would inflict as he sought "to kill Boche and to terrify Boche."[104]

In December 1940, Harris had been working at the Air Ministry in London when the *Luftwaffe* had attacked the capital. Harris had gone up on to the roof of the building and watched as the German incendiaries fell on to the buildings below and did their work. The sight of "St. Paul's cathedral standing out in the midst of an ocean of fire"[105] had moved Harris to utter the phrase that would guide him for the rest of the war. "They sowed the wind," he exclaimed. "They will reap the whirlwind."[106]

One man who questioned the policies that were adopted by the British government during the war was Richard Stokes, who won the Ipswich seat in a by-election in 1938. Stokes, who had served with the Royal Artillery during the first world war,[107] stood up in the House of Commons on 19th May 1942 and said,

> I want now to say a few words about the whole question of night bombing. I believe the major strategical error in the war - and again my right hon. and learned Friend can tear me up on this particular point when he winds up the Debate, and I shall be glad to be torn up if I am wrong - was made when the Prime Minister decided in 1940 that the way to win this war was by bombing aeroplanes and tanks, when those who thought differently considered the right way was by more ships and fighting aeroplanes. I question very much the policy which is now being pursued with regard to telling people in this country that they are going to win the war by bombing Germany. I do not believe that for a single moment. I have been through practically every raid in London, and to most of the places which have been badly blitzed, and I do not believe for a single moment that you are ever going to destroy the morale of the people by bombing from the air. You will do terrific destruction to property - and thank God some slums have gone west as a result of what has happened in this territory - but to think that you are going to bring down Germany by bombing from the air is absolutely puerile. One of our more noted strategic critics described strategical bombing the other day as contagious lunacy, and I think there is a good deal in what he said. I question very much whether the losses we incur in the process are worth the material damage which is done.[108]

Stokes asked about the casualties of the area bombing offensive on several occasions in the House of Commons and on 6th March 1945, he wondered what visiting so much destruction upon the cities of Germany had achieved:

> I raise this issue of bombing because I have always doubted the advantages of what I call strategic bombing. In anything I am going to say please let it be clearly understood that I am not criticising, for a single moment, any of the actions of the men who go and do these things, or their great loyalty, devotion, courage and determination. Nothing of the sort. I am merely criticising on the higher level as to what is the right policy. I questioned the usefulness of bombing on strategic grounds alone, at an early stage, and whether the manufacture of these vast machines was not deflecting war production from other more important aims. I also questioned whether the "blanket" bombing could really ever win a war. It is very noticeable that the Russians do not seem to indulge in it. The answer, of course, may be that we are doing it all for them, but I cannot really swallow that.[109]

17 Consequences

The British attempt to destroy the city of Hamburg did not end with the firestorm in the early hours of 28th July 1943. The bombers returned two nights later, following the same attack routes as before.[1] The *Luftwaffe* had adapted their tactics after the first use of Window, and their fighters were free to attack the incoming bombers on sight.[2] When the British pathfinders dropped red flares to mark the route to the city, this not only allowed the following bombers to aim at their designated target. The German fighter pilots knew that the bombers would be passing over that area.[3]

The British bombers were attacked as soon as they crossed the coastline, and seven of them were shot down. As they headed farther inland, three more were shot down by the German fighters.[4] When the bombers arrived over their target, they found that there were more anti-aircraft searchlights operating than that had been on the earlier raids.[5] Once a bomber was "coned" by these searchlights, they could be targeted by the anti-aircraft gunners. This was not the only danger the bomber crews had to contend with. Some of the German fighters were now flying high enough to see the bombers outlined against the fires burning in the city below, and when the bombers were visible, the German fighters would swoop down and open fire. Nine of the British bombers were shot down over the city, three of them being hit by anti-aircraft fire from the ground as well as taking fire from German fighters employing these new high-risk tactics.[6]

The British had intended to target the north-west of Hamburg on this occasion but the pathfinders had been blown off course, and they ended up dropping their target indicators farther east.[7] As a result, the districts of Eilbek and Barmbek, which were both east of the Outer Alster lake, were bombed heavily during the raid.[8] Survivors who left their shelters the next morning and walked out into the streets where they had lived were faced with a scene of utter devastation.[9] The chief of police in Hamburg said later that the level of destruction was as bad as it had been after the raid on 27th July.[10]

The following Monday, a storm was beginning to gather over the German coast.[11] The clouds had been over England the night before and the final attack of Operation Gomorrah, which had been scheduled for 1st August, had been postponed.[12] A Mosquito was sent out from RAF Wyton in Cambridgeshire at 6.45 p.m. in the evening to report on the conditions over the north of Germany. After Harris received a weather report from the Meteorological Office at 10 p.m., he authorised the raid on Hamburg.[13] The bombers left England and after crossing the North Sea, they flew straight into the storm, which had drifted east across Europe and was now directly over the city, with predictable results.[14] The planes began to ice up in the freezing temperatures, and visibility was so poor that the targets were not visible.[15] The German flak was being laid down at a maximum level of 4,500 metres, which meant that the bomber pilots would have to fly through the exploding anti-aircraft fire if they descended. If they tried to say on course, then they would have to fly through the darkened clouds in the middle of a raging storm, hoping all the while that they would not be struck by lightning, and try to avoid the German night fighters that were trying to shoot them down.[16] The British commanders had sent thousands of brave young men into this situation on this fourth and final raid, with little chance of them even hitting their target, let alone achieving a worthwhile military objective. The chief of police in Hamburg reported after the raid that there were fewer fatalities than there had been in the previous raids, and the bombs had been scattered over such a wide area that it was difficult to discern what the actual target had been.[17]

Churchill had promised Stalin when the two met in August 1942 that Germany's cities were going to be bombed, and the raids on Hamburg in July and August of 1943 showed that he had every intention of making good on that promise. Churchill had spoken about forming a "Grand Alliance" with the Soviet Union as early as 3rd April 1939, and when fortune's wheel turned around and he became Prime Minister, it fell to Churchill to make that alliance a reality. Churchill showed throughout his premiership that he would go to any lengths to maintain his country's wartime relationship with the Soviet Union. When Bomber Command was sent back to attack Hamburg again after the city had already been devastated by the firestorm raid, that showed how committed the British were to the area bombing campaign against Germany. The bombing of Hamburg may have been a significant event in the timeline of the second world war, demonstrating as it did a willingness on the part of the British government to act with the utmost ruthlessness in a time of war, but it should not be forgotten that it was not Churchill who made the fateful decision that led to Britain's involvement in a war against Germany in the first place.

When Neville Chamberlain issued his verbal guarantee to Poland on 31st March 1939, he understood very well the risk he was taking. At a Cabinet meeting held on 20th March, Chamberlain had acknowledged that if any arrangement was made with the Polish leadership, "they would be tempted to adopt a very rigid line about minor matters, and this might precipitate the very situation we wished to avoid."[18] In the mistaken belief that the British government would honour their guarantee, the Poles dug their heels in and refused to consider making a deal with Germany over which country's flag would end up flying over Danzig or whether a road to East Prussia could ever be built. This set the stage for a military conflict between the two countries. When the British sent a delegation to the Soviet Union without first making sure that the Soviet forces had permission to cross Polish territory so they would be able to engage with the *Wehrmacht* on the German border, the likelihood of the Soviets agreeing to fight against Germany was precisely zero. Despite knowing that the verbal guarantee he had given to the Poles could not, and therefore would not, be honoured, Chamberlain issued a hard copy of the guarantee on 25th August 1939, the day after the Nazi-Soviet pact was signed. A war against Germany was now inevitable.

The Chiefs of Staff had said in February 1937 that the only way Britain could prevail in that conflict was to recruit the Soviet Union and the United States then use the economic resources of the British Empire to fight a long war.[19] When the Americans acted as the "arsenal of democracy"[20] at the beginning of the war, they demanded payment in advance for any materiel they supplied. Once the Lend-Lease system came online in March 1941, the British government was able to place orders in America without having to pay for anything up front. By the time the war ended, Britain had run up so much debt that it was not completely paid off until December 2006.[21]

There were other long-term consequences to the second world war. As Churchill acknowledged on 5th June 1946, the Atlantic Charter had proven to be "an unattainable ideal." The peoples of the Baltic States were "no longer recognisable as those which existed before the war," he said. "They have suffered a double liquidation, both at German hands and at Russian hands."[22]

Churchill stated that there was "a broad band of territory containing all the capitals of Eastern and Central Europe and many ancient States and nations, in which dwell nearly one-third of the population of Europe" and "all this is ruled or actively directed by that same group of very able men, the Commissars in the Kremlin, which already disposes with despotic power of the fortunes of its own mighty Empire. It is here in this great band or belt, if anywhere, that the seeds of a new world war are being sown."[23]

The country whose independence Britain was supposed to have gone to war to protect was, as Churchill said, being "held in strict control by a Soviet-dominated Government" and "denied all free expression of her national will."[24] The attitude of the British government towards the Poles could not have been made clearer when the Polish soldiers who had fought alongside British and Commonwealth forces during the war were banned from participating in the victory parade held in London on 8th June 1946.[25]

According to Churchill, when Chamberlain issued a guarantee to Poland on 31st March 1939, "No one who understood the situation could doubt that it meant in all human probability a major war, in which we should be involved."[26] The Chiefs of Staff had argued in February 1937 that the only way Britain could wage war against Germany would be to fight a long war, and to recruit the Soviet Union and the United States to the cause. When Poland was invaded in September 1939, all the British government could do was adopt a defensive posture, and hope that fortune would allow that long war to be fought against Germany.

Machiavelli believed that fortune is the arbiter of much of human affairs, although we can still exercise some control over our lives. According to Machiavelli, fortune is like a river that can break its banks and flood the area, forcing everyone in its path to flee. However, it is possible to build defences and barriers when everything is peaceful so that when the water rises again, it can be controlled and the risk of damage can be minimised.[27] In the years prior to the outbreak of hostilities in the west, a fighter force had been created in Britain to defend the country against a German air attack. Since achieving air superiority was a necessary condition of the enemy being able to cross the English Channel, the success of the British fighters in the summer of 1940 meant that a German invasion was no longer possible.

The RAF may have minimised the likelihood of the people of Britain ever being exposed to an invasion, but the country was still at risk. Britain had no allies at that time, so the prospect of ever being able to implement the last phase of the long war foreseen by the Chiefs of Staff in 1937 could only be a long-term goal. Machiavelli argued that a leader with virtue would be able to adapt their "way of proceeding"[28] to suit whatever circumstances obtained after each turn of fortune's wheel. When Churchill accepted the challenge of leading his country, he was faced with a military disaster in France and a possible invasion by the enemy, but he was still able to act effectively. When he ordered the attack on the French fleet at Mers-el-Kébir, that not only prevented those ships from falling into German hands, it also convinced Roosevelt that the British should be provided with American materiel. When Churchill sent PQ16 out on the Murmansk run, that helped keep the Soviets onside until the Anglo-Soviet Treaty was signed on 26th May 1942. Whenever Churchill gave an order to have something done that was "not good" it served an important purpose, and it was done out of necessity. Churchill's predecessor had shown that he did not have it in him to be a war leader, and the only other candidate for the job had turned it down. Only someone with Churchill's strength of character could have done what was necessary to keep on fighting against Germany. The use of Britain's industrial resources to create a fleet of heavy bombers, and the use of these heavy bombers to engage in an area bombing campaign that intentionally targeted the "morale" of the German people by de-housing them or burning them to death, was for years the only way that Britain could take the war to the enemy. When Churchill flew out to Moscow in August 1942, he promised Stalin that Bomber Command would be used to attack Germany and "if need be, as the war went on, we hoped to shatter almost every dwelling in almost every German city."[29] The bombing attack on the coastal port of Hamburg in July 1943 was an exemplary use of a weapon that had been created to ensure "the proper application of overwhelming force."[30]

The second world war is sometimes seen as a fundamentally moral conflict, where the forces of good prevailed over the forces of darkness in the world. When Chamberlain issued his war guarantee to Poland, it is possible that he was trying to forestall German territorial expansion. However, the British government's promise to give "all the support and assistance in its power"[31] to a country in Eastern Europe inevitably affected how the leaders of that country acted towards their neighbours. The Poles refused to negotiate a deal with Germany over which flag should fly over the city of Danzig, or whether a road to East Prussia should be built. Without that guarantee, the Polish leaders would have had no option but to reach an arrangement with Germany over these "minor matters,"[32] and if Germany had wanted to attack the Soviet Union to secure *Lebensraum* in the east at some point in the future, then the Poles would have had to choose a side in that conflict. That could have been Hitler's only war. Instead of sitting back and watching as Germany and the Soviet Union fought against one another, Chamberlain had involved Britain in what became a global war that lasted for five and a half years, which his country could only participate in as a junior partner of the United States of America and the Soviet Union. The British membership in what Churchill called the "Grand Alliance"[33] may have allowed the claim to be made after the war that Great Britain had helped to defeat the Nazis, but it could just as easily be argued that the second world war helped transform the Soviet Union into a superpower. Stalin always intended to lay claim to more territory in Eastern Europe and the Baltics, and when the war finally came to an end in 1945, millions of people were trapped behind the "iron curtain"[34] with no possibility of escape. These people would remain under Soviet control for more than four decades. If one disregards the intentions of the politicians who involved Britain in the war, and one sets aside everything that has been said about it and considers what really happened, both during the war and after it ended, then the second world war cannot be said to have been a good war. It was a war just like any other – and in the final analysis, there are no good wars.

Notes

Epigraph

1. Boethius, *The Consolations of Philosophy*, translated by H.R. James, Project Gutenberg, p. 45, accessed 27th March 2021: https://www.gutenberg.org/files/14328/14328-h/14328-h.htm#Page_45
2. Niccolo Machiavelli, *Il Principe*, Chapter 15 (Oxford, Clarendon Press, 1891) Online Library of Liberty, accessed 20th October 2021: https://oll.libertyfund.org/title/acton-il-principe

Chapter One

1. Hansard, Commons Sitting, 31st March 1939, accessed 6th October 2020: https://hansard.parliament.uk/Commons/1939-03-31/debates/1524fe0b-019d-48fd-982d-99547a359ec6/EuropeanSituation
2. Hansard, Commons Sitting, 3rd April 1939, accessed 6th October 2020: https://hansard.parliament.uk/Commons/1939-04-03/debates/817ee449-6976-4e08-b600-1d08461b1e27/EuropeanSituation#contribution-d405de37-3756-4025-b717-43c10dc3ce35
3. Captain G.C. Wynne, *Stopping Hitler: An Official Account of How Britain Planned to Defend Itself in The Second World War* (Barnsley, Frontline Books, 2017) pp. 11-12.
4. Wynne, *Stopping Hitler*, p. 1; Alan Allport, *Browned Off and Bloody-Minded: The British Soldier Goes to War 1939-1945* (London, Yale University Press, 2015) p. 26.
5. Allport, *Browned Off and Bloody-Minded*, p. xxii, p. 19.
6. Allport, *Browned Off and Bloody-Minded*, p. 21.
7. Volker Ullrich, *Hitler: Volume 1: Ascent 1889-1939* (London, Vintage, 2017) p. 480.
8. Allport, *Browned Off and Bloody-Minded*, pp. 3-5.
9. Hansard, Commons Sitting, 3rd April 1939, accessed 2nd November 2020: https://hansard.parliament.uk/Commons/1939-04-03/debates/817ee449-6976-4e08-b600-1d08461b1e27/EuropeanSituation#contribution-f915a505-8440-4f29-b35c-be8385d0d5f0
10. Hansard, Commons Sitting, 3rd April 1939, accessed 2nd November 2020: https://hansard.parliament.uk/Commons/1939-04-03/debates/817ee449-6976-4e08-b600-

1d08461b1e27/EuropeanSituation#contribution-9ca44a17-ac7d-41a2-b2e1-8757b006998f
11. Hansard, Commons Sitting, 3rd April 1939, accessed 2nd November 2020: https://hansard.parliament.uk/Commons/1939-04-03/debates/817ee449-6976-4e08-b600-1d08461b1e27/EuropeanSituation#contribution-411a3c55-f6a3-4a2e-8cc9-db07ddfd1167
12. Hansard, Commons Sitting, 3rd April 1939, accessed 2nd November 2020: https://hansard.parliament.uk/Commons/1939-04-03/debates/817ee449-6976-4e08-b600-1d08461b1e27/EuropeanSituation#contribution-411a3c55-f6a3-4a2e-8cc9-db07ddfd1167
13. Hansard, Commons Sitting, 3rd April 1939, accessed 2nd November 2020: https://hansard.parliament.uk/Commons/1939-04-03/debates/817ee449-6976-4e08-b600-1d08461b1e27/EuropeanSituation#contribution-411a3c55-f6a3-4a2e-8cc9-db07ddfd1167
14. Hansard, Commons Sitting, 3rd April 1939, accessed 2nd November 2020: https://hansard.parliament.uk/Commons/1939-04-03/debates/817ee449-6976-4e08-b600-1d08461b1e27/EuropeanSituation#contribution-ad9ad7f5-2f2e-4939-b212-0b7308aae650
15. Hansard, Commons Sitting, 6th April 1939, accessed 2nd November 2020: https://hansard.parliament.uk/Commons/1939-04-06/debates/00576de1-3321-4b93-92dc-41ff5b352f7f/EuropeanSituation#contribution-202958e7-bf08-41ee-9544-bb6039f6ba0c
16. "Planning for a war with Germany," memorandum by the British Chiefs of Staff, 15th February 1937, quoted by Wynne, *Stopping Hitler*, pp. 8-11.
17. Hansard, Commons Sitting, 6th April 1939, accessed 2nd November 2020: https://hansard.parliament.uk/Commons/1939-04-06/debates/00576de1-3321-4b93-92dc-41ff5b352f7f/EuropeanSituation#contribution-0cdefe19-941b-4146-b191-bb70673c000d
18. Hansard, Commons Sitting, 3rd April 1939, accessed 2nd November 2020: https://hansard.parliament.uk/Commons/1939-04-03/debates/817ee449-6976-4e08-b600-1d08461b1e27/EuropeanSituation#contribution-ff720333-7e46-48f1-854d-5742472b1767
19. Hansard, Commons Sitting, 3rd April 1939, accessed 2nd November 2020: https://hansard.parliament.uk/Commons/1939-04-03/debates/817ee449-6976-4e08-b600-

1d08461b1e27/EuropeanSituation#contribution-ff720333-7e46-48f1-854d-5742472b1767
20. Hansard, Commons Sitting, 3rd April 1939, accessed 2nd November 2020: https://hansard.parliament.uk/Commons/1939-04-03/debates/817ee449-6976-4e08-b600-1d08461b1e27/EuropeanSituation#contribution-ff720333-7e46-48f1-854d-5742472b1767
21. Winston Churchill, *The Second World War Volume I: The Gathering Storm* (London, Penguin Classics, 2005) pp. 310-312.
22. National Archives, CAB 23/98/3.
23. Alan Bullock, *Hitler: A Study in Tyranny* (London, Penguin, 1990) p. 491.

Chapter Two

1. Ullrich, *Hitler: Volume 1: Ascent*, p. 161.
2. William Shirer, *The Rise and Fall of the Third Reich* (London, Arrow Books, 1991) p.43.
3. Shirer, *The Rise and Fall of the Third Reich*, p. 319.
4. Documents on German Foreign Policy (DGFP) Series D, Volume V (Washington, United States Government Printing Office, 1953) p. 105.
5. DGFP, Series D, Volume V, pp. 105-106.
6. DGFP, Series D, Volume V, pp. 105-106.
7. DGFP, Series D, Volume V, pp. 20-21.
8. DGFP, Series D, Volume V, p. 114.
9. DGFP, Series D, Volume V, pp. 38-39.
10. DGFP, Series D, Volume V, pp. 153-156.
11. Bullock, *Hitler*, p. 491.
12. J. Noakes and G. Pridham, *Nazism 1919-1945 Volume 3: Foreign Policy, War and Racial Extermination* (Liverpool, Liverpool University Press, 2014) p. 65.
13. Andrew Roberts, *The Holy Fox: The Life of Lord Halifax* (London, Head of Zeus, 2014) Kindle loc. 132.
14. Roberts, *The Holy Fox*, Kindle loc. 1040.
15. Roberts, *The Holy Fox*, Kindle loc. 1423; Noakes and Pridham, *Nazism*, p. 80.
16. National Archives, CAB 23/90A/5.
17. DGFP, Series D, Volume I, pp. 55 ff. quoted by Noakes and Pridham, *Nazism*, pp. 81-82.

18. Basil Liddell Hart, *A History of the Second World War* (Basingstoke, Pan, 2015) Kindle loc. 302.
19. Liddell Hart, *A History of the Second World War*, Kindle loc. 305.
20. National Archives, CAB 23/98/11.
21. Shirer, *The Rise and Fall of the Third Reich*, pp. 466-467.
22. Shirer, *The Rise and Fall of the Third Reich*, p. 467.
23. Shirer, *The Rise and Fall of the Third Reich*, pp. 467-468.
24. Bullock, *Hitler*, p. 497; Volker Ullrich, *Hitler: Downfall 1939-45* (London, The Bodley Head, 2020) p. 14.
25. Robert M. Citino, *The Path to Blitzkrieg: Doctrine and Training in the German Army, 1920-39* (Mechanicsburg, Stackpole Books, 2008) p. 9; Robert Forczyk, *Case White: The Invasion of Poland 1939* (Oxford, Osprey Publishing, 2019) p. 75.
26. Citino, *The Path to Blitzkrieg*, p. 11; Niklas Zetterling, *Blitzkrieg from The Ground Up* (Oxford, Casemate, 2017) p. 20.
27. Citino, *The Path to Blitzkrieg*, p. 13.
28. Forczyk, *Case White*, pp. 75-76; Zetterling, *Blitzkrieg From The Ground Up*, p. 16.
29. Forczyk, *Case White*, p. 77.
30. Forczyk, *Case White*, p. 78.
31. Forczyk, *Case White*, p. 82.
32. Forczyk, *Case White*, pp. 81-82.
33. Forczyk, *Case White*, p. 82.
34. Forczyk, *Case White*, p. 83.
35. Zetterling, *Blitzkrieg From The Ground Up*, p. 28; p. 36; Lloyd Clark, *Blitzkrieg: Myth, Reality and Hitler's Lightning War – France 1940* (London, Atlantic Books, 2017) p. 149; Two light German tanks in the Ardennes (*Bundesarchiv, Bild 101I-382-0248-33A)*, Illustrations, Section 2.
36. Clark, *Blitzkrieg*, p. 21.
37. Bullock, *Hitler*, p. 525.
38. "Donovan Nuremberg Trials Collection: Second Speech by The Führer on 22 Aug. '39. / Translation of Document 1014-PS / Office of U.S. Chief of Counsel," Cornell University Library: Law Library, 2015, accessed 25th January 2020: http://lawcollections.library.cornell.edu/nuremberg/catalog/nur:00459
39. "Donovan Nuremberg Trials Collection: Second Speech by The Führer on 22 Aug. '39. / Translation of Document 1014-PS / Office of U.S. Chief of Counsel," Cornell University Library: Law Library, 2015, accessed 25th January 2020: http://lawcollections.library.cornell.edu/nuremberg/catalog/nur:00459
40. Bullock, *Hitler*, p. 536.

41. "Donovan Nuremberg Trials Collection: Second Speech by The Führer on 22 Aug. '39. / Translation of Document 1014-PS / Office of U.S. Chief of Counsel," Cornell University Library: Law Library, 2015, accessed 25th January 2020:
http://lawcollections.library.cornell.edu/nuremberg/catalog/nur:00459
42. "Donovan Nuremberg Trials Collection: Second Speech by The Führer on 22 Aug. '39. / Translation of Document 1014-PS / Office of U.S. Chief of Counsel," Cornell University Library: Law Library, 2015, accessed 25th January 2020:
http://lawcollections.library.cornell.edu/nuremberg/catalog/nur:00459

Chapter Three

1. Robin Prior, *When Britain Saved the West: The Story of 1940* (London, Yale University Press, 2015) pp. 9-10.
2. Churchill, *The Gathering Storm*, p. 325.
3. Churchill, *The Gathering Storm*, p. 325.
4. National Archives, CAB 23/100/6.
5. National Archives, CAB 23/100/6.
6. Roberts, *The Holy Fox*, Kindle loc. 3615.
7. Roberts, *The Holy Fox*, Kindle loc. 3626.
8. Roberts, *The Holy Fox*, Kindle loc. 3625; Shirer, *The Rise and Fall of the Third Reich*, p. 504.
9. Shirer, *The Rise and Fall of The Third Reich*, p. 504.
10. Shirer, *The Rise and Fall of The Third Reich*, p. 533.
11. Shirer, *The Rise and Fall of The Third Reich*, p. 533.
12. Shirer, *The Rise and Fall of The Third Reich*, pp. 533-534.
13. Shirer, *The Rise and Fall of The Third Reich*, p. 534.
14. Shirer, *The Rise and Fall of The Third Reich*, p. 534.
15. Shirer, *The Rise and Fall of The Third Reich*, p. 535.
16. Shirer, *The Rise and Fall of The Third Reich*, p. 536.
17. Shirer, *The Rise and Fall of The Third Reich*, p. 537.
18. Churchill, *The Gathering Storm*, p. 310.
19. Shirer, *The Rise and Fall of The Third Reich*, pp. 536-537.
20. Shirer, *The Rise and Fall of The Third Reich*, p. 538.
21. Moorhouse, *The Devils' Alliance*, Kindle loc. 813.
22. Churchill, *The Gathering Storm*, p. 325.
23. Rees, *World War Two: Behind Closed Doors*, Kindle loc. 328.
24. DGFP, Series D, Volume VII, pp. 245-247, quoted by Noakes and Pridham, *Nazism*, pp. 135-136.

25. National Archives, CAB 23/100/6.
26. Hansard, Commons Sitting, 24th August 1939, accessed 6th November 2020: https://hansard.parliament.uk/Commons/1939-08-24/debates/50fe91c4-54cd-441c-9573-6dea0f05e385/InternationalSituation#contribution-2e1f3269-2a9a-4abf-bf1a-76b88c23cc07
27. National Archives, PREM 3/352/8.
28. Hansard, Commons Sitting, 24th August 1939, accessed 6th November 2020: https://hansard.parliament.uk/Commons/1939-08-24/debates/50fe91c4-54cd-441c-9573-6dea0f05e385/InternationalSituation#contribution-7f7eabf4-784d-4098-b317-fb5873282c0d
29. Churchill, *The Gathering Storm*, p. 325.
30. Churchill, *The Gathering Storm*, p. 325.

Chapter Four

1. Ullrich, *Hitler: Volume 1: Ascent,* p. 54.
2. Ullrich, *Hitler: Volume 1: Ascent,* pp. 54-55.
3. Ullrich, *Hitler: Volume 1: Ascent,* pp. 55-56.
4. Ullrich, *Hitler: Volume 1: Ascent,* p. 56.
5. Ullrich, *Hitler: Volume 1: Ascent*, pp. 60-61.
6. Ullrich, *Hitler: Volume 1: Ascent*, p. 61.
7. "Nuremberg Trial Proceedings Volume 4, Twenty-Third Day, Wednesday 19th December 1945," Yale Law School: The Avalon Project, 2008, 184, accessed 8th February 2020: http://avalon.law.yale.edu/imt/12-19-45.asp#ss
8. Rossino, *Hitler Strikes Poland: Blitzkrieg, Ideology and Atrocity* (Kansas, University Press of Kansas, 2003) p. 10, lines 35-37.
9. Timothy Snyder, *Bloodlands: Europe Between Hitler and Stalin* (London, The Bodley Head, 2010) Kindle loc. 2578.
10. Rossino, *Hitler Strikes Poland,* p. 10, lines 21-25; p. 11, lines 28-35; p. 12, lines 1-4.
11. Rossino, *Hitler Strikes Poland,* p. 15, lines 6-10; p. 43, lines 19-23.
12. Rossino, *Hitler Strikes Poland*, p. 15.
13. Rossino, *Hitler Strikes Poland*, pp. 15-16.
14. Forczyk, *Case White,* pp. 360-366.
15. Zetterling, *Blitzkrieg From The Ground Up,* p. 44.
16. Forczyk, *Case White,* p. 179.
17. Rossino, *Hitler Strikes Poland,* pp. 59-60.
18. Rossino, *Hitler Strikes Poland,* pp. 63-64.

19. Rossino, *Hitler Strikes Poland,* p. 68.
20. Rossino, *Hitler Strikes Poland,* pp. 70-71.
21. Rossino, *Hitler Strikes Poland,* pp. 71-72.
22. Rossino, *Hitler Strikes Poland,* p. 72, lines 2-5.
23. Richard Evans, *The Third Reich at War: How the Nazis Led Germany from Conquest to Disaster* (London, Penguin, 2012) Kindle loc. 572.
24. Martin Gilbert, *The Second World War: A Complete History* (New York, RosettaBooks, 2014) Kindle loc. 285.
25. Rossino, *Hitler Strikes Poland,* pp. 183-184.
26. Noakes and Pridham, *Nazism,* pp. 322-323.
27. Heinrich Himmler, Document 1919-PS, USA-304, quoted in Major Warren F. Farr, "Nuremberg Trial Proceedings Volume 4, Twenty-Third Day, 19th December 1945," Yale Law School: The Avalon Project, 2008, 178, accessed 8th February 2020: http://avalon.law.yale.edu/imt/12-19-45.asp#ss
28. Noakes and Pridham, *Nazism,* pp, 322-323; Heinrich Fraenkel & Roger Manvell, *Heinrich Himmler: The Sinister Life of The Head of The SS and Gestapo* (Barnsley, Frontline Books, 2017) p. 85.
29. Noakes and Pridham, *Nazism,* pp. 316-317.
30. Moorhouse, *The Devils' Alliance,* loc. 1123.
31. Noakes and Pridham, *Nazism,* p. 317.
32. Ullrich, *Hitler: Volume 1: Ascent,* loc. 1865; Snyder, *Bloodlands,* loc. 2610.
33. Noakes and Pridham, *Nazism,* pp. 329-330; Snyder, *Bloodlands,* loc. 2722.
34. "Extracts from speeches concerning the SS and the conduct of the war," Harvard Law School Library - Nuremberg Trials Project, NMT2 (USA v. Erhard Milch), HLSL No. 2974, accessed 8th February 2020: http://nuremberg.law.harvard.edu/documents/2974-extracts-from-speeches-concerning?q=Himmler+1919-PS#p.1
35. "Polish Premier Denounces Germany's Atrocities," The Nottingham Journal, 30th November 1939.
36. National Archives, CAB 65/2/19.
37. Arthur Harris, *Bomber Offensive* (Barnsley, Pen & Sword, 2005) Kindle loc. 146.
38. National Archives, CAB 65/1/1/, p. 3.
39. Gilbert, *The Second World War,* loc. 260; National Archives, CAB 65/1/1, p. 3.
40. National Archives, CAB 65/1/3, p. 21; CAB 65/1/8, p. 53.
41. National Archives, CAB 65/1/8, p. 53.
42. National Archives, CAB 65/6/26.
43. National Archives, CAB 65/11/22.

44. Gilbert, *The Second World War,* loc. 264; James Holland, *The War in the West: A New History: Volume I: Germany Ascendant 1939-1941* (London, Transworld, 2015) loc. 1454.
45. Rees, *World War Two: Behind Closed Doors*, Kindle loc. 415.
46. Ivan Maisky, *The Maisky Diaries: Red Ambassador to the Court of St. James's 1932-1943* (New Haven, Yale University Press, 2015) p. 226.
47. Hansard, Commons Sitting, 20th September 1939, accessed 16th November 2020: https://hansard.parliament.uk/Commons/1939-09-20/debates/7cc5ed4c-74bc-47a6-ba81-c0682a73ddce/WarSituation
48. Moorhouse, *The Devils' Alliance*, Kindle loc. 1114.
49. Moorhouse, *The Devils' Alliance,* Kindle loc. 1120.
50. Moorhouse, *The Devils' Alliance*, Kindle loc. 1162.
51. Rees, *World War Two: Behind Closed Doors*, Kindle loc. 496.
52. Maisky, *The Maisky Diaries*, pp. 227-228.
53. Eugenia Maresch, *Katyn 1940: The Documentary Evidence of the West's Betrayal* (Cheltenham, The History Press, 2020) p. 12.
54. Rees, *World War Two: Behind Closed Doors*, Kindle loc. 862.
55. Maresch, *Katyn 1940*, p. 12.
56. Maresch, *Katyn 1940*, p. 13.
57. Rees, *World War Two: Behind Closed Doors*, Kindle loc. 965; Institute of National Remembrance, "Decision to commence investigation into Katyn massacre," 1st December 2014, accessed 28th January 2022: https://ipn.gov.pl/en/news/77,dok.html
58. Rees, *World War Two: Behind Closed Doors*, loc. 977-998; Snyder, *Bloodlands*, loc. 2794-2814.
59. Rees, *World War Two: Behind Closed Doors*, loc. 998, loc. 1013.
60. Moorhouse, *The Devils' Alliance*, loc. 1203.
61. Maresch, *Katyn 1940*, p. 14.
62. Reuters, ""Phantom Train of Dead" in Soviet-Occupied Poland," The Nottingham Journal, 6th April 1940; ""Reign of Terror" in Soviet-Occupied Poland," The Scotsman, 6th April 1940.
63. Hansard, Commons Sitting, 3rd April 1939, accessed 2nd November 2020: https://hansard.parliament.uk/Commons/1939-04-03/debates/817ee449-6976-4e08-b600-1d08461b1e27/EuropeanSituation#contribution-ff720333-7e46-48f1-854d-5742472b1767
64. National Archives, WO 32/15548, quoted by Maresch, *Katyn 1940*, pp. 15-16.

<u>Chapter Five</u>

1. Gilbert, *The Second World War,* Kindle loc. 1523.
2. Churchill, *The Gathering Storm*, p. 599.
3. Lord Moran, *Churchill at War 1940-1945* (London, Robinson, 2002) p. 3.
4. Max Hastings, *Finest Years: Churchill as Warlord 1940-1945* (New York, Harper Collins, 2009) loc. 190.
5. Robin Prior, *When Britain Saved the West: The Story of 1940* (London, Yale University Press) p. 75.
6. Prior, *When Britain Saved the West*, p. 74.
7. Prior, *When Britain Saved the West*, p. 77.
8. Clark, *Blitzkrieg,* pp. 140-141.
9. Clark, *Blitzkrieg,* p. 153.
10. Gilbert, *The Second World War*, loc. 1574.
11. Prior, *When Britain Saved the West*, p. 74.
12. Prior, *When Britain Saved the West*, p. 77.
13. Prior, *When Britain Saved the West*, pp. 77-78.
14. Prior, *When Britain Saved the West*, p. 72.
15. Prior, *When Britain Saved the West*, p. 79.
16. Prior, *When Britain Saved the West*, p. 82.
17. National Archives, CAB 65/13/12, p. 1.
18. National Archives, CAB 65/13/12, p. 1.
19. National Archives, CAB 65/13/12, p. 1.
20. National Archives, CAB 65/13/12, p. 2.
21. National Archives, CAB 65/13/12, p. 4.
22. Gilbert, *The Second World War*, Kindle loc. 1685.
23. Gilbert, *The Second World War*, Kindle loc. 1703.
24. Gilbert, *The Second World War*, Kindle loc. 1686.
25. Gilbert, *The Second World War*, Kindle loc. 1733.
26. Prior, *When Britain Saved the West*, p. 110.
27. Stewart Mitchell, *St Valéry and Its Aftermath* (Barnsley, Pen & Sword, 2017) p. 25.
28. Mitchell, *St Valéry and Its Aftermath*, p. 28-29.
29. Mitchell, *St Valéry and Its Aftermath*, p. 36.
30. Mitchell, *St Valéry and Its Aftermath*, p. 37.
31. Mitchell, *St Valéry and Its Aftermath*, p. 37.
32. Mitchell, *St Valéry and Its Aftermath*, p. 38.
33. Mitchell, *St Valéry and Its Aftermath*, p. 40.
34. Mitchell, *St Valéry and Its Aftermath*, p. 40.
35. Mitchell, *St Valéry and Its Aftermath*, p. 42.

36. Mitchell, *St Valéry and Its Aftermath*, p. 44; Gilbert, *The Second World War*, Kindle loc. 2205.
37. Mitchell, *St Valéry and Its Aftermath*, p. 50.
38. Hansard, Commons Sitting, 4th June 1940, accessed 29th October 2020: https://hansard.parliament.uk/Commons/1940-06-04/debates/60ee1caa-abcf-48e5-8c55-c4e587b94de7/WarSituation
39. Hansard, Commons Sitting, 4th June 1940.
40. Hansard, Commons Sitting, 4th June 1940.
41. Hansard, Commons Sitting, 4th June 1940.
42. Hansard, Commons Sitting, 4th June 1940.
43. National Archives, CAB 65/13/49, p. 2.
44. National Archives, CAB 65/13/49, p. 2.
45. National Archives, CAB 65/13/49, p. 4.
46. National Archives, CAB 65/13/53, p. 1.
47. National Archives, CAB 65/13/53, pp. 1-2.
48. National Archives, CAB 65/13/53, p. 2.
49. National Archives, CAB 65/13/53, p. 2.
50. National Archives, CAB 65/13/53, p. 3.
51. Martin Gilbert, *Winston S. Churchill: Finest Hour, 1939-1941 (Volume VI)* (New York, RosettaBooks, 2015) Kindle loc. 12273.
52. Gilbert, *Winston S. Churchill: Finest Hour, 1939-1941*, Kindle loc. 12304.
53. Gilbert, *Winston S. Churchill: Finest Hour, 1939-1941*, Kindle loc. 12279.
54. Gilbert, *Winston S. Churchill: Finest Hour, 1939-1941*, Kindle loc. 12350.
55. Gilbert, *Winston S. Churchill: Finest Hour, 1939-1941*, Kindle loc. 12376.
56. Gilbert, *Winston S. Churchill: Finest Hour, 1939-1941,* Kindle loc. 12381.
57. Gilbert, *Winston S. Churchill: Finest Hour, 1939-1941*, Kindle loc. 12386.
58. Gilbert, *Winston S. Churchill: Finest Hour, 1939-1941,* Kindle loc. 12387.
59. National Archives, CAB 65/14/5, p. 1.
60. National Archives, CAB 65/14/6, p. 3.
61. Niccolo Machiavelli, *Il Principe*, Chapter 15 (Oxford, Clarendon Press, 1891) (translation by Kenneth Duthie), Online Library of Liberty, accessed 20th October 2021: https://oll.libertyfund.org/title/acton-il-principe

Chapter Six

1. Press Conference #622, Executive Offices of the White House, February 9th, 1940, 10.50am, p. 1, Press Conferences of President Franklin D. Roosevelt, 1933-1945, Franklin D. Roosevelt Presidential Library and Museum, accessed 23rd April 2017: http://www.fdrlibrary.marist.edu/archives/collections/franklin/?p=collections/findingaid&id=508
2. Welles Report pt. 2 – 12th March 1940, p. 20, PSF files, Safe File, Box 6, Franklin D. Roosevelt Presidential Library and Museum, accessed 23rd April 2017, http://www.fdrlibrary.marist.edu/archives/collections/franklin/?p=collections/findingaid&id=502&q=&rootcontentid=139882#id139882
3. Welles Report pt. 2, 12th March 1940, p. 21.
4. Welles Report pt. 2, 12th March 1940, p. 22.
5. Simon Berthon and Joanna Potts, *Warlords: An Extraordinary Re-creation of World War II Through the Eyes and Minds of Hitler, Churchill, Roosevelt and Stalin* (London, Thistle Publishing, 2013) Kindle loc. 146.
6. Gavin J. Bailey, *The Arsenal of Democracy: Aircraft Supply and the Evolution of the Anglo-American Alliance, 1938-1942* (Edinburgh, Edinburgh University Press, 2013) Kindle loc. 1573.
7. National Archives, PREM 3/468, folios 204-21, quoted by Martin Gilbert, *Winston S. Churchill: Volume VI: Finest Hour 1939-1941* (Hillsdale, Hillsdale College Press, 2018) pp. 345-346; Winston Churchill, *The Second World War Volume II: Their Finest Hour* (London, Penguin Classics, 2005) pp. 22-23.
8. Wynne, *Stopping Hitler*, p. 11.
9. Wynne, *Stopping Hitler*, p. 11.
10. National Archives, CAB 66/7/48.
11. National Archives, CAB 66/7/48.
12. Bailey, *Arsenal of Democracy*, Kindle loc. 731.
13. Bailey, *Arsenal of Democracy*, Kindle loc. 760.
14. Bailey, *Arsenal of Democracy*, Kindle loc. 849; Patrick Bishop, *Battle of Britain: A Day-by-Day Chronicle 10 July-31 October 1940* (London, Quercus Editions Ltd., 2020) p. 23.
15. Stephen Bungay, *The Most Dangerous Enemy: A History of the Battle of Britain* (London, Aurum Press Ltd., 2015) p. 59.
16. National Archives, CAB 23/93/8.
17. Bailey, *Arsenal of Democracy*, Kindle loc. 937.
18. Harris, *Bomber Offensive*, Kindle loc. 432.
19. Bailey, *Arsenal of Democracy*, Kindle loc. 945.
20. Harris, *Bomber Offensive*, Kindle loc. 456.

21. Bailey, *Arsenal of Democracy*, Kindle loc. 951.
22. National Archives, CAB 23/93/13.
23. National Archives, AVIA 10/120; Bailey, *Arsenal of Democracy*, Kindle loc. 1100.
24. Bailey, *Arsenal of Democracy*, Kindle loc. 1100.
25. National Archives, PREM 3/468, folios 194-5, quoted by Gilbert, *Winston S. Churchill: Volume VI: Finest Hour 1939-1941*, pp. 367-368; Churchill, *Their Finest Hour*, pp. 50.
26. National Archives, CAB 85/14/6.
27. National Archives, CAB 85/14/6.
28. National Archives, PREM 3/468, folios 194-5, quoted by Gilbert, *Winston S. Churchill: Volume VI: Finest Hour 1939-1941*, pp. 367-368; Churchill, *Their Finest Hour*, pp. 50-51.
29. Bailey, *Arsenal of Democracy*, Kindle loc. 2070.
30. Bailey, *Arsenal of Democracy*, Kindle loc. 873.
31. Bailey, *Arsenal of Democracy*, Kindle loc. 837.
32. John Nichol, *Spitfire: A Very British Love Story* (London Simon & Schuster, 2018) p. 19.
33. Bungay, *The Most Dangerous Enemy*, p. 76.
34. Nichol, *Spitfire*, p. 22.
35. Nichol, *Spitfire*, p. 22.
36. Nichol, *Spitfire*, p. 22.
37. Nichol, *Spitfire*, p. 25.
38. Churchill, *Their Finest Hour*, p. 12; Holland, *The War in the West: Volume I*, Kindle loc. 5480.
39. Churchill, *Their Finest Hour*, p. 12.
40. Holland, *The War in the West: Volume I*, Kindle loc. 5492.
41. Holland, *The War in the West: Volume I*, Kindle loc. 5496.
42. Bungay, *The Most Dangerous Enemy*, p. 61; Bishop, *Battle of Britain*, p. 22.
43. Bungay, *The Most Dangerous Enemy*, p. 62.
44. Bungay, *The Most Dangerous Enemy*, p. 64.
45. Bishop, *Battle of Britain*, p. 54.
46. Bungay, *The Most Dangerous Enemy*, p. 67.
47. Bishop, *Battle of Britain*, p. 57.
48. Raymond E. Lee, *The London Observer: The Journal of General Raymond E. Lee 1940-1941* (London, Hutchinson & Co. Ltd., 1972) p. 30.
49. Churchill, *Their Finest Hour*, p. 281.
50. Churchill, *Their Finest Hour*, pp. 282-283.
51. Hansard, Commons Sitting, 20th August 1940, accessed 19th October 2020: https://hansard.parliament.uk/Commons/1940-08-

20/debates/ebe6c652-0e92-46d7-978c-7a49003c589e/WarSituation quoted by Churchill, *Their Finest Hour*, p. 288.
52. Bungay, *The Most Dangerous Enemy*, pp. 423-426.
53. Bungay, *The Most Dangerous Enemy*, pp. 79-80.
54. Bailey, *Arsenal of Democracy*, Kindle loc. 1174.
55. Bailey, *Arsenal of Democracy*, Kindle loc. 364.
56. National Archives, PREM 3/468, folios 204-21, quoted by Gilbert, *Winston S. Churchill: Volume VI: Finest Hour 1939-1941*, p. 346; Churchill, *Their Finest Hour*, p. 353.
57. National Archives, PREM 3/468, folios 170-72, quoted by Gilbert, *Winston S. Churchill: Volume VI: Finest Hour 1939-1941*, p. 493; Churchill, *Their Finest Hour*, p. 353.
58. National Archives, CAB 65/7/36.
59. National Archives, CAB 65/7/36.
60. Churchill, *Their Finest Hour*, p. 357.
61. Churchill, *Their Finest Hour*, p. 363.
62. Churchill, *Their Finest Hour*, p. 357.
63. Gilbert, *Winston S. Churchill: Volume VI: Finest Hour 1939-1941*, p. 974.
64. Hansard, Commons Sitting, 20th August 1940, accessed 19th October 2020: https://hansard.parliament.uk/Commons/1940-08-20/debates/ebe6c652-0e92-46d7-978c-7a49003c589e/WarSituation
65. "Press Conference #702," Executive Offices of the White House, December 17th 1940, 4.10 pm, p. 1, Press Conferences of President Franklin D. Roosevelt, 1933-1945, Franklin D. Roosevelt Presidential Library and Museum, accessed 10th October 2018: http://www.fdrlibrary.marist.edu/archives/collections/franklin/?p=collections/findingaid&id=508
66. "Fireside Chat No. 16," December 29th 1940, Master Speech File 1898-1945, Box 58, Franklin D. Roosevelt Library and Museum, accessed 16th October 2020: http://www.fdrlibrary.marist.edu/archives/collections/franklin/index.php?p=collections/findingaid&id=582
67. "Fireside Chat No. 16," December 29th 1940.
68. Welles Report pt.2 - 19th March 1940, p. 131.
69. Winston Churchill, *The Grand Alliance* (London, Weidenfeld & Nicolson, 2015) p. 33.
70. Hastings, *Finest Years: Churchill as Warlord*, Kindle loc. 3022.
71. Churchill, *The Grand Alliance*, p. 34.
72. National Archives, CAB 65/14/3.
73. John Colville, quoted in Warren Tute, *The Deadly Stroke* (Barnsley, Pen & Sword, 2007) Kindle loc. 168.

Chapter Seven

1. Gilbert, *The Second World War,* Kindle loc. 4540.
2. Evans, *The Third Reich at War*, Kindle loc. 3426.
3. Andrew Roberts, *The Storm of War: A New History of the Second World War* (London, Penguin, 2009) Kindle loc. 2974.
4. Gilbert, *The Second World War,* Kindle loc. 4542.
5. Laurence Rees, *The Nazis: A Warning from History* (London, BBC Digital, 2012) Kindle loc. 2424; Liddell Hart, *A History of the Second World War*, Kindle loc. 2984-2989.
6. DGFP, Series D, Vol. XII, pp. 1066 ff., quoted by Noakes and Pridham, *Nazism*, p. 209.
7. Gilbert, *Winston S. Churchill: Finest Hour, 1939-1941,* Kindle loc. 21239.
8. Hastings, *Finest Years: Churchill as Warlord,* Kindle loc. 2562; Gilbert, *Winston S. Churchill: Finest Hour, 1939-1941*, Kindle loc. 21257.
9. Winston Churchill, "Alliance with Russia, 22nd June 1941, Broadcast, London," in *Never Give In! Winston Churchill's Speeches* (London, Bloomsbury, 2013) p. 240.
10. Winston Churchill, "Alliance with Russia, 22nd June 1941, Broadcast, London," in *Never Give In! Winston Churchill's Speeches*, pp. 241-242.
11. Winston Churchill, "Alliance with Russia, 22nd June 1941, Broadcast, London," in *Never Give In! Winston Churchill's Speeches*, p. 242.
12. David Reynolds and Vladimir Pechatnov, *The Kremlin Letters: Stalin's Wartime Correspondence with Churchill and Roosevelt* (New Haven, Yale University Press, 2018) p. 23.
13. National Archives, PREM 3/401/1, Prime Minister's Personal Telegram T.377, quoted by Gilbert, *Winston S. Churchill: Finest Hour 1939-1941* Kindle loc. 21503; Reynolds and Pechatnov, *The Kremlin Letters*, p. 23.
14. Berthon and Potts, *Warlords*, Kindle loc. 1706; Reynolds and Pechatnov, *The Kremlin Letters*, p. 24.
15. National Archives, CAB 65/19/3.
16. "Agreement Between the United Kingdom and the Union of Soviet Socialist Republics: July 12, 1941," Yale Law School, Avalon Project, 2008, accessed 14th December 2019: http://avalon.law.yale.edu/wwii/brsov41.asp
17. Hansard, Commons Sitting, 15th July 1941, accessed 14th December 2019: https://api.parliament.uk/historic-hansard/commons/1941/jul/15/war-situation
18. Churchill, *The Grand Alliance*, pp. 290-292.
19. Gilbert, *The Second World War*, Kindle loc. 4623.

20. Winston Churchill, *The Second World War Volume IV: The Hinge of Fate* (London, Penguin, 2005) p. 228.
21. Maisky, *The Maisky Diaries*, p. 374.
22. Jonathan Fenby, *Alliance: The Inside Story of How Roosevelt, Stalin and Churchill Won One War and Began Another* (New York, Simon and Schuster, 2015) Kindle loc. 922.
23. Fenby, *Alliance*, Kindle loc. 925.
24. Fenby, *Alliance*, Kindle loc. 928.
25. Harry Hopkins, correspondence with Roosevelt, 25th July 1941, p. 8, Franklin D. Roosevelt, Papers as President, PSF File, Safe File, Box 3, FDR Presidential Library & Museum, accessed 10th October 2018: http://www.fdrlibrary.marist.edu/archives/collections/franklin/?p=collections/findingaid&id=502
26. Franklin Roosevelt, correspondence with Hopkins, 26th July 1941, p. 6, Franklin D. Roosevelt, Papers as President, PSF File, Safe File, Box 3, FDR Presidential Library & Museum, accessed 10th October 2018: http://www.fdrlibrary.marist.edu/archives/collections/franklin/?p=collections/findingaid&id=502
27. Sumner Welles, correspondence with Steinhardt, 27th July 1941, United States Department of State: Foreign relations of the United States diplomatic papers, 1941, p. 797. General, The Soviet Union (1941), University of Wisconsin-Madison Libraries, accessed 13th August 2017: http://digicoll.library.wisc.edu/cgi-bin/FRUS/FRUS-idx?type=turn&entity=FRUS.FRUS1941v01.p0809&id=FRUS.FRUS1941v01&isize=M
28. Harry Hopkins, Memorandum, 30th July 1941, United States Department of State: Foreign relations of the United States diplomatic papers, 1941, pp. 802-803. General, The Soviet Union (1941), University of Wisconsin-Madison Libraries, accessed 13th August 2017: http://digicoll.library.wisc.edu/cgi-bin/FRUS/FRUS-idx?type=turn&entity=FRUS.FRUS1941v01.p0815&id=FRUS.FRUS1941v01&isize=M
29. Josef Stalin, quoted in Harry Hopkins, Memorandum, 30th July 1941, United States Department of State: Foreign relations of the United States diplomatic papers, 1941, p. 803. General, The Soviet Union (1941), University of Wisconsin-Madison Libraries, accessed 13th August 2017: http://digicoll.library.wisc.edu/cgi-bin/FRUS/FRUS-idx?type=turn&entity=FRUS.FRUS1941v01.p0815&id=FRUS.FRUS1941v01&isize=M
30. Stalin, quoted in Harry Hopkins, Memorandum, 30th July 1941, p. 804.
31. Stalin, quoted in Harry Hopkins, Memorandum, 30th July 1941, p. 804.

32. The Atlantic Conference Between President Roosevelt and Prime Minister Churchill, August 9-12, 1941, United States Department of State: Foreign relations of the United States diplomatic papers, 1941, p. 341. General, The Soviet Union (1941), University of Wisconsin-Madison Libraries, accessed 5th July 2018: http://digicoll.library.wisc.edu/cgi-bin/FRUS/FRUS-idx?type=goto&id=FRUS.FRUS1941v01&isize=M&submit=Go+to+page&page=341
33. Hastings, *Finest Years: Churchill as Warlord*, Kindle loc. 3211.
34. Churchill, *The Grand Alliance*, p. 343.
35. H.V. Morton, *Atlantic Meeting* (London, Methuen & Co Ltd., 1943) pp. 35-37.
36. National Archives, PREM 3/485/6 fo. 16, quoted by Hastings, *Finest Years: Churchill as Warlord*, Kindle loc. 3205.
37. Gilbert, *Winston S. Churchill: Finest Hour, 1939-1941*, Kindle loc. 22006.
38. Franklin Roosevelt, Campaign Speech, Philadelphia, 23rd October 1940, FDR Audio Recordings, FDR Library, accessed 14th December 2019: https://www.fdrlibrary.org/utterancesfdr#afdr205
39. Nigel Hamilton, *The Mantle of Command: FDR at War, 1941-1942* (London, Biteback Publishing, 2016) p. 6; Wapshott, *The Sphinx*, p. 318; Fenby, *Alliance*, Kindle loc. 781.
40. Hamilton, *The Mantle of Command*, pp. 5-6.
41. Hamilton, *The Mantle of Command*, pp. 14-15.
42. Hamilton, *The Mantle of Command*, pp. 15-16; Fenby, *Alliance*, Kindle loc. 801.
43. Fenby, *Alliance*, Kindle loc. 1047.
44. Fenby, *Alliance*, Kindle loc. 1053.
45. Hamilton, *The Mantle of Command*, p. 23.
46. Churchill, *The Grand Alliance*, p. 346.
47. Hamilton, *The Mantle of Command*, p. 36.
48. "Atlantic Charter," Yale Law School: The Avalon Project, 2008, accessed 8th February 2021: https://avalon.law.yale.edu/wwii/atlantic.asp
49. "Atlantic Charter," Yale Law School: The Avalon Project, 2008, accessed 8th February 2021: https://avalon.law.yale.edu/wwii/atlantic.asp
50. "Winston's Parents," National Churchill Museum, Westminster College, Fulton, Missouri, 2018, accessed 14th December 2019: https://www.nationalchurchillmuseum.org/winston-churchills-parents.html
51. "Atlantic conference with Churchill and Roosevelt (1941)," British Pathé, YouTube, accessed 31st August 2021: https://youtu.be/s_Gae3AUs4U

52. "Inter-Allied Council Statement on the Principles of the Atlantic Charter: September 24, 1941," Yale Law School: The Avalon Project, 2008, accessed 14th December 2019: http://avalon.law.yale.edu/wwii/interall.asp

53. Gilbert, *The Second World War*, Kindle loc. 5136; Reynolds and Pechatnov, *The Kremlin Letters*, p. 37.

54. National Archives, FO 954/24B/488-9, quoted by Reynolds and Pechatnov, *The Kremlin Letters*, p. 65.

55. Reynolds and Pechatnov, *The Kremlin Letters*, pp. 66-67.

56. Reynolds and Pechatnov, *The Kremlin Letters*, p. 68.

57. National Archives, FO 954/24B/517.

58. Reynolds and Pechatnov, *The Kremlin Letters*, p. 74.

59. Rees, *World War Two: Behind Closed Doors*, Kindle loc. 2043.

60. Rees, *World War Two: Behind Closed Doors*, Kindle loc. 2053.

61. National Archives, FO 371/29655 Telegram No. 13 HECTIC.

62. National Archives, FO 371/29655 Telegram No. 22 HECTIC.

63. Churchill, *The Grand Alliance*, p. 493.

64. Prime Minister to Lord Privy Seal, 20th December 1941, quoted by Churchill, *The Grand Alliance*, p. 493.

Chapter Eight

1. William R. Trotter, *The Winter War: The Russo-Finnish War of 1939-40* (London, Aurum Press, 2013) p. 14; "Secret Additional Protocol," The Avalon Project, Yale Law School, 2008, accessed 8th February 2021: https://avalon.law.yale.edu/20th_century/addsepro.asp

2. Moorhouse, *The Devils' Alliance,* Kindle loc. 1114.

3. Moorhouse, *The Devils' Alliance*, Kindle loc. 1537-1584.

4. Moorhouse, *The Devils' Alliance*, Kindle loc. 1598.

5. Moorhouse, *The Devils' Alliance*, Kindle loc. 1601-1610.

6. Moorhouse, *The Devils' Alliance*, Kindle loc. 1610-1615.

7. Moorhouse, *The Devils' Alliance*, Kindle loc. 1621-1640.

8. Moorhouse, *The Devils' Alliance*, Kindle loc. 1945-1962.

9. Moorhouse, *The Devils' Alliance*, Kindle loc. 1962-1973.

10. Moorhouse, *The Devils' Alliance*, Kindle loc. 1973; Kindle loc. 1979-1983; Roberts, *The Storm of War,* Kindle loc. 686.

11. Moorhouse, *The Devils' Alliance*, Kindle loc. 2108-2815; Kindle loc. 2126-2136.

12. Moorhouse, *The Devils' Alliance*, Kindle loc. 2146-2161.

13. Trotter, *The Winter War*, p. 39.

14. Trotter, *The Winter War*, p. 42.

15. Trotter, *The Winter War*, pp. 43-44.
16. Bair Irincheev, *War of the White Death: Finland Against the Soviet Union 1939-40* (Barnsley, Pen & Sword, 2011) p. 8.
17. Trotter, *The Winter War*, p. 38; Irincheev, *War of the White Death*, pp. 10-11.
18. Trotter, *The Winter War*, pp. 45-46.
19. Trotter, *The Winter War*, pp. 62-66.
20. Trotter, *The Winter War*, pp. 41-42.
21. Trotter, *The Winter War*, p. 42; pp. 75-76.
22. Trotter, *The Winter War*, p. 39.
23. Vesa Nenye, Peter Munter, Toni Wirtanen, Chris Birks, *Finland at War: The Winter War 1939-40* (Oxford, Osprey, 2015) p. 49; Trotter, *The Winter War*, p. 15.
24. Trotter, *The Winter War*, p. 15.
25. Trotter, *The Winter War*, pp. 15-16.
26. Trotter, *The Winter War*, pp. 15-16.
27. Trotter, *The Winter War*, p, 18.
28. Nenye et al., *Finland at War: The Winter War 1939-40*, pp. 50-51.
29. Nenye et al., *Finland at War: The Winter War 1939-40*, p. 53.
30. Trotter, *The Winter War*, p. 21.
31. Irincheev, *War of the White Death*, p. 2.
32. Nenye et al., *Finland at War: The Winter War 1939-40*, p. 53.
33. National Archives, CAB 65/2/30.
34. National Archives, CAB 65/2/30.
35. National Archives, CAB 65/2/32.
36. National Archives, CAB 65/2/32.
37. Maisky, *The Maisky Diaries*, p. 242.
38. Trotter, *The Winter War*, p. 48.
39. Trotter, *The Winter War*, p. 50.
40. National Archives, CAB 65/2/33, p. 265.
41. Hansard, Commons Sitting, 3rd April 1939, accessed 26th February 2019:
https://api.parliament.uk/historic-hansard/commons/1939/apr/03/european-situation-1#S5CV0345P0_19390403_HOC_311
42. National Archives, CAB 65/2/33, p. 266.
43. National Archives, CAB 65/2/33, p. 266.
44. National Archives, CAB 65/2/33, p. 266.
45. National Archives, CAB 65/2/33, p. 266.
46. National Archives, CAB 65/2/33, p. 266.

47. Hansard, Commons Sitting, 30th November 1939, accessed 26th November 2020: https://hansard.parliament.uk/Commons/1939-11-30/debates/6821e9bd-75a2-4609-909a-4e1b45dd1b17/RussiaAndFinland
48. Hansard, Commons Sitting, 30th November 1939, accessed 26th November 2020: https://hansard.parliament.uk/Commons/1939-11-30/debates/6821e9bd-75a2-4609-909a-4e1b45dd1b17/RussiaAndFinland
49. Hansard, Commons Sitting, 14th December 1939, accessed 26th November 2020: https://hansard.parliament.uk/Commons/1939-12-14/debates/42812234-bff2-474a-9b91-f9707bd4e56b/TheWar#contribution-95833764-a5ae-4286-8e6e-1a52d37084b5
50. Hansard, Commons Sitting, 14th December 1939, accessed 26th November 2020: https://hansard.parliament.uk/Commons/1939-12-14/debates/42812234-bff2-474a-9b91-f9707bd4e56b/TheWar#contribution-e309bc3c-633e-4d24-a77d-3eefb842acb9
51. Press Conference #602, Executive Offices of the White House, December 1st, 1939, p. 2, Press Conferences of President Franklin D. Roosevelt, 1933-1945, FDR Presidential Library and Museum, accessed 27th February 2019: http://www.fdrlibrary.marist.edu/archives/collections/franklin/?p=collections/findingaid&id=508
52. Press Conference #602, Executive Offices of the White House, December 1st, 1939.
53. Press Conference #605, Executive Offices of the White House, December 12th, 1939, pp. 2-3, Press Conferences of President Franklin D. Roosevelt, 1933-1945, FDR Presidential Library and Museum, accessed 27th February 2019: http://www.fdrlibrary.marist.edu/archives/collections/franklin/?p=collections/findingaid&id=508
54. Herbert Hoover, *Freedom Betrayed: Herbert Hoover's Secret History of the Second World War and Its Aftermath* (Stanford, Hoover Institution Press, 2011), Kindle loc. 6608.
55. Winston Churchill, *The Power of Words: His Remarkable Life Recounted Through His Writings and Speeches* (London, Transworld, 2012) p. 372.
56. Trotter, *The Winter War*, p. 68
57. Trotter, *The Winter War*, p. 75.
58. Trotter, *The Winter War*, p. 75.
59. Trotter, *The Winter War*, p. 75-76.
60. Trotter, *The Winter War*, p. 77-78.
61. Trotter, *The Winter War*, p. 79; pp. 83-84.

62. Trotter, *The Winter War*, p. 80.
63. Trotter, *The Winter War*, pp. 80-81.
64. Trotter, *The Winter War*, p. 82.
65. Trotter, *The Winter War*, p. 82.
66. Trotter, *The Winter War*, p. 81.
67. "Navajo Code Talkers and the Unbreakable Code," News and Information, Central Intelligence Agency, accessed 27th February 2019: https://www.cia.gov/news-information/featured-story-archive/2008-featured-story-archive/navajo-code-talkers/
68. Trotter, *The Winter War*, p. 37.
69. Trotter, *The Winter War*, pp 144-145.
70. Trotter, *The Winter War*, p. 145.
71. Trotter, *The Winter War*, p. 145.
72. Trotter, *The Winter War*, p. 147.
73. Trotter, *The Winter War*, p. 38; pp. 147-148.
74. Trotter, *The Winter War*, p. 146.
75. Nenye et al. *Finland at War: The Winter War 1939-40*, p. 231.
76. Trotter, *The Winter War*, p. 209.
77. Trotter, *The Winter War*, p. 108.
78. Trotter, *The Winter War*, p. 206.
79. Trotter, *The Winter War*, p. 51.
80. Gilbert, *The Second World War,* Kindle loc. 1081.
81. Gilbert, *The Second World War*, Kindle loc. 1091.
82. Gilbert, *The Second World War*, Kindle loc. 1099.
83. Gilbert, *The Second World War*, Kindle loc. 1206.
84. Gilbert, *The Second World War*, Kindle loc. 1210-1213.
85. Trotter, *The Winter War*, p. 263.
86. Nenye et al. *Finland at War: The Winter War 1939-40*, p. 288.
87. Vesa Nenye, Peter Munter, Toni Wirtanen, Chris Birks, *Finland at War: The Continuation and Lapland Wars 1941-45* (Oxford, Osprey, 2016) p. 41.

Chapter Nine

1. Arthur Schoenfeld, telegram to Secretary of State, February 7th, 1941, Foreign Relations of the United States Diplomatic Papers, 1941, General, The Soviet Union, Volume I, p. 10, The Office of the Historian, accessed 10th December 2020: https://history.state.gov/historicaldocuments/frus1941v01/pg_10
2. Arthur Schoenfeld, telegram to Secretary of State, June 25th, 1941, Foreign Relations of the United States Diplomatic Papers, 1941, General,

The Soviet Union, Volume I, p. 42, The Office of the Historian, accessed 10th December 2020:
https://history.state.gov/historicaldocuments/frus1941v01/pg_42
3. Sumner Welles, memorandum of conversation, June 26th, 1941, Foreign Relations of the United States Diplomatic Papers, 1941, General, The Soviet Union, Volume I, p. 43, The Office of the Historian, accessed 10th December 2020:
https://history.state.gov/historicaldocuments/frus1941v01/pg_43
4. National Archives, CAB 65/18/42.
5. National Archives, CAB 65/18/43.
6. Sumner Welles, memorandum of conversation, June 28th, Foreign Relations of the United States Diplomatic Papers, 1941, General, The Soviet Union, Volume I, pp. 43-44, The Office of the Historian, accessed 10th December 2020:
https://history.state.gov/historicaldocuments/frus1941v01/pg_43
7. Arthur Schoenfeld, telegram to the Secretary of State, July 4, 1941, Foreign Relations of the United States Diplomatic Papers, 1941, General, The Soviet Union, Volume I, p. 48, The Office of the Historian, accessed 10th December 2020:
https://history.state.gov/historicaldocuments/frus1941v01/pg_48
8. Hamilton, *The Mantle of Command,* pp. 20-21; Gilbert, *Winston S. Churchill: Finest Hour, 1939-1941,* loc. 22067.
9. Gilbert, *Winston S. Churchill: Finest Hour, 1939-1941,* Kindle loc. 22919; Footnote 3680.
10. Fenby, *Alliance,* Kindle loc. 1494; Reynolds and Pechatnov, *The Kremlin Letters*, p. 61.
11. Vesa Nenye, Peter Munter, Toni Wirtanen, Chris Birks, *Finland at War: The Continuation and Lapland Wars 1941-45* (Oxford, Osprey, 2016) pp. 53-54.
12. Nenye et al., *Finland at War: The Continuation and Lapland Wars*, pp. 51-52.
13. Nenye et al., *Finland at War: The Continuation and Lapland Wars*, pp. 55-56.
14. Nenye et al., *Finland at War: The Continuation and Lapland Wars*, p. 57.
15. Nenye et al., *Finland at War: The Continuation and Lapland Wars*, pp. 57-58.
16. Nenye et al., *Finland at War: The Continuation and Lapland Wars*, p. 61.
17. Nenye et al., *Finland at War: The Continuation and Lapland Wars*, pp. 52-53.

18. Nenye et al., *Finland at War: The Continuation and Lapland Wars*, p. 58.
19. Nenye et al., *Finland at War: The Continuation and Lapland Wars*, pp. 58-59.
20. The Secretary of State to the Minister in Finland (Schoenfeld), October 25th, 1941, Foreign Relations of the United States Diplomatic Papers, 1941, General, The Soviet Union, Volume I, p. 81, The Office of the Historian, accessed 10th December 2020:
https://history.state.gov/historicaldocuments/frus1941v01/pg_81
21. The Minister in Finland (Schoenfeld) to the Secretary of State, October 27th, 1941, Foreign Relations of the United States Diplomatic Papers, 1941, General, The Soviet Union, Volume I, p. 83, The Office of the Historian, accessed 10th December 2020:
https://history.state.gov/historicaldocuments/frus1941v01/pg_83
22. The Minister in Finland (Schoenfeld) to the Secretary of State, October 27th, 1941, Foreign Relations of the United States Diplomatic Papers, 1941, General, The Soviet Union, Volume I, pp. 83-84, The Office of the Historian, accessed 10th December 2020:
https://history.state.gov/historicaldocuments/frus1941v01/pg_83
23. National Archives, CAB 65/2/19.
24. "The British War Bluebook: Statement by the Prime Minister in the House of Commons on March 31, 1939," The Avalon Project, Yale Law School, 2008, accessed 23rd December 2019,
http://avalon.law.yale.edu/wwii/blbk17.asp
25. Bullock, *Hitler*, p. 505; Liddell Hart, *A History of the Second World War*, loc. 356; AJP Taylor, *The Origins of the Second World War*, (Penguin, London, 2001) loc. 3937.
26. National Archives, PREM 3/352/8.
27. Churchill, *The Grand Alliance*, pp. 412-413.
28. National Archives, FO 945/24B/394.
29. National Archives, FO 945/24B/439.
30. National Archives, CAB 66/19/18.
31. National Archives, FO 954/24B/517.
32. National Archives, FO 954/24B/521.
33. National Archives, CAB 65/24/10.
34. Churchill, *The Grand Alliance*, p. 419; Nenye et al., *Finland at War: The Continuation and Lapland Wars*, p. 133.
35. Steven Merritt Miner, *Between Churchill and Stalin: The Soviet Union, Great Britain and the Origins of the Grand Alliance* (Chapel Hill, University of North Carolina Press, 1988) p. 191.
36. National Archives, FO 954/25A/3, p. 1.
37. National Archives, FO 954/25A/3, p. 13.

38. National Archives, FO 954/25A/3, p. 18.
39. National Archives, FO 954/25A/3, p. 18.
40. National Archives, FO 954/25A/3, p. 18.
41. National Archives, FO 954/25A/3, p. 18.
42. National Archives, FO 954/25A/3, pp. 18-19.
43. National Archives, FO 954/25A/3, p. 19.
44. National Archives, FO 954/25A/3, p. 21.
45. National Archives, FO 954/25A/3, p. 21.
46. Miner, *Between Churchill and Stalin*, p. 193.
47. National Archives, CAB 66/21/28, p. 1.
48. National Archives, CAB 66/21/28, pp. 1-2.
49. National Archives, CAB 66/21/28, p. 3.
50. National Archives, CAB 66/21/28, p. 3.
51. National Archives, CAB 66/21/28, p. 2.
52. National Archives, CAB 66/21/28, p. 3.
53. National Archives, CAB 66/21/28, p. 3.

Chapter Ten

1. Roger Hermiston, *All Behind You, Winston: Churchill's Great Coalition 1940-45* (London, Aurum, 2016) pp. 123-124.
2. Hermiston, *All Behind You, Winston*, pp. 124-125.
3. Sumner Welles, memorandum of conversation, February 18th, 1942, Foreign Relations of the United States Diplomatic Papers, 1942, Europe, Volume 3, The Office of the Historian, accessed 10th December 2020: https://history.state.gov/historicaldocuments/frus1942v03/d430
4. Welles, memorandum of conversation, February 18th, 1942: https://history.state.gov/historicaldocuments/frus1942v03/d430
5. Welles, memorandum of conversation, February 18th, 1942: https://history.state.gov/historicaldocuments/frus1942v03/d430
6. Welles, memorandum of conversation, February 18th, 1942: https://history.state.gov/historicaldocuments/frus1942v03/d430
7. Hamilton, *Mantle of Command*, p. 91.
8. Hamilton, *Mantle of Command*, p. 94.
9. Hamilton, *Mantle of Command*, p. 135.
10. "1946-47 Part 1: The United Nations. Section 1: Origin and Evolution, Chapter A: The Declaration by United Nations," The Yearbook of The United Nations, accessed 15th February 2020: http://www.unmultimedia.org/searchers/yearbook/page.jsp?volume=1946-47&page=36

11. Welles, memorandum of conversation, February 18th 1942: https://history.state.gov/historicaldocuments/frus1942v03/d430
12. Nigel Hamilton, *Commander in Chief: FDR's Battle with Churchill, 1943* (London, Biteback Publishing, 2016), p. 279; Gregory J. Wallance, "Sex and the Secret Service," Los Angeles Times, 3rd May 2012, accessed 15th February 2020: http://articles.latimes.com/2012/may/03/opinion/la-oe-wallance-secret-service-20120503; Sumner Welles, correspondence with Roosevelt, 16th August 1943, pp. 48-49, Franklin D. Roosevelt, Papers as President, The President's Secretary's File (PSF) 1933-1945, Box 77, FDR Presidential Library & Museum, accessed 15th February 2020: http://www.fdrlibrary.marist.edu/archives/collections/franklin/?p=collections/findingaid&id=502&rootcontentid=140402&q=Sumner+Welles#id140612
13. National Archives, CAB 65/29/11.
14. National Archives, CAB 65/29/11.
15. National Archives, CAB 65/29/11.
16. National Archives, FO 954/25A/52.
17. Michael G. Walling, *Forgotten Sacrifice: The Arctic Convoys of World War II* (Oxford, Osprey Publishing, 2012) pp. 38-39.
18. Walling, *Forgotten Sacrifice,* p. 41.
19. Walling, *Forgotten Sacrifice,* p. 41.
20. Walling, *Forgotten Sacrifice,* p. 48.
21. Walling, *Forgotten Sacrifice,* p. 53; Churchill, *The Hinge of Fate*, p. 229.
22. Walling, *Forgotten Sacrifice,* p. 96.
23. Walling, *Forgotten Sacrifice,* pp. 97-98.
24. Walling, *Forgotten Sacrifice,* p. 102-104.
25. Walling, *Forgotten Sacrifice,* p. 104.
26. Walling, *Forgotten Sacrifice,* p. 104.
27. Rees, *World War Two: Behind Closed Doors,* loc. 2343.
28. Churchill, *The Hinge of Fate,* pp. 230-231.
29. National Archives, FO 954/25A/59.
30. Prime Minister to General Ismay, for C.O.S. Committee, quoted by Churchill, *The Hinge of Fate*, pp. 233-234.
31. Berthon and Potts, *Warlords,* Kindle loc. 2730.
32. Berthon and Potts, *Warlords,* Kindle loc. 2740.
33. Oleg Rzheshevsky (ed.), *War and Diplomacy: The Making of the Grand Documents from Stalin's Archives*, Amsterdam, 1996, Document 38, quoted by Berthon and Potts, *Warlords,* Kindle loc. 2760.
34. National Archives, HW 1/593.
35. Walling, *Forgotten Sacrifice,* p. 131.

36. Twenty Year Mutual Assistance Agreement Between the United Kingdom and the Union of Soviet Socialist Republics: May 26, 1942, Yale Law School: The Avalon Project, 2008, accessed 16th February 2020: http://avalon.law.yale.edu/wwii/brsov42.asp
37. Walling, *Forgotten Sacrifice,* pp. 131-132.
38. Walling, *Forgotten Sacrifice,* p. 133.
39. Walling, *Forgotten Sacrifice,* p. 133.
40. Walling, *Forgotten Sacrifice,* p. 138.
41. Walling, *Forgotten Sacrifice,* p. 143.
42. Walling, *Forgotten Sacrifice,* p. 144.
43. Walling, *Forgotten Sacrifice*, p. 149; Hastings, *Finest Years: Churchill as Warlord 1940-1945,* Kindle loc. 5361.

Chapter Eleven

1. Arthur Harris, *Bomber Offensive* (Barnsley, Pen & Sword, 2005) Kindle loc. 146.
2. Harris, *Bomber Offensive*, Kindle loc. 149.
3. Leo McKinstry, *Lancaster: The Second World War's Greatest Bomber* (John Murray, London, 2009) Kindle loc. 491.
4. McKinstry, *Lancaster*, Kindle loc. 492.
5. McKinstry, *Lancaster*, Kindle loc. 494.
6. McKinstry, *Lancaster*, Kindle loc. 503.
7. John Nichol, *Lancaster: The Forging of a Very British Legend* (London, Simon & Schuster UK, 2020) p. 49.
8. Nichol, *Lancaster*, p. 52; McKinstry, *Lancaster*, Kindle loc. 811.
9. Nichol, *Lancaster*, pp. 52-53.
10. Nichol, *Lancaster*, p. 53.
11. McKinstry, *Lancaster*, Kindle loc. 1609.
12. McKinstry, *Lancaster*, Kindle loc. 1683.
13. McKinstry, *Lancaster*, Kindle loc. 1475; Nichol, *Lancaster*, p. 54.
14. McKinstry, *Lancaster*, Kindle loc. 1492-1527.
15. McKinstry, *Lancaster*, Kindle loc. 1549.
16. "Cologne But a Beginning," Press and Journal, 10th June 1942; British Pathé, "On The Chin 1942," YouTube, accessed 31st August 2020: https://youtu.be/to4djmDqJRI
17. Lowe, *Inferno*, pp. 54-55.
18. Sir Charles Webster and Noble Frankland, *The Strategic Air Offensive Against Germany 1939-1945: Volume 1: Preparation* (Uckland, The Naval & Military Press, 2006) p. 144.
19. Lowe, *Inferno*, p. 55.

20. Webster and Frankland, *The Strategic Air Offensive Against Germany*, p. 145.
21. Webster and Frankland, *The Strategic Air Offensive Against Germany*, p. 149.
22. Webster and Frankland, *The Strategic Air Offensive Against Germany*, p. 150.
23. Webster and Frankland, *The Strategic Air Offensive Against Germany*, p. 150.
24. Lowe, *Inferno*, p. 56.
25. John Colville, *The Fringes of Power: Downing Street Diaries 1939-1955* (London, Phoenix, 2005) p. 192.
26. Lowe, *Inferno*, p. 56; Ullrich, *Hitler: Downfall 1939-45*, p. 128.
27. Shirer, *The Rise and Fall of The Third Reich*, p. 778.
28. Shirer, *The Rise and Fall of The Third Reich*, p. 778.
29. Shirer, *The Rise and Fall of The Third Reich*, pp. 779-780.
30. Shirer, *The Rise and Fall of The Third Reich*, pp. 780-781.
31. Webster and Frankland, *The Strategic Air Offensive Against Germany*, p. 153.
32. Webster and Frankland, *The Strategic Air Offensive Against Germany*, pp. 153-154.
33. Webster and Frankland, *The Strategic Air Offensive Against Germany*, p. 154.
34. Webster and Frankland, *The Strategic Air Offensive Against Germany*, p. 154.
35. Webster and Frankland, *The Strategic Air Offensive Against Germany*, pp. 154-155.
36. Webster and Frankland, *The Strategic Air Offensive Against Germany*, pp. 156-157.
37. Webster and Frankland, *The Strategic Air Offensive Against Germany*, p. 157.
38. Webster and Frankland, *The Strategic Air Offensive Against Germany*, p. 163.
39. Webster and Frankland, *The Strategic Air Offensive Against Germany*, pp. 163-164.
40. Webster and Frankland, *The Strategic Air Offensive Against Germany*, p. 165.
41. Harris, *Bomber Offensive*, Kindle loc. 1525.
42. Webster and Frankland, *The Strategic Air Offensive Against Germany*, p. 323; Max Hastings, *Bomber Command* (London, Pan Macmillan, 2010) p. 161.
43. Webster and Frankland, *The Strategic Air Offensive Against Germany*, p. 324; McKinstry, *Lancaster*, Kindle loc. 1689; Hastings, *Bomber*

Command, p. 162; Jörg Friedrich, *The Fire: The Bombing of Germany 1940-1945* (New York, Colombia University Press, 2006) p. 70.
44. Harris, *Bomber Offensive*, Kindle loc. 1295.
45. Harris, *Bomber Offensive*, Kindle loc. 1612.
46. McKinstry, *Lancaster*, Kindle loc. 1578-1587; Patrick Bishop, *Bomber Boys: Fighting Back 1940-1945* (London, Harper Perennial, 2008) p. 91.
47. McKinstry, *Lancaster*, Kindle loc. 1570.
48. A.C. Grayling, *Among the Dead Cities* (Bloomsbury, London 2011) Kindle loc. 712.
49. Hastings, *Bomber Command*, pp. 126-127.
50. Webster and Frankland, *The Strategic Air Offensive Against Germany*, p. 178; p. 247.
51. Webster and Frankland, *The Strategic Air Offensive Against Germany*, p. 178.
52. Webster and Frankland, *The Strategic Air Offensive Against Germany*, p. 178.
53. Webster and Frankland, *The Strategic Air Offensive Against Germany*, p. 180.
54. Harris, *Bomber Offensive*, loc. 1617.
55. Harris, *Bomber Offensive*, loc. 1616.
56. Harris, *Bomber Offensive*, loc. 1621.
57. National Archives, AIR 27/449/4.
58. Harris, *Bomber Offensive*, loc. 1622.
59. Harris, *Bomber Offensive*, loc. 1628.
60. Friedrich, *The Fire*, p. 70.
61. Harris to David Irving, quoted by Hastings, *Bomber Command*, p. 180.
62. Randall Hansen, *Fire and Fury: The Allied Bombing of Germany and Japan* (London, Faber & Faber, 2020) p. 76.
63. Hastings, *Bomber Command*, p. 180.
64. Bishop, *Bomber Boys*, p. 95.
65. Hansen, *Fire and Fury*, p. 75.
66. McKinstry, *Lancaster*, loc. 1720; Bishop, *Bomber Boys*, p. 95; Friedrich, *The Fire*, p. 71.
67. National Archives, AIR 27/626/5.
68. Bishop, *Bomber Boys*, p. 95.
69. Hastings, *Bomber Command*, p. 182.
70. Hansen, *Fire and Fury*, p. 91.
71. National Archives, AIR 27/449/6; McKinstry, *Lancaster*, Kindle loc. 1800.
72. National Archives, AIR 27/449/6; McKinstry, *Lancaster*, Kindle loc. 1802-1826.
73. National Archives, AIR 27/449/6.

74. McKinstry, *Lancaster*, Kindle loc. 1845; Nichol, *Lancaster*, p. 80.
75. Vannoy, *Deep Strike on Augsburg*, Warfare History Network, accessed 16th December 2020:
https://warfarehistorynetwork.com/2016/09/13/deep-strike-on-augsburg/
76. Nichol, *Lancaster*, p. 79; McKinstry, *Lancaster*, Kindle loc. 1826; Vannoy, *Deep Strike on Augsburg*, Warfare History Network.
77. Webster and Frankland, *The Strategic Air Offensive Against Germany*, p. 177.
78. Webster and Frankland, *The Strategic Air Offensive Against Germany*, p. 402.
79. Webster and Frankland, *The Strategic Air Offensive Against Germany*, p. 402.
80. Webster and Frankland, *The Strategic Air Offensive Against Germany*, p. 402; Grayling, *Among the Dead Cities*, loc. 821.
81. McKinstry, *Lancaster*, Kindle loc. 1853; Hansen, *Fire and Fury*, p. 92; Bishop, *Bomber Boys*, p. 97.
82. Hansen, *Fire and Fury*, p. 92.
83. Hansen, *Fire and Fury*, p. 93; McKinstry, *Lancaster*, Kindle loc. 1871.
84. Hansen, *Fire and Fury*, p. 93.
85. Harris, *Bomber Offensive*, Kindle loc. 1905; Hansen, *Fire and Fury*, pp. 93-94.
86. Bishop, *Bomber Boys*, p. 98.
87. National Archives, AIR 27/143/10.
88. National Archives, AIR 27/449/8.
89. Hastings, *Bomber Command*, pp. 153-159; Grayling, *Among the Dead Cities*, loc. 831.
90. Harris, *Bomber Offensive*, Kindle loc. 1258.
91. Roberts, *The Storm of War*, Kindle loc. 7966.
92. Rees, *World War Two: Behind Closed Doors*, loc. 2555.
93. Churchill, The Hinge of Fate, p. 241.
94. National Archives, FO 371/32911, quoted by Rees, *World War Two: Behind Closed Doors*, Kindle loc. 2608.
95. Rees, *World War Two: Behind Closed Doors,* Kindle loc. 2613.
96. Rees, *World War Two: Behind Closed Doors*, Kindle loc. 2620.
97. Churchill, *The Hinge of Fate*, p. 428.
98. National Archives, CAB 66/28/3.
99. National Archives, CAB 66/28/3.
100. National Archives, CAB 66/28/3.
101. National Archives, CAB 66/28/3.
102. National Archives, CAB 66/28/3.
103. National Archives, CAB 66/28/3.
104. Churchill, *The Hinge of Fate*, p. 433.

105. Churchill, *The Hinge of Fate*, p. 435.
106. National Archives, CAB 66/21/28, p. 3.
107. National Archives, CAB 66/28/3.
108. "The Fallen," UK Parliament, accessed 23rd March 2021: https://www.parliament.uk/business/publications/research/olympic-britain/crime-and-defence/the-fallen/
109. Welles, memorandum of conversation, February 18th 1942: https://history.state.gov/historicaldocuments/frus1942v03/d430

Chapter Twelve

1. Max Hastings, *All Hell Let Loose: The World at War 1939 – 1945* (London, William Collins, 2011) Kindle loc. 2789.
2. David Glantz, *Operation Barbarossa: Hitler's Invasion of Russia 1941* (The History Press, Cheltenham, 2011) Kindle loc. 210.
3. Glantz, *Operation Barbarossa*, Kindle loc. 213.
4. Chris Bellamy, *Absolute War: Soviet Russia in the Second World War* (London, Pan Books, 2009) pp. 166-167.
5. Stephen G. Fritz, *The First Soldier: Hitler as Military Leader* (London, Yale University Press, 2018) p. 7.
6. Fritz, *The First Soldier*, p. 31.
7. Fritz, *The First Soldier*, pp. 30-31, p. 33; Roberts, *The Storm of War*, Kindle loc. 2755.
8. Fritz, *The First Soldier*, p. 55.
9. David Stahel, *Operation Barbarossa and Germany's Defeat in the East* (Cambridge, Cambridge University Press) Kindle loc. 1078.
10. Stahel, *Operation Barbarossa*, loc. 1087; Fritz, *The First Soldier*, p. 133.
11. Fritz, *The First Soldier*, p. 133.
12. Fritz, *The First Soldier*, p. 134; Stahel, *Operation Barbarossa*, Kindle loc. 1105.
13. Stahel, *Operation Barbarossa*, Kindle loc. 1108.
14. Fritz, *The First Soldier*, p. 134.
15. Stahel, *Operation Barbarossa*, Kindle loc. 1111.
16. Stahel, *Operation Barbarossa*, Kindle loc. 1117.
17. Stahel, *Operation Barbarossa*, Kindle loc. 1143-1152.
18. Stahel, *Operation Barbarossa*, Kindle loc. 1159-1164.
19. Stahel, *Operation Barbarossa*, Kindle loc. 1232.
20. Stahel, *Operation Barbarossa*, Kindle loc. 1256.
21. Stahel, *Operation Barbarossa*, Kindle loc. 1236.
22. Stahel, *Operation Barbarossa*, Kindle loc. 1265.
23. Stahel, *Operation Barbarossa*, Kindle loc. 1275.

24. Stahel, *Operation Barbarossa*, Kindle loc. 1349.
25. Bellamy, *Absolute War*, p. 165.
26. Distance from Czyzew to Moscow, DistanceFromTo, accessed 12th April 2020: https://www.distancefromto.net/
27. Evans, *The Third Reich at War*, Kindle loc. 3089; Andrew Nagorski, *The Greatest Battle: Stalin, Hitler and the Desperate Struggle for Moscow That Changed the Course of World War II* (Nagorski, 2007) Kindle loc. 476.
28. Glantz, *Operation Barbarossa*, Kindle loc. 224.
29. Keith Cumins, *Cataclysm: The War on the Eastern Front 1941-45* (Solihull, Helion & Company Ltd, 2011) p. 307.
30. Glantz, *Operation Barbarossa*, Kindle loc. 488.
31. Cumins, *Cataclysm*, pp. 12-13; Stahel, *Operation Barbarossa*, Kindle loc. 4099.
32. Cumins, *Cataclysm*, p. 11; Holland, *The War in the West: Volume 1*, Kindle loc. 3624.
33. Holland, *The War in the West: Volume 1*, Kindle loc. 3641.
34. Stahel, *Operation Barbarossa*, Kindle loc. 3393; Hastings, *All Hell Let Loose*, Kindle loc. 2800.
35. Glantz, *Operation Barbarossa*, Kindle loc. 254-255; Liddell Hart, *A History of the Second World War*, Kindle loc. 2952; V.E. Tarrant, Stalingrad (London, Leo Cooper, 1992) p. 15.
36. Glantz, *Operation Barbarossa*, Kindle loc. 194; Liddell Hart, *A History of the Second World War*, Kindle loc. 2994.
37. Stahel, *Operation Barbarossa*, Kindle loc. 4102.
38. Stahel, *Operation Barbarossa*, Kindle loc. 4430.
39. Stahel, *Operation Barbarossa*, Kindle loc. 4120.
40. Stahel, *Operation Barbarossa*, Kindle loc. 4126.
41. Nagorski, *The Greatest Battle*, Kindle loc. 1152; Stahel, *Operation Barbarossa*, Kindle loc. 4170-4174; James Lucas, *War on the Eastern Front: The German Soldier in Russia 1941-1945* (Frontline Books, Barnsley, 2014) Kindle loc. 2377.
42. Glantz, *Operation Barbarossa*, loc. 284.
43. James Holland: *The War in the West, Volume II: The Allies Fight Back 1941-1943* (London, Corgi Books, 2017) pp. 24-25.
44. Len Deighton, *Blitzkrieg: From the Rise of Hitler to the Fall of Dunkirk* (London, William Collins, 2014) p. 179; Stahel, *Operation Barbarossa*, Kindle loc. 3347.
45. Deighton, *Blitzkrieg*, p. 178.
46. Hastings, *All Hell Broke Loose*, loc. 2800-2802; Antony Beevor, *Stalingrad* (London, Penguin, 2007) Kindle loc. 369.
47. Stahel, *Operation Barbarossa*, Kindle loc. 3359.

48. Stahel, *Operation Barbarossa*, Kindle loc. 3363.
49. Tarrant, *Stalingrad*, pp. 5-6.
50. Evans, *The Third Reich at War*, Kindle loc. 3837.
51. Stahel, *Operation Barbarossa*, Kindle loc. 4216.
52. Stahel, *Operation Barbarossa*, Kindle loc. 4242-4256.
53. Cumins, *Cataclysm*, p. 304; Stahel, *Operation Barbarossa*, Kindle loc. 4430.
54. Stahel, *Operation Barbarossa*, Kindle loc. 4445.
55. Cumins, *Cataclysm*, p. 305.
56. Stahel, *Operation Barbarossa*, Kindle loc. 4460.
57. Cumins, *Cataclysm*, p. 18.
58. Bellamy, *Absolute War*, p. 190.
59. Stahel, *Operation Barbarossa*, Kindle loc. 4577.
60. Bellamy, *Absolute War*, p. 193; Glantz, *Operation Barbarossa*, Kindle loc. 546.
61. Gilbert, *The Second World War*, Kindle loc. 4650.
62. Nagorski, *The Greatest Battle*, Kindle loc. 1343-1348.
63. Nagorski, *The Greatest Battle*, Kindle loc. 1584-1589.
64. "The Execution of Admiral Byng," History Today, accessed 27th April 2020: https://www.historytoday.com/archive/months-past/execution-admiral-byng
65. Voltaire, *Candide* (Project Gutenberg, 2006) p. 122, accessed 23rd September 2021: https://www.gutenberg.org/cache/epub/19942/pg19942-images.html#Page_122
66. Voltaire, *Candide*, p. 123, accessed 23rd September 2021: https://www.gutenberg.org/cache/epub/19942/pg19942-images.html#Page_123
67. Holland, *The War in the West: Volume 2*, Kindle loc. 491-493; Hastings, *All Hell Let Loose*, Kindle loc. 2828.
68. Glantz, *Operation Barbarossa*, Kindle loc. 538-540; 3251.
69. Gilbert, *The Second World War*, Kindle loc. 4600.
70. Stahel, *Operation Barbarossa*, Kindle loc. 4937.
71. Stahel, *Operation Barbarossa*, Kindle loc. 5057.
72. Gilbert, *The Second World War*, Kindle loc. 4576.
73. Hastings, *All Hell Let Loose*, Kindle loc. 3019.
74. Stahel, *Operation Barbarossa*, Kindle loc. 3498.
75. Stahel, *Operation Barbarossa*, Kindle loc. 5547.
76. Stahel, *Operation Barbarossa*, Kindle loc. 5546.
77. Stahel, *Operation Barbarossa*, Kindle loc. 5584-5590.
78. Stahel, *Operation Barbarossa*, Kindle loc. 5601.
79. Stahel, *Operation Barbarossa*, Kindle loc. 5619.
80. Stahel, *Operation Barbarossa*, Kindle loc. 5626-5631.

81. Stahel, *Operation Barbarossa*, Kindle loc. 5676.
82. Stahel, *Operation Barbarossa*, Kindle loc. 6849.
83. Bellamy, *Absolute War*, p. 243.
84. Stahel, *Operation Barbarossa*, Kindle loc. 7892.
85. Stahel, *Operation Barbarossa*, Kindle loc. 8040.
86. Stahel, *Operation Barbarossa*, Kindle loc. 8054.
87. Stahel, *Operation Barbarossa*, Kindle loc. 7881.
88. Stahel, *Operation Barbarossa*, Kindle loc. 7884; 8049; 8069.
89. Stahel, *Operation Barbarossa*, Kindle loc. 8135.
90. Stahel, *Operation Barbarossa*, Kindle loc. 8076; 8138.
91. Stahel, *Operation Barbarossa*, Kindle loc. 7901.
92. Stahel, *Operation Barbarossa*, Kindle loc. 7903.

Chapter Thirteen

1. National Archives, FO 954/24B/346.
2. National Archives, FO 954/24B/248.
3. Stahel, *Operation Barbarossa*, Kindle loc. 1147.
4. Wynne, *Stopping Hitler*, p. 11.
5. Hansard, Commons Sitting, 3rd April 1939, accessed 13th January 2021: https://hansard.parliament.uk/Commons/1939-04-03/debates/817ee449-6976-4e08-b600-1d08461b1e27/EuropeanSituation#contribution-ff720333-7e46-48f1-854d-5742472b1767
6. Michael Jones, *The Retreat: Hitler's First Defeat* (John Murray, London, 2009) Kindle loc. 471.
7. Jones, *The Retreat*, Kindle loc. 485.
8. Jones, *The Retreat*, Kindle loc. 508.
9. Jones, *The Retreat*, Kindle loc. 506; loc. 516-531; Beevor, *Stalingrad*, Kindle loc. 629.
10. Jones, *The Retreat*, Kindle loc. 536.
11. Alan Clark, *Barbarossa: The Russian-German Conflict 1941-45* (London, Cassell, 2005) pp. 147-148.
12. Nagorski, *The Greatest Battle*, Kindle loc. 2135; loc. 2438; Beevor, *Stalingrad*, Kindle loc. 710.
13. Jones, *The Retreat*, Kindle loc. 760.
14. Jones, *The Retreat*, Kindle loc. 890.
15. Jones, *The Retreat*, Kindle loc. 880.
16. Nagorski, *The Greatest Battle*, Kindle loc. 2517.
17. Nagorski, *The Greatest Battle*, Kindle loc. 3091.
18. Nagorski, *The Greatest Battle*, Kindle loc. 3134.
19. Nagorski, *The Greatest Battle*, Kindle loc. 3363.

20. Nagorski, *The Greatest Battle*, Kindle loc. 3368.
21. Nagorski, *The Greatest Battle*, Kindle loc. 3370.
22. Rees, *World War Two: Behind Closed Doors*, Kindle loc. 1869.
23. Beevor, *Stalingrad*, Kindle loc. 722.
24. Evans, *The Third Reich at War*, Kindle loc. 3939; 3943.
25. Evans, *The Third Reich at War*, Kindle loc. 3950.
26. Evans, *The Third Reich at War*, Kindle loc. 3952.
27. Lucas, *War on The Eastern Front*, Kindle loc. 1800.
28. Lucas, *War on The Eastern Front*, Kindle loc. 1817.
29. Lucas, *War on The Eastern Front*, Kindle loc. 1819.
30. Lucas, *War on The Eastern Front*, Kindle loc. 1840.
31. Jones, *The Retreat*, Kindle loc. 1257.
32. Jones, *The Retreat*, Kindle loc. 2067.
33. Nagorski, *The Greatest Battle*, Kindle loc. 4460; Jones, *The Retreat*, Kindle loc. 2230.
34. Jones, *The Retreat*, Kindle loc. 2237.
35. Nagorski, *The Greatest Battle*, Kindle loc. 4619.
36. Nagorski, *The Greatest Battle*, Kindle loc. 4465.
37. Evans, *The Third Reich at War*, Kindle loc. 4024.
38. Evans, *The Third Reich at War*, Kindle loc. 4026.
39. Evans, *The Third Reich at War*, Kindle loc. 4027.
40. Evans, *The Third Reich at War*, Kindle loc. 4029.
41. Evans, *The Third Reich at War*, Kindle loc. 4036.
42. Evans, *The Third Reich at War*, Kindle loc. 4038; Ullrich, *Hitler: Downfall 1939-45*, p. 226.
43. Ullrich, *Hitler: Downfall 1939-45*, p. 227.
44. Gilbert, *The Second World War*, p. 270.
45. Clark, *Barbarossa*, pp. 180-181.
46. Churchill, *The Grand Alliance*, pp. 476-477.

Chapter Fourteen

1. William Craig, *Enemy at the Gates: The Battle for Stalingrad* (Old Saybrook, Konecky & Konecky, 1973) p. 36; Cumins, *Cataclysm*, pp. 105-106.
2. Craig, *Enemy at the Gates*, p. 37; Tarrant, *Stalingrad*, p. 49.
3. Craig, *Enemy at the Gates*, p. 33; Tarrant, *Stalingrad*, p. 51.
4. Joel S. A. Hayward, *Stopped at Stalingrad: The Luftwaffe and Hitler's Defeat in the East 1942-1943* (Lawrence, University Press of Kansas, 1998) p. 188.

5. Tarrant, *Stalingrad*, p. 48.
6. Craig, *Enemy at the Gates*, pp. 58-59; Tarrant, *Stalingrad*, p. 54; Cumins, *Cataclysm*, pp. 104-105; Clark, *Barbarossa*, pp. 217-218; Ullrich, *Hitler: Downfall 1939-1945*, p. 320.
7. Hayward, *Stopped at Stalingrad*, p. 188.
8. Hayward, *Stopped at Stalingrad*, p. 187.
9. Hayward, *Stopped at Stalingrad*, pp. 134-135.
10. Beevor, *Stalingrad*, pp. 106-107.
11. Tarrant, *Stalingrad*, p. 52; Craig, *Enemy at the Gates*, p. 51; Hayward, *Stopped at Stalingrad*, p. 187.
12. Tarrant, *Stalingrad*, p. 52.
13. Tarrant, *Stalingrad*, p. 52.
14. Tarrant, *Stalingrad*, pp. 51-52; Hayward, *Stopped at Stalingrad*, p. 189.
15. Tarrant, *Stalingrad*, p. 54; Beevor, *Stalingrad*, p. 110.
16. Hayward, *Stopped at Stalingrad*, p. 143.
17. Hayward, *Stopped at Stalingrad*, p. 131.
18. Hayward, *Stopped at Stalingrad*, pp. 188-189.
19. Clark, *Barbarossa*, p. 218; Cumins, *Cataclysm*, p. 106.
20. *Fuehrer Directives and Other Top-Level Directives of The German Armed Forces, 1942-1945* (Washington, U.S. Office of Naval Intelligence, 1948) p. 17.
21. *Fuehrer Directives*, p. 17.
22. *Fuehrer Directives*, p. 18.
23. *Fuehrer Directives*, p. 18.
24. Noakes and Pridham, *Nazism*, p. 231; Hayward, *Stopped at Stalingrad*, p. 24.
25. *Fuehrer Directives*, p. 18.
26. Hayward, *Stopped at Stalingrad*, p. 24.
27. *Fuehrer Directives*, p. 18.
28. *Fuehrer Directives*, p. 19; Hayward, *Stopped at Stalingrad*, p. 24.
29. *Fuehrer Directives*, p. 19.
30. Hayward, *Stopped at Stalingrad*, p. 23.
31. Hayward, *Stopped at Stalingrad*, pp. 19-20; Fritz, *The First Soldier*, p. 242.
32. Peter Longerich, *Hitler: A Life* (Oxford, Oxford University Press, 2019) p. 781.
33. Longerich, *Hitler: A Life*, pp. 781-782.
34. Hayward, *Stopped at Stalingrad*, p. 15.
35. Longerich, *Hitler: A Life*, pp. 797-798; Fritz, *The First Soldier*, p. 240.
36. Hayward, *Stopped at Stalingrad*, p. 18.
37. Hayward, *Stopped at Stalingrad*, pp. 18-19.
38. Hayward, *Stopped at Stalingrad*, p. 19.

39. Galeazzo Ciano, *The Ciano Diaries 1939-1943* (Safety Harbor, Simon Publications, 2001) p. 477.
40. Ciano, *The Ciano Diaries*, p. 478.
41. Hayward, *Stopped at Stalingrad*, p. 18; Shirer, *The Rise and Fall of The Third Reich*, p. 909.
42. Hayward, *Stopped at Stalingrad*, p. 130.
43. Hayward, *Stopped at Stalingrad*, p. 130.
44. Ciano, *The Ciano Diaries*, p. 440.
45. Shirer, *The Rise and Fall of The Third Reich*, p. 910.
46. Shirer, *The Rise and Fall of The Third Reich*, p. 911.
47. Cumins, *Cataclysm*, p. 311.
48. Cumins, *Cataclysm*, p. 92.
49. Hayward, *Stopped at Stalingrad*, pp. 133-134.
50. Hayward, *Stopped at Stalingrad*, pp. 136-137.
51. Hayward, *Stopped at Stalingrad*, p. 137.
52. Hayward, *Stopped at Stalingrad*, p. 137.
53. Cumins, *Cataclysm*, p. 312.
54. Hayward, *Stopped at Stalingrad*, p. 137.
55. Cumins, *Cataclysm*, p. 312.
56. Hayward, *Stopped at Stalingrad*, p. 137.
57. Hayward, *Stopped at Stalingrad*, p. 138.
58. Hayward, *Stopped at Stalingrad*, p. 138.
59. Hayward, *Stopped in Stalingrad*, p. 138.
60. Hayward, *Stopped in Stalingrad*, p. 138.
61. Hayward, *Stopped in Stalingrad*, p. 139.
62. Hayward, *Stopped in Stalingrad*, pp. 139-140; Cumins, *Cataclysm*, pp. 311-312.
63. Cumins, *Cataclysm*, p. 96; Clark, *Barbarossa*, pp. 209-210.
64. Clark, *Barbarossa*, p. 212.
65. Hayward, *Stopped at Stalingrad*, p. 141.
66. Cumins, *Cataclysm*, p. 92.
67. *Fuehrer Directives*, p. 42.
68. *Fuehrer Directives*, p. 42.
69. *Fuehrer Directives*, p. 42.
70. *Fuehrer Directives*, p. 42.
71. Clark, *Barbarossa*, p. 191.
72. Clark, *Barbarossa*, p. 211.
73. Clark, *Barbarossa*, p. 212.
74. Fritz, *The First Soldier*, p. 259.
75. Hayward, *Stopped at Stalingrad*, pp. 186-187.
76. Hayward, *Stopped at Stalingrad*, p. 186; Beevor, *Stalingrad*, pp. 113-114.

77. Beevor, *Stalingrad*, p. 112.
78. Beevor, *Stalingrad*, p. 115.
79. Tarrant, *Stalingrad*, p. 60; Hayward, *Stopped at Stalingrad*, p. 191.
80. Tarrant, *Stalingrad*, p. 60.
81. Hayward, *Stopped at Stalingrad*, p. 191; Tarrant, *Stalingrad*, p. 62.
82. Tarrant, *Stalingrad*, p. 62.
83. Tarrant, *Stalingrad*, pp. 62-63.
84. Hayward, *Stopped at Stalingrad*, p. 191.
85. Hayward, *Stopped at Stalingrad*, p. 192.
86. Tarrant, *Stalingrad*, p. 74; Clark, *Barbarossa*, p. 223.
87. Clark, *Barbarossa*, p. 225.
88. Clark, *Barbarossa*, p. 226; Tarrant, *Stalingrad*, pp. 77-78.
89. Clark, *Barbarossa*, pp. 225-226; Tarrant, *Stalingrad*, p. 78.
90. Clark, *Barbarossa*, p. 228.
91. Clark, *Barbarossa*, p. 232; Beevor, *Stalingrad*, p. 159.
92. Clark, *Barbarossa*, p. 232.
93. Beevor, *Stalingrad*, p. 161.
94. Beevor, *Stalingrad*, p. 163.
95. Beevor, *Stalingrad*, p. 164.
96. Clark, *Barbarossa*, p. 224.
97. Tarrant, *Stalingrad*, p. 60.
98. Beevor, *Stalingrad*, p. 221.
99. Tarrant, *Stalingrad*, p. 98; Beevor, *Stalingrad*, p. 226.
100. Tarrant, *Stalingrad*, pp. 87-89.
101. Tarrant, *Stalingrad*, p. 90.
102. Tarrant, *Stalingrad*, pp. 102-103.
103. Beevor, *Stalingrad*, pp. 241-242.
104. Craig, *Enemy at the Gates*, p. 160; Tarrant, *Stalingrad*, p. 105.
105. Beevor, *Stalingrad*, p. 244; Tarrant, *Stalingrad*, p. 106.
106. Tarrant, *Stalingrad*, p. 106.
107. Tarrant, *Stalingrad*, p. 106.
108. Tarrant, *Stalingrad*, p. 107.
109. Tarrant, *Stalingrad*, p. 107.
110. Clark, *Barbarossa*, pp 247-248.
111. Tarrant, *Stalingrad*, pp. 107-110.
112. Tarrant, *Stalingrad*, pp. 117-118.
113.Shirer, *The Rise and Fall of the Third Reich*, p. 922.
114. Shirer, *The Rise and Fall of the Third Reich*, pp. 925-926.
115. Ullrich, *Hitler: Downfall 1939-45*, p. 331.
116. Shirer, *The Rise and Fall of the Third Reich*, p. 926.
117. Hayward, *Stopped in Stalingrad*, p. 235.
118. Shirer, *The Rise and Fall of the Third Reich*, pp. 925-926.

119. Shirer, *The Rise and Fall of the Third Reich*, p. 926.
120. Shirer, *The Rise and Fall of the Third Reich*, pp. 925-928.
121. Shirer, *The Rise and Fall of the Third Reich*, p. 928.
122. Shirer, *The Rise and Fall of the Third Reich*, pp. 928-929; Ciano, *The Ciano Diaries*, pp. 555-556.
123. Ciano, *The Ciano Diaries*, pp. 556-557.
124. Shirer, *The Rise and Fall of the Third Reich*, p. 929.
125. Shirer, *The Rise and Fall of the Third Reich*, p. 931.
126. Shirer, *The Rise and Fall of the Third Reich*, p. 932.
127. Hansard, Commons Sitting, 2nd August 1944, accessed 12th September 2021: https://hansard.parliament.uk/Commons/1944-08-02/debates/915a1711-27da-45c8-bae7-d47f8133a3fa/WarSituation#contribution-3181d331-cd68-46d2-b3e0-4b99d02de900

Chapter Fifteen

1. Bailey, *Arsenal of Democracy*, Kindle loc. 3716.
2. Bailey, *Arsenal of Democracy*, Kindle loc. 3734.
3. Memorandum by Prime Minister for Chiefs of Staff Committee, quoted by Churchill, *The Grand Alliance*, pp. 508-509.
4. Churchill, *The Grand Alliance*, pp. 508-509.
5. Webster and Frankland, *The Strategic Air Offensive Against Germany*, pp. 168-169.
6. Bishop, *Bomber Boys*, pp. 7-8.
7. Webster and Frankland, *The Strategic Air Offensive Against Germany*, pp. 169-170.
8. "Fireside Chat No. 15," May 26th, 1940, Master Speech File 1898-1945, Box 52, Franklin D. Roosevelt Library and Museum, accessed 25th January 2021: http://www.fdrlibrary.marist.edu/archives/collections/franklin/index.php?p=collections/findingaid&id=582
9. Herman, *Freedom's Forge*, pp. 66-67.
10. Herman, *Freedom's Forge*, pp. 18-19.
11. Herman, *Freedom's Forge*, pp 21-22.
12. Herman, *Freedom's Forge*, p. 31.
13. Herman, *Freedom's Forge*, p. 21.
14. Herman, *Freedom's Forge*, p. 24-25.
15. Herman, *Freedom's Forge*, p. 32.
16. Herman, *Freedom's Forge*, pp. 33-35.
17. Herman, *Freedom's Forge*, p. 36.

18. Herman, *Freedom's Forge*, pp. 69-70.
19. Herman, *Freedom's Forge*, pp. 70-71.
20. Herman, *Freedom's Forge*, p. 76.
21. Herman, *Freedom's Forge*, p. 113.
22. Herman, *Freedom's Forge*, pp. 114-115.
23. Herman, *Freedom's Forge*, pp. 114-115.
24. Maury Klein, *A Call to Arms: Mobilizing America for World War II* (New York, Bloomsbury, 2013) p. 459.
25. Klein, *A Call to Arms*, p. 459.
26. Herman, *Freedom's Forge*, p. 219.
27. Herman, *Freedom's Forge*, p. 221.
28. Herman, *Freedom's Forge*, pp. 225-226.
29. Herman, *Freedom's Forge*, pp. 228-229.
30. Herman, *Freedom's Forge*, p. 227.
31. Klein, *A Call to Arms*, p. 531.
32. Herman, *Freedom's Forge*, p. 229.
33. Roy Brazier, *The USAAF in Suffolk* (Stroud, Fonthill Media, 2017) Kindle loc. 261.
34. Herman, *Freedom's Forge*, p. 236.
35. Herman, *Freedom's Forge*, pp. 238-239.
36. Herman, *Freedom's Forge*, p. 239.
37. Herman, *Freedom's Forge*, p. 242.
38. "Building Bechtel: Projects and Partnerships Throughout our History," bechtel.com, accessed 16th July 2020: https://www.bechtel.com/who-is-bechtel/timeline.html#d1940
39. Herman, *Freedom's Forge*, p. 200.
40. Herman, *Freedom's Forge*, p. 247.
41. Klein, *A Call to Arms*, p. 675; "Willow Run B-24 Bombers – The Henry Ford's Innovation Nation," YouTube, accessed 16th July 2020: https://www.youtube.com/watch?v=zWAWuTlUpO4
42. Churchill, *The Grand Alliance*, pp. 476-477.
43. Hansen, *Fire and Fury*, pp. 58-60.
44. Norden Retirees Club, "History," nordenretireesclub.org, accessed 16th July 2020: http://nordenretireesclub.org/norden_bio.htm
45. Hansen, *Fire and Fury*, pp. 61-62.
46. Hansen, *Fire and Fury*, p. 70.
47. Hansen, *Fire and Fury*, p. 71.
48. Hansen, *Fire and Fury*, p. 72.
49. Keith Lowe, *Inferno: The Devastation of Hamburg, 1945* (London, Penguin, 2007) pp. 64-65.
50. Lowe, *Inferno*, p. 67.

51. Webster and Frankland, *The Strategic Air Offensive Against Germany*, p. 355.
52. Webster and Frankland, *The Strategic Air Offensive Against Germany*, pp. 358-359.
53. Webster and Frankland, *The Strategic Air Offensive Against Germany*, pp. 360-361.
54. Webster and Frankland, *The Strategic Air Offensive Against Germany*, p. 361.
55. Webster and Frankland, *The Strategic Air Offensive Against Germany*, p. 361.
56. Webster and Frankland, *The Strategic Air Offensive Against Germany*, p. 366.
57. Webster and Frankland, *The Strategic Air Offensive Against Germany*, p. 366.
58. Webster and Frankland, *The Strategic Air Offensive Against Germany*, p. 366.
59. Webster and Frankland, *The Strategic Air Offensive Against Germany*, pp. 366-367.
60. Webster and Frankland, *The Strategic Air Offensive Against Germany*, p. 373.
61. Webster and Frankland, *The Strategic Air Offensive Against Germany*, pp. 372-373.
62. Webster and Frankland, *The Strategic Air Offensive Against Germany*, p. 371.
63. Webster and Frankland, *The Strategic Air Offensive Against Germany*, p. 374.
64. Hoover, *Freedom Betrayed,* Kindle loc. 8094.
65. Webster and Frankland, *The Strategic Air Offensive Against Germany*, p. 377.
66. Webster and Frankland, *The Strategic Air Offensive Against Germany*, p. 378.
67. Webster and Frankland, *The Strategic Air Offensive Against Germany*, p. 379.
68. Webster and Frankland, *The Strategic Air Offensive Against Germany*, p. 379.
69. Hansen, *Fire and Fury*, p. 150.

Chapter Sixteen

1. Winston Churchill, "War Leader," International Churchill Society, accessed 5th October 2020: https://winstonchurchill.org/the-life-of-churchill/war-leader/
2. Machiavelli, *Il Principe*, Chapter 15 (translation by Kenneth Duthie.)
3. National Archives, FO 954/25A/59.
4. Peter Hitchens, *The Rage Against God* (London, Bloomsbury, 2011) Kindle loc. 791; Winston Churchill, "Their Finest Hour," International Churchill Society, accessed 2nd February 2021: https://winstonchurchill.org/resources/speeches/1940-the-finest-hour/their-finest-hour/
5. Machiavelli, *Il Principe*, Chapter 18 (translation by Kenneth Duthie.)
6. Rees, *World War Two: Behind Closed Doors*, loc. 3087.
7. Berthon and Potts, *Warlords*, loc. 3429.
8. Winston Churchill, correspondence with Franklin Roosevelt dated 13th August 1943, available at: Franklin D. Roosevelt, Papers as President: The President's Secretary's File (PSF), 1933-1945 | Franklin D. Roosevelt Presidential Library & Museum, Box 37, Great Britain, - Churchill, Winston, 1942-1943, p. 59, accessed 27th August 2020: http://www.fdrlibrary.marist.edu/archives/collections/franklin/?p=collections/findingaid&id=502
9. Sir Owen O'Malley, British Embassy to Poland, correspondence with Anthony Eden dated 24th May 1943, available at: Franklin D. Roosevelt, Papers as President: The President's Secretary's File (PSF), 1933-1945 | Franklin D. Roosevelt Presidential Library & Museum, Box 37, Great Britain, - Churchill, Winston, 1942-1943, p. 61, accessed 27th August 2020: http://www.fdrlibrary.marist.edu/archives/collections/franklin/?p=collections/findingaid&id=502
10. Sir Owen O'Malley, correspondence with Anthony Eden, pp. 61-62.
11. Sir Owen O'Malley, correspondence with Anthony Eden, p. 62.
12. Sir Owen O'Malley, correspondence with Anthony Eden, p. 62.
13. Churchill, *The Hinge of Fate*, p. 678.
14. Churchill, *The Hinge of Fate*, p. 679; Sir Owen O'Malley, correspondence with Anthony Eden, p. 62.
15. Sir Owen O'Malley, correspondence with Anthony Eden, p. 62.
16. Sir Owen O'Malley, correspondence with Anthony Eden, pp. 62-63.
17. Sir Owen O'Malley, correspondence with Anthony Eden, p. 63.
18. Sir Owen O'Malley, correspondence with Anthony Eden, p. 63.
19. Sir Owen O'Malley, correspondence with Anthony Eden, p. 63.
20. Sir Owen O'Malley, correspondence with Anthony Eden, p. 63.
21. Sir Owen O'Malley, correspondence with Anthony Eden, p. 63.

22. Sir Owen O'Malley, correspondence with Anthony Eden, p. 63.
23. Sir Owen O'Malley, correspondence with Anthony Eden, p. 63.
24. Sir Owen O'Malley, correspondence with Anthony Eden, pp. 63-65.
25. Berthon and Potts, *Warlords*, p. 185.
26. Rees, *World War Two: Behind Closed Doors*, p. 4.
27. Berthon and Potts, *Warlords*, pp;. 185-186; William Manchester, *The Last Lion: Winston Spencer Churchill, Defender of The Realm, 1940-1965* (Bello, London, 2015) Kindle loc. 14428.
28. Manchester, *The Last Lion, 1940-1965*, Kindle loc. 14429.
29. Manchester, *The Last Lion, 1940-1965*, Kindle loc. 14432.
30. Churchill, *The Hinge of Fate*, pp. 233-234.
31. Machiavelli, *Il Principe*, Chapter 18 (translation by Kenneth Duthie.)
32. National Archives, FO 371/34577, quoted by Eugenia Maresch, *Katyn 1940: The Documentary Evidence of The West's Betrayal* (Cheltenham, The History Press, 2020) pp. 68-69.
33. Maresch, *Katyn*, p. 43.
34. Reynolds and Pechatnov, *The Kremlin Letters*, pp. 237-238.
35. Reynolds and Pechatnov, *The Kremlin Letters*, pp. 243-244.
36. Sir Owen O'Malley, correspondence with Anthony Eden, p. 66.
37. Sir Owen O'Malley, correspondence with Anthony Eden, p. 66.
38. Churchill, *The Hinge of Fate*, pp. 680-681.
39. Churchill, *The Hinge of Fate*, p. 681.
40. National Archives, CAB 66/28/3.
41. Hansen, *Fire and Fury*, pp. 155-156.
42. McKinstry, *Lancaster*, Kindle loc. 6070.
43. R.V. Jones, *Most Secret War* (London, Penguin, 2009) Kindle loc. 297.
44. Hansen, *Fire and Fury*, p. 155.
45. McKinstry, *Lancaster*, Kindle loc. 6149; Hastings, *Bomber Command*, p. 258.
46. National Archives, AIR 27/687/14.
47. Hansen, *Fire and Fury*, p. 157.
48. McKinstry, *Lancaster*, Kindle loc. 6173.
49. National Archives, AIR 27/450/13.
50. National Archives, CAB 65/1/11.
51. Hastings, *Bomber Command*, p. 259.
52. Hastings, *Bomber Command*, p. 259.
53. Lowe, *Inferno*, p. 129.
54. Lowe, *Inferno*, p. 133.
55. Lowe, *Inferno*, p. 133.
56. Lowe, *Inferno*, p. 145.
57. Lowe, *Inferno*, p. 135.
58. Lowe, *Inferno*, p. 150.

59. Lowe, *Inferno*, p. 147.
60. Lowe, *Inferno*, p. 147.
61. Lowe, *Inferno*, p. 149.
62. Lowe, *Inferno*, p. 149.
63. Lowe, *Inferno*, p. 150.
64. Lowe, *Inferno*, p. 151.
65. Lowe, *Inferno*, p. 155.
66. Lowe, *Inferno*, p. 154.
67. Lowe, *Inferno*, p. 161.
68. Lowe, *Inferno*, p. 162.
69. Lowe, *Inferno*, p. 162.
70. Lowe, *Inferno*, p. 164.
71. Lowe, *Inferno*, p. 165.
72. Lowe, *Inferno*, p. 166.
73. Lowe, *Inferno*, p. 167.
74. Lowe, *Inferno*, p. 169.
75. Lowe, *Inferno*, p. 169-170.
76. Lowe, *Inferno*, p. 172.
77. Lowe, *Inferno*, p. 172-173.
78. Lowe, *Inferno*, p. 165.
79. Lowe, *Inferno*, p. 173.
80. Lowe, *Inferno*, p. 186.
81. Lowe, *Inferno*, p. 187.
82. McKinstry, *Lancaster*, Kindle loc. 6200; Lowe, *Inferno*, pp. 200-201.
83. Friedrich, *The Fire*, pp. 166-167.
84. Lowe, *Inferno*, p. 201; McKinstry, *Lancaster*, Kindle loc. 6206.
85. McKinstry, *Lancaster*, Kindle loc. 6209.
86. Evans, *The Third Reich at War*, p. 444.
87. Lowe, *Inferno*, p. 216.
88. Lowe, *Inferno*, p. 211.
89. Lowe, *Inferno*, p. 219.
90. National Archives, AIR 27/1930/14.
91. National Archives, AIR 27/1041/36.
92. National Archives, AIR 27/1041/36.
93. Churchill, *The Gathering Storm*, p. 133.
94. Marquess of Salisbury to Sinclair, 26th November 1943, RAF Museum, Harris Papers H79, quoted by McKinstry, Lancaster, Kindle loc. 7259.
95. Hastings, *All Hell Let Loose*, Kindle loc. 109.
96. Lowe, *Inferno*, p. 236.
97. Lowe, *Inferno*, p. 236.
98. Lowe, *Inferno*, p. 237.
99. Lowe, *Inferno*, pp. 238-239; McKinstry, *Lancaster*, Kindle loc. 6250.

100. Lowe, *Inferno*, p. 238.
101. Lowe, *Inferno*, p. 240-241.
102. Lowe, *Inferno*, p. 235.
103. Lowe, *Inferno*, p. 247.
104. Harris to Freeman, 29th April 1942, RAF Museum, Harris Papers H16, quoted by McKinstry, *Lancaster*, Kindle loc. 1760.
105. Harris, *Bomber Offensive*, Kindle loc. 853.
106. "Cologne But a Beginning," Press and Journal, 10th June 1942; British Pathé, "On The Chin 1942," YouTube, accessed 31st August 2020: https://youtu.be/to4djmDqJRI
107. "Richard Rapier Stokes," Grace's Guide to British Industrial History, 1st March 2015, accessed 28th August 2020: https://www.gracesguide.co.uk/Richard_Rapier_Stokes
108. Hansard, Commons Sitting, 19th May 1942, accessed 28th August 2020: https://api.parliament.uk/historic-hansard/commons/1942/may/19/war-situation#S5CV0380P0_19420519_HOC_423
109. Hansard, Commons Sitting, 6th March 1945, accessed 28th August 2020: https://api.parliament.uk/historic-hansard/commons/1945/mar/06/air-estimates-1945#column_1898

Chapter Seventeen

1. Lowe, *Inferno*, pp. 249-250.
2. Lowe, *Inferno*, p. 251.
3. Lowe, *Inferno*, p. 250.
4. Lowe, *Inferno*, pp. 251-252.
5. Lowe, *Inferno*, p. 254.
6. Lowe, *Inferno*, p. 254.
7. Lowe, *Inferno*, p. 257.
8. Lowe, *Inferno*, pp. 257-258.
9. Lowe, *Inferno*, pp. 260-261.
10. Lowe, *Inferno*, p. 257.
11. Lowe, *Inferno*, pp. 266-267.
12. Lowe, *Inferno*, p. 268.
13. Lowe, *Inferno*, p. 269.
14. Lowe, *Inferno*, p. 271.
15. Lowe, *Inferno*, p. 273.
16. Lowe, *Inferno*, pp. 278-279.
17. Lowe, *Inferno*, pp. 281-282.

18. National Archives, CAB 23/98/3.
19. "Planning for a war with Germany," memorandum by the British Chiefs of Staff, 15th February 1937, quoted by Wynne, *Stopping Hitler*, pp. 8-11.
20. "Fireside Chat No. 16," December 29th 1940.
21. "For the British Treasury, only today is the war over," The Guardian, 29th December 2006, accessed 5th February 2021: https://www.theguardian.com/business/2006/dec/29/politics.secondworlddwar
22. Hansard, Commons Sitting, 5th June 1946, accessed 5th February 2020: https://api.parliament.uk/historic-hansard/commons/1946/jun/05/foreign-affairs
23. Hansard, Commons Sitting, 5th June 1946, accessed 5th February 2020: https://api.parliament.uk/historic-hansard/commons/1946/jun/05/foreign-affairs
24. Hansard, Commons Sitting, 5th June 1946, accessed 5th February 2020: https://api.parliament.uk/historic-hansard/commons/1946/jun/05/foreign-affairs
25. Hansard, Commons Sitting, 5th June 1946, accessed 5th February 2020: https://api.parliament.uk/historic-hansard/commons/1946/jun/05/foreign-affairs
26. Churchill, *The Gathering Storm*, p. 310.
27. Niccolo Machiavelli, *The Prince*, translated by W.K. Marriot, Gutenberg Press, Chapter 25, accessed 8th March 2021: https://www.gutenberg.org/files/1232/1232-h/1232-h.htm#chap25
28. Machiavelli, *Il Principe*, Chapter 25 (translation by Kenneth Duthie.)
29. National Archives, CAB 66/28/3.
30. Churchill, *The Grand Alliance*, pp. 476-477.
31. National Archives, PREM 3/352/8.
32. National Archives, CAB 23/98/3.
33. Hansard, Commons Sitting, 3rd April 1939, accessed 8th March 2021: https://hansard.parliament.uk/Commons/1939-04-03/debates/817ee449-6976-4e08-b600-1d08461b1e27/EuropeanSituation#contribution-ff720333-7e46-48f1-854d-5742472b1767
34. Hansard, Commons Sitting, 16th August 1945, accessed 8th March 2021: http://hansard.millbanksystems.com/commons/1945/aug/16/debate-on-the-address#column_84

Printed in Great Britain
by Amazon

20651285R00138